500 Live Ideas

FOR THE GRADE TEACHER

By
BETTY LOIS ECKGREN
VIVIAN FISHEL

Illustrations by DOROTHY TODD
Cover by DATY HEALY

HARPER & ROW, PUBLISHERS
NEW YORK, EVANSTON, AND LONDON

B-P

FOREWORD

Teachers face a constant need for fresh, appealing material in their work. They feel a need for ideas that add zest, variety, and fun to subject matter and to play activities both in the classroom and on the playground. Even the most ingenious and creative teachers feel that they are feeding a relentless funnel. It is to help meet these needs that we present *500 Live Ideas*.

500 Live Ideas for the Grade Teacher is a collection of activities, handicraft projects, puzzles, riddles, and games that has grown out of our own teaching experiences and associations. The emphasis is on the practical, on the inexpensive, and on the easy way of making and doing.

Betty Lois Eckgren
Vivian Fishel

TABLE OF CONTENTS

The items in this book are arranged in alphabetical order according to title. For this reason, the book does not contain a table of contents. The subject matter, however, is indexed and arranged in a General Index in the back of the book (pages 313–20).

Lists, entitled "Materials To Save for Handicraft Projects" and "Where To Write for Free Materials," are given on pages 307–12.

ACROSTICS

FOR THE UPPER ELEMENTARY GRADES

The acrostic is an entertaining vocabulary builder. It is a word square in which the words read the same down as across. To start the class off, the teacher may need to work an acrostic with the class or to supply the first word. Many of the children, however, soon will enjoy making up their own acrostics.

On the blackboard make a blank copy of the squares below and of the numbers in the squares. Ask the pupils to copy the squares and the numbers in the squares on paper. Then write the clues to the acrostic on the blackboard so that the pupils can solve the acrostic. The squares below were filled out as a time-saver for the teacher.

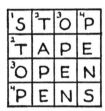

ACROSS AND DOWN

1. To halt
2. Adhesive ———
3. Not closed
4. Tools used for writing with ink

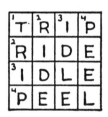

ACROSS AND DOWN

1. Journey
2. To sit on something and make it go
3. Not busy
4. To take off the skin from an apple

7

ACTING OUT WORDS

A GAME FOR THE PRIMARY GRADES

Prepare a goodly number of flash cards bearing action words. Select words that can be acted out easily, such as "jump," "sing,"  "hop," "run," "walk," "skip," "talk," "whisper," "tiptoe," "limp," "march," "cry."

Divide the class into two sides or teams, and choose a leader for each team. The teams take turns in acting out a word. Play begins with the leader of one team setting several flash cards along the chalk tray. The leader calls on a volunteer from his team to choose a word from the flash cards. The player goes to the front of the room to act out the word for the group. If he performs satisfactorily, he scores a point for his team. If he wishes, a player may keep the flash card as a reward for his efforts.

Play now passes to the other team. The team that scores the larger number of points wins.

AIRPLANE

AN OUTDOOR GAME FOR ANY NUMBER OF PLAYERS

Airplane is a game of tag. One of the players is chosen to be "it." He serves as the airplane. The other players find safety off the ground on objects, such as steps, swings, slides, and boxes. The "airplane" may tag any player who is caught on the ground. The players dare the airplane to catch them by capering about on the ground or by running from one safety zone to another. The first person to be caught becomes the next "it."

AN ALPHABET BOOK

FOR THE PRIMARY GRADES

The alphabet becomes a topic of lively interest when the class sets out to make an alphabet book. Plan to make the book about 12 x 18 inches. Use butcher paper for pages and tagboard or cardboard for the covers. To hold the pages in place, punch holes in one side of the pages and lace together with shoestring, yarn, or narrow ribbon.

To illustrate the letters of the alphabet, cut pictures of objects from old magazines and paste the pictures in place. Some of the children may want to draw their own pictures. Plan several pictures for each letter. Suggestions for pictures for the letters *A, B, C, D, E, F* are given below.

airplane	balloon	cat	daisy	eagle	fish
anchor	banana	carrot	deer	egg	flag
apple	bird	chair	dog	elephant	flower
automobile	boat	cherries	drum	envelope	frog

ALPHABET CARDS

FOR THE INTERMEDIATE GRADES

Sometimes an upper-grade class enjoys assembling an alphabet for a primary grade. An interesting variation of the previous project is to illustrate the alphabet on cards and to compose rhymes for some or all of the letters. Below is an example.

A is for apricot
Golden and sweet
Round as a ball
And delicious to eat.

Plan to use large cards made from thin cardboard. A good size is 8½ x 11 inches. Put only one letter and the accompanying illustration on a card. The cards may be arranged into a wall border or displayed in any way that space permits.

ALPHABET GARDEN

A GAME FOR ANY NUMBER OF PLAYERS

To play Alphabet Garden, two captains choose sides and line up their teams facing each other. The captains take turns at calling out names of fruits and vegetables beginning with the first letter of the alphabet, such as apple, apricot, artichoke, asparagus, avocado, alligator pear.

A captain has fifteen seconds in which to think of a word Players may whisper suggestions to their captains; but, if a player speaks aloud, he goes to the foot of the line. Each fruit or vegetable can be named only once. When he fails to come up with a word during the allotted time, the captain goes to the foot of the line. The second player moves into the captain's place. The two captains now alternate in calling fruits and vegetables beginning with *b*, such as bananas, beans, beets, blackberries, black-eyed beans, blueberries, broccoli, Brussels sprouts.

Each team scores a point for sending the rival captain to the foot of the line. One of the players or the teacher may act as timekeeper and scorer. Skip letters, such as *i, u, v, z*, for which no one can think of a fruit or vegetable. Suggestions for the other letters follow.

cabbage	eggplant	lettuce	persimmon	shaddock
cantaloupe	elderberry	lima bean	peppers	soybean
carrot	endive	lime	pineapple	spinach
cauliflower	fig	loganberry	plum	squash
celery	gooseberry	medlar	plumcot	strawberry
cherry	grapes	muskmelon	pomegranate	sweet potato
citrange	grapefruit	nectarine	pomelo	Swiss chard
citron	guava	okra	potato	tangelo
corn	horseradish	olive	prune	tangerine
cranberry	jujube	onion	pumpkin	tepary bean
cress	kale	orange	quince	tomato
cucumber	kohlrabi	parsley	radish	turnip
currants	kumquat	parsnip	raisin	watercress
dates	leek	peach	raspberry	watermelon
dewberry	lemon	peas	rhubarb	yam
drupe	lentil	pear	rutabaga	youngberry

ANAGRAMS

FOR THE UPPER GRADES

There is nothing new about anagrams. People through the ages have enjoyed making them. The Hebrews, the Greeks, the Romans, the people of the Middle Ages and modern times have enjoyed working with these brain teasers.

To make an anagram, you take a word, or phrase, rearrange its letters, and form a new word, as for example:

> *Rage* is an anagram for *gear.*
> *Resist* is an anagram for *sister.*
> *Brain teasers* may be rearranged to spell *bat in erasers.*

Making up anagrams offers a challenge to students who finish their work ahead of the others and who always are ready for more work. It is an excellent activity for odd moments.

ANIMAL BLINDMAN'S BUFF

A GAME FOR ANY NUMBER OF PLAYERS

In the game of Animal Blindman's Buff, the players form a circle. Someone is chosen to be "it." He is blindfolded and takes his position in the center of the circle. All the other players are animal actors. The teacher, or leader, secretly assigns to each player the part of an animal, such as a dog, cat, lion, hen, rooster, pony, or mouse.

The blind man tries to identify one of the animal actors and to make him "it." He calls upon each animal by saying, "Speak Dog, speak," or "Speak Lion, speak." The animal answers in his characteristic vocal sound; that is, with a growl, bark, bray, whinny, cackle, moo, mew, or squeak (for a mouse). The blind man has three guesses in which to identify the animal. If he succeeds, the blind man and the actor change places, and the actor is the new "it." If he fails, the blind man calls on another animal to speak.

11

ANIMAL STAND-UPS

Animal stand-ups may be made from orange or lemon crates or apple boxes. The pupil draws an animal—bear, giraffe, elephant, donkey, dog, goose—on colored paper. He puts two sheets together so that when he cuts out his drawing he will have duplicate figures, one for each side of the stand-up.

Use one of the figures as a pattern. Lay it on the wood and trace the silhouette of the animal. With the help of the teacher and a coping saw, the child cuts along the lines of the drawing. The colored pictures are then glued to the wood and shellacked, and the animal is ready for the parade!

ANIMAL TRACK STORIES

To encourage the writing of original stories, draw tracks of animals on the blackboard. Include fowl—chickens, ducks, and geese—if you wish to have variety. Ask the class to identify the tracks and label the drawings as you proceed.

Hold a lively class discussion about the habits of the animals, about their food, shelter, nesting habits if any, enemies, and prey. This usually serves as an incentive for the class to write stories about the adventures of the animals as suggested by their tracks. The tracks on page 12 are those of a chicken, duck, horse, and dog.

ARITHMETIC TAG

AN INDOOR OR OUTDOOR GAME FOR ANY NUMBER OF PLAYERS

Arithmetic Tag is a game that gives drill in the fundamentals of arithmetic. To play the game the players form a circle. Two or three children volunteer to be in the "mush pot," which is anywhere inside the circle. Another person is chosen to be "it." He skips around the circle stopping suddenly behind a player to challenge him with a problem. He, for example, may ask, "Two and four are how many?" or "Eight from twelve is how much?" or "Three nine's are how many?" or "How many four's in eight?" The type of problem will depend upon the grade level of the players.

The player who is being challenged must give the correct answer before someone in the mush pot does. If he succeeds, he becomes "it" and goes skipping around the circle stopping suddenly to challenge someone else. If he fails, he must exchange places with the winner in the mush pot. Players in the mush pot try to work their way out by calling out the answer ahead of the one being challenged on the perimeter of the circle.

AN ART COLLECTION

Boys and girls enjoy building up an art collection for the classroom. Encourage them to add only pictures that have some artistic merit. Usually the children have magazines at home which they may want to bring to school to be used for clipping.

Some of the commercial art; that is, advertising art, in the magazines has shown a marked improvement in recent years. Reproductions of photographs and works of art may be found in the daily and Sunday newspapers if a person is diligent in his search. In towns and cities that have art and bookshops, reproductions of famous works of art may be purchased from postcard size up. Small prints can also be purchased cheaply at art museums.

Pupils enjoy organizing their art collection and putting it in a large scrapbook or in folders, and in keeping both the scrapbook and folder as repositories.

BABY PICTURE CONTEST

Baby pictures provide an opportunity for an hilarious contest. Children are always delighted with snapshots of one another.

Teacher and pupils bring pictures of their babyhood and childhood to school. Arrange the pictures on the bulletin board low enough for everyone to see. During the course of the day, children take turns in going to the bulletin board to identify the pictures. They write their answers on a piece of paper. After everyone has finished, the teacher supplies the right answers. The contestant with the highest score wins.

BACK-TO-BACK RACE

AN OUTDOOR GAME

For a back-to-back race appoint two leaders who choose up sides. Establish a starting point and two goal posts about 10 feet apart and 25 feet from the starting point. Ask the players to take turns at serving as posts. They thoroughly enjoy it.

The players on each team stand back to back in pairs, link elbows, and run in relays in this position. The first pair on each team moves up to the starting line. At the word "Go!" each pair races toward its goal post, circles it, races back to the starting line, and tags the next couple which has moved into the starting position. No couple may start until it has been tagged by the returning couple. The race continues until each couple has participated. The team to finish first wins.

BAGS FOR MARBLES

To help boys (and girls, too) to keep their marbles off the floor, have the players make bags for their marbles. Ask the marble players to bring old socks to school.

Use the top of the sock for the bag. Cut off and discard the foot. Sew up the bottom end of the leg of the sock and hem the top to form a casing for the drawstring. Use a heavy string or cord. A ½-inch strip cut from a piece of discarded cotton cloth makes an excellent drawstring, too. Draw the string through the hem and the marble bag is ready.

A BASEBALL SPELLING GAME

FOR THE INTERMEDIATE AND UPPER GRADES

To have fun with a review in spelling, make the lesson into a baseball game occasionally. Have the children choose sides. If this is too time consuming, divide the class into two teams. Designate one side as the Home Team and the other as Visitors. Appoint a scorekeeper to keep track of the strikeouts and runs. Designate the corner of the room near the blackboard as home base. Counterclockwise from home base, assign first, second, and third base to the remaining three corners.

15

To start the first inning, the Visitors have the first turn at bat. The first batter steps to the blackboard. The teacher pronounces a word from the review list. The batter pronounces the word aloud and writes it on the blackboard. If he does both correctly, the batter makes a hit, and he goes to first base. If he either mispronounces or misspells a word, the batter is called "Out" by the teacher. He takes his seat, and the next batter goes to the board. As soon as another batter gets a hit, the first runner advances to second base. If a third batter gets on base, the first two advance to second and third bases. If a fourth batter gets on, the first runner comes home from third base to score a run for his team.

The Visitors continue at bat until three men are out. When the side is retired, the players take their seats, and the Home Team comes to bat. To end the game fairly, allow each team the same number of turns at bat.

A BEACH BAG

A very satisfactory beach bag may be made from old inner tubing. Cut open the tubing. Fold it once to make a rectangle the size desired for the bag. Punch a row of small holes in the ends of the bag and lace together with a shoestring or heavy string.

Paint or paste pictures on the front of the bag or decorate with sealing wax. Make a handle from inner tubing. Sew it on with heavy thread or fasten with roundheads (brass paper fasteners).

A BEAD LOOM

To make a loom on which to weave beads, cut a rectangle from cardboard the size of the article that you plan to make. For a napkin ring, for example, you will need a loom 3 x 7 inches. Use stiff cardboard and cut small notches across both ends of the cardboard to hold the thread in place as in the illustration at the left. Space the notches so that the threads will be as far apart as the beads are wide. Thread the loom and a needle with strong thread and weave in the beads. When the loom is full, reinforce the ends of the beadwork by weaving a thread through the ends and sides. Then break the cardboard to release the beadwork.

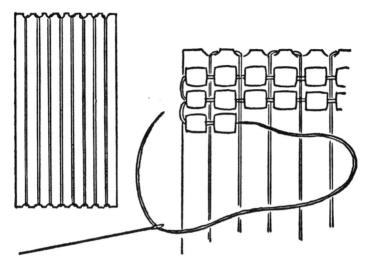

Macaroni may be used instead of beads. Color the macaroni by dipping it into calcimine paint. Cut it into the size of beads and spread on newspapers to dry.

Articles that may be made with beadwork are napkin rings, belts, and small purses. For an article as long as a belt, weave several short pieces and sew them together.

A BEAN BAG

A small bag filled with beans is a handy item to have on hand in the primary classroom. It may be used in games as a substitute for a ball; or in relay races as an object that is passed from hand to hand.

To make a bean bag, cut out two 5 x 5-inch squares from burlap, canvas, or flour sacking. Place one square upon the other. Seam together on three sides. Turn the bag inside out and fill it with navy beans. To close the bag whip the fourth side together.

BEAN THROW

AN INDOOR GAME

To play Bean Throw, place several boxes or bowls of graduated sizes inside one another. Assign a different scoring value to each bowl or box. Assign the highest value to the largest bowl since it is on the outside and the hardest to hit. The easiest to hit, of course, is the empty bowl in the center.

Establish a foul line a specified distance from the bowls across which the players may not step while throwing the beans. The distance, of course, will depend upon the age group of the children. Establish the foul line far enough away to provide a real challenge. Give each player fifty beans. As soon as he has finished, a player totals his score. One or two others check his arithmetic as he proceeds.

Several sets of bowls or boxes may be kept in play to accommodate more players.

BEAUTY IN EVERYDAY SURROUNDINGS

FOR THE INTERMEDIATE GRADES

Children's appreciation of beauty may be easily increased. Point out, for example, the artistic merits of objects that children see in their everyday surroundings. Call their attention to a flower, a delicate fern frond, a maple leaf, a well-shaped tree, the tints in a sea shell. Other objects, of course, may be selected depending upon the region.

Call their attention to good and not so good design in the industrial arts. Observe color, line, and design in a vase, draperies, wallpaper, room furnishings, fabrics. Notice pleasing examples of architecture and architectural features. Look for a well-designed building, an attractive factory building, a water pumping station, a barn, a garage, a beautiful church spire or bell tower, a steep gable roof, an attractive window display in a store, a well-bound book, a carefully planned photograph.

BELLE THE CAT

A GAME FOR THE PRIMARY GRADES

This is a game in which one of the players is chosen to be the cat. All of the other players are mice. Everyone, including the cat, is blindfolded. The cat is a mouser and goes hunting for mice. She carries a bell to warn the blind mice of her whereabouts. The mice scurry about bumping into one another as they try to keep out of the cat's way. When she catches a mouse, the cat cries, "Meow! I've got you." Then everyone takes off his blindfold to see who has been caught. The mouse who has been caught becomes the next cat. The blindfolds are put on again and the game is resumed.

BERRY AND TWIG FIGURES

Stick figures and tiny furniture may be made from a variety of berries and thin twigs or dried fern stems. Cranberries lend themselves especially well to this type of work.

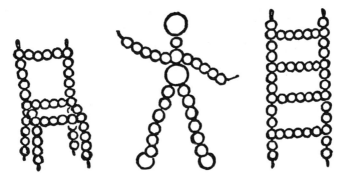

Cut the twigs the desired length and string the berries on the sticks. To hold the sticks together at the corners, use a berry to serve as a joint. The corners will be strengthened as the berries dry. Peas and toothpicks may be used instead of berries and twigs. To thread the peas, pierce them with a needle.

BIG BROTHERS

If older boys and girls are annoyed by younger children entering into their games, the teacher may point out that the younger children regard them as experts and leaders. Encourage the older group to act as big brothers and sisters and to help the younger children organize their own games and activities.

BIG SISTERS

A constant vigilance against carelessness about matters of hygiene and health needs to be kept with boys and girls on the elementary school level. Teachers of the upper elementary grades may encourage the class to discuss ways of improving standards of cleanliness and health. They can make check sheets and include items, such as brushing teeth twice daily, drinking six glasses of water and milk every day, and using a handkerchief when sneezing.

Upper grade pupils can help to assume responsibility in hygiene matters for their younger brothers and sisters at home. They can, in addition to keeping a check sheet for themselves, make one for the younger members of the family, take it home, and put it to use. This type of approach is often quite effective.

A BIRDBATH

To make a small, cement birdbath, you will need two pie tins, one somewhat smaller than the other one. Mix enough cement to fill the larger pie tin. Press the smaller tin into the cement and brush off the excess cement from the sides. The top pan may be left as a permanent part of the birdbath, or it may be removed after the cement has begun to harden. Do not remove the bottom pan. For instructions for mixing cement mortar, see page 41.

If you care to do so, place a mirror on the floor of the bath and birds will reward your effort by putting on a good show.

A BIRD COSTUME

A bird costume is often needed for a classroom play or for a Halloween costume. An inexpensive one can be made from newspapers. Use a discarded slip or plain dress for the foundation. With calcimine or tempera paint, paint five sections of newspaper the color of feathers. The number of sections of newspaper, of course, will vary with the length of the costume that is needed.

Take one section of newspaper, fold it lengthwise and cut a fringe of feathers as shown in the illustration at the left. If you are proficient at this sort of thing, you may try folding and cutting two newspapers at a time. Sew a band of feathers to the bottom of the foundation, and arrange the others in tiers as in the illustration at the right.

BIRD MIGRATION MAP

FOR THE INTERMEDIATE GRADES

One of the best introductions to the study of bird migrations is to plot the route of migratory birds. Draw an outline map of North America, Mexico, Central, and South America. Gather information about the migrations of birds, such as the reason they migrate, the routes or air passageways they follow, and the distances they travel. One of the greatest travelers, for example, is the golden plover which nests in the Arctic Circle and migrates to South America.

Choose several birds, or more if you like, for your study. Choose birds that follow different routes. Select one that follows the Mississippi Valley route, another the Pacific Coast route, or perhaps an ocean route. If you have chosen a bird that migrates through the area in which you live, keep a record of the date when you notice the bird. Be careful to note that not all birds follow the same route in the fall as in the spring.

Perhaps you would like to chart the routes of some of the birds that spend the summers only in your region. Find out where they go for the winter and plot the route on the map.

BIRTHDAY CARDS

Friendliness is encouraged among the members of a class by the exchange of birthday cards. Birthdays occur so frequently, however, that it may not be practical to celebrate each one separately. One day a month may be set aside to take care of the birthdays that come within that period.

One type of card that may be prepared by the class as a group is a large single greeting. Select a paper varying in thickness from butcher paper to tagboard. Make the card any size and color that you like. For a design or for a border across the top choose a decoration appropriate to the month. Peach blossoms, for example, may be used for April, a snowman for January, children on their way to school for September, colored leaves for October, a gobbler for November. Allow for enough space so that everyone can sign his name.

If the birthday card activity is to be carried on as an art lesson, the members of the class will want to make individual cards and use their own ingenuity.

Linoleum-block printing described on page 153 and blue printing on page 24 are effective methods of printing designs on cards.

BLACKBOARD ANAGRAMS

To play Blackboard Anagrams, the teacher writes a letter of the alphabet on the blackboard. A volunteer may add a letter if the letter makes a new word. If the teacher writes an "A," the volunteer may add T to form AT. Additional letters may be added to make ATE, HEAT, WHEAT. As soon as no more letters can be added to change the word, the game begins again with a new letter.

Another form of Blackboard Anagrams is to add letters which prepare for a new word. The new letters do not necessarily complete the word as it progresses, as in C, CA, CAT. The word may turn out differently from the one that the originator had in mind. The next player, for example, may add R instead of T to make CAR. Each child scores a point for every word he completes.

BLACKBOARD DRAWING GAME

The teacher and children cover the blackboard with pictures of as many different objects as they can draw, such as eyeglasses, scissors, light bulb, lamp, bed, birthday cake, giraffe, caterpillar. Someone with an artistic aptitude, for instance, may begin the drawing game. Others volunteer, and soon everyone is contributing to the game. Children soon discover that they can draw a variety of objects easily. Colored chalk adds interest.

BLOTTER AND PENWIPER

To make a blotter and penwiper, cut blotting paper and soft absorbent felt into rectangles of graduated sizes. Use the blotting paper for the bottom layer, and make this layer the larger. The felt, of course, will serve as a penwiper. Lay the layers concentrically one on top of the other and fasten them in the middle with a staple. Or punch two holes close together in button fashion. Draw a ribbon through the holes and tie in a bow.

BLUEPRINT PICTURES OF FLOWERS AND LEAVES

Some beautiful silhouettes of flowers and leaves may be made with blueprint paper. Select a flat flower like a pansy or any leaf, such as oak, maple, chestnut, elm, butternut, sycamore. Lay it on a piece of blueprint paper. Put a glass on the flower or leaf to hold it down. Lay the paper, specimen, and glass out in strong sunshine for about a minute. Then take it inside and apply a fixative of potassium bichromate. Blueprint paper and potassium bichromate may be obtained from dealers in blueprint supplies. Large office supply houses usually carry blueprint paper.

Blueprint pictures are excellent for decorating scrapbooks, greeting cards, stationary, and friezes. Blueprint pictures of flowers and leaves make beautiful displays for a science exhibit.

A BOOK BORDER

One way of giving credit for reading books is to give children recognition in a "book border." Make a four-page book; that is, a booklet with two leaves. Take a rectangular sheet of colored paper and fold it crosswise to make four pages.

The reader writes the title of the book and the name of the author on the cover. He may arrange the title and name as it appears on the title page of the book. Then he writes his own name in the lower, right-hand corner. With a paper punch, punch several holes in the fold of the booklet. Thread colored string or ribbon through the holes and tie in a bow.

Hang the booklets into a border. Not all of the books need to be the same size. The border may be a yard long or it may extend around the room.

BOOK COVERS

Children should be encouraged to cover their books in order to protect them from soil and wear. Attractive covers may be made from chintz, printed cotton cloth, small figured wallpaper, or colored shelf paper.

To make a cover, cut a piece of material or paper in the shape of a rectangle large enough to cover the outside of the book and to allow for a 2-inch overlap all around. Place the rectangle flat on a table and fold in two inches all around. Slit the overlap at the top and bottom to accommodate the back of the book. Slip the covers of the book into the folds.

To make a finished job, miter the corners of the overlap; that is, form an angle by cutting out a triangular piece to avoid bulkiness. If the cover is made from cloth sew together the cut edges.

BOOKENDS

An attractive pair of bookends can be made from an orange crate. Before you begin, study the illustration on the next page to determine the size and therefore the dimensions of the bookends that you want to make. Note that the bottom of the bookend is larger and thicker than the upright part. Use the heavier endboards of the orange crate for the bottom of the bookend and the thinner sideboards of the crate for the uprights of the bookends.

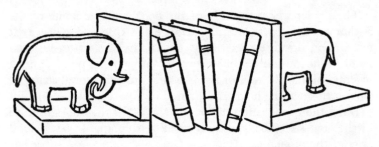

Saw the boards to the size desired and nail the pieces together at a right angle. On paper draw an elephant. Cut it out, lay it on the board, and trace around it. Cut out the wooden figure with a coping saw. Sandpaper the figure and bookends smooth. With India ink or paint, draw in the eyes, ears, parts of the tusks, and the tail. Glue the figure to the base and side. Paint and then lacquer the entire job.

BOOK MARKS

A simple kind of book mark can be made by fitting a marker in hat fashion over the corner of a page. Copy the drawing on this page on construction paper. Cut on the curved dotted line and fold on the dashed lines. Then glue the flap marked "Paste" to the back of the marker. Fancier and more durable books marks may be made from ribbon or felt. Work the design with embroidery floss on ribbon and with yarn on felt.

PASTE

BOTTLE CAP WRISTWATCH

FOR THE PRIMARY GRADES

The proud distinction of wearing a wristwatch is often an incentive for children in the primary grades to learn to tell time. Here is a type of watch that can be made easily and handily in the classroom.

Collect caps from soda pop bottles and remove the linings from the caps. Use one of the caps as a base for a watch. Cut a slit on opposite edges of the top of the cap. To cut the slit, fasten the bottle cap firmly in a clamp and use a can opener or a combination ice pick and an old penknife.

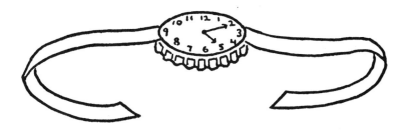

Have the children paint the face of the clock on the top of the bottle cap with white enamel or lacquer. When this is dry, write the numerals on the clock with India ink. Or, instead of painting the face of the clock, you may prefer to paste on a paper dial. Make a paper dial by having the children cut out white paper circles the size of the bottle cap. With India ink draw the hands of the clock and write on the numerals. Paste the dial on the bottle cap with rubber cement.

To give the appearance of a watch crystal, stick on a layer of clear, colorless Scotch tape. Thread a ribbon or band through the slits for a watch bracelet. Another way of fastening the ribbon to the bottle cap is to glue the ribbon to the underside of the cap. To add a finishing touch, glue the cork back into place. If the cork was destroyed in the process of removing it, substitute circles cut from cardboard.

BOTTLE FIGURINES

Here is a use for old bottles. They may be turned into figurines such as those in the illustrations.

A MUSKETEER

For the musketeer figurine select a squat, attractively shaped bottle about 8 inches high. You also need a cork for the bottle,

an ice-cream bar stick, colored crepe paper, bits of cardboard, and white paper.

Fashion the uniform from crepe paper and glue it in place on the bottle. Make the collar from white paper and match the necktie with the uniform. With India ink draw the features—eyes, ears, nose, mouth, hairline. Indicate the legs and trousers with ink as in the picture. The cork, of course, forms the pillbox cap. Paint it any color you like. Make the uniform from crepe paper. Draw the arms and right hand. Make the left hand from cardboard so that it holds the musket and glue it to the bottle. Whittle the ice-cream bar stick into a musket. Hold the musket in place with the musketeer's hand and by tacking it to the suit with thread.

A PETITE MISS

To make the petite miss select a round slender bottle. Try to find one that is smaller in the middle than at the ends, one that will form the base for an hourglasslike figure! You will need a low flat cork to which you can anchor the hair, one or two paper doilies depending upon their size, about a yard of yarn, and a piece of colored cloth or tiny figured material large enough to make a long dress.

Cover the stopper part of the cork with a scrap of pink paper or cloth to give a flesh-colored effect through the glass. With

India ink draw the outline of the girl's face and the features as in the picture. Fashion the hair from yarn by cutting it into short lengths. Glue the hair to the top of the cork.

It will be helpful to make a pattern for the dress on tissue paper so that you can adjust the pattern to the size of the figurine. This helps you to determine how large to cut the dress. Make the dress generously large and allow for seams. Cut the front and back alike; that is, cut the material double. The hands and arms are cut in one piece as a part of the dress. Stitch up the seams and turn the dress right side out. Stuff the hands and arms with cotton.

Slip the dress on the figurine and fit it by tying it at the waist and neck. Add a starched apron. Cut the ruffles for the bonnet, collar, sleeves, and for around the hem of the dress from crisp, white paper doilies. Gather the ruffles with needle and thread and sew them in place.

A GAY LITTLE PIG

To make a piggy figurine you need a round, stocky bottle, a cork that fits the bottle, four small corks, a scrap of small-figured wallpaper, a pipe cleaner, glue, and cellophane tape. For the body of the pig, cover the bottle with wallpaper. Use glue to stick on the paper. Make a curly tail with the pipe cleaner and fasten it with cellophane tape. Fit a tall cork into the neck of the bottle for the snout. Draw the eyes with ink or crayon. Notch and whittle four small corks into hoofs and legs and glue them on. Make the ears of wallpaper. Draw a triangle with a slightly rounded base and use as a pattern for fashioning the ear.

A BOWL GARDEN

Making a garden in a bowl offers an opportunity for originality. Select a large flat bowl or a small tray with a high rim. Mix a
small amount of cement. (For cement mortar, see page 41.) Model
an interesting terrain, molding hills, valleys, and perhaps a river
or a lake.

Use your ingenuity in making people, trees and other vegetation, a house, fence, river, or a lake. These may be made with

toothpicks, burned kitchen matches, hairpins, clothespins, or pipe
cleaners. Dress the figurines in cloth or crepe paper. Printed
chintz is especially attractive.

Adapt the vegetation to the type of garden that you are making. Fir trees and evergreen shrubbery make a beautiful garden.
Use small branches of evergreens for trees in this type of scene.
For a desert garden use Joshua trees, cacti, Sedums, yuccas, and
other succulent plants. In a tropical garden use palm trees, perhaps vines, and large leafy plants, flowers. Adorn some of the
trees with Spanish moss. Use a wood-fibered packing material for
moss. Paint the moss green with calcimine paint.

A BRAIDED RUG

To collect the material for a braided rug, encourage the children to bring old stockings and scraps of colored cloth to school. Have them cut the material into strips one inch wide. Sew the ends of the strips together until you have many yards. Wind the strips into three balls for convenience in braiding. When you have braided a goodly amount, start the rug at the center by arranging the braid into an oval coil. Sew the edges of the braids together. Continue to wind and sew the braids until the rug is the size desired. Then press the rug by putting it under a heavy object for several days. The rug may be used in the schoolroom, in a playhouse, or for a gift.

BREADBOARD

To make a breadboard, use the thick end of an orange crate or apple box. Cut a board 12 inches long and 7½ inches wide. Sandpaper it smooth. A breadboard makes a useful gift for any occasion, as for a birthday, Christmas, or Mother's Day.

BUILDING A HOUSE OF GOOD DEEDS

If they are given encouragement, boys and girls enjoy fostering a friendly and courteous atmosphere in the classroom. They begin to notice nice things about one another.

One way to encourage a feeling of friendliness is to "build" a brick house and to name each brick for the person who does a courteous deed. Draw the outline of a large brick house or castle on Manila or wrapping paper. Indicate the bricks distinctly, and post the drawing on the wall, or move it to the bulletin board for a few days. Each time that a child reports a kind and courteous deed that someone in the group has performed, the doer of the deed writes his name on a brick. If he is too modest, someone else may write it for him.

BULLETIN BOARD

A teacher who finds that she needs to supply a bulletin board for the schoolroom can make one easily from various kinds of materials. A small linoleum rug, turned wrong side out and tacked on the wall, makes a good one. Tagboard and beaverboard are suitable materials, too. A wide strip of felt makes a handy bulletin board. Felt letters and felt decorations will stick to the felt board without pins or thumbtacks. Use a contrasting color for the letters and decorations. Cardboard salvaged from large cartons is another inexpensive material. A folding screen makes an adaptable bulletin board since it can be moved from place to place. It can also be used for displaying illustrative materials to the class during a recitation period.

BUTTON PICTURES

FOR THE PRIMARY AND INTERMEDIATE GRADES

To make the man below, you will need two buttons, a very large one for the body and a smaller one for the head. Spend

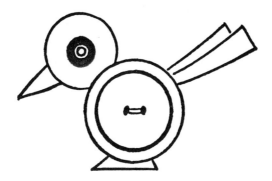

time in selecting just the right buttons. Cut the cardboard large enough, about 5 x 6 inches, so that you will have plenty of space around the picture. Place the buttons in position and indicate their positions with a pencil. Then sew them on. Complete the figure by pasting on cutouts made from paper or fabric. Draw in any missing details with ink.

To make the bird above, sew a large button on a 6 x 5-inch cardboard. Place the picture on the cardboard so that the margins are well balanced. Allow for a wider margin at the bottom than at the top. Draw the bird's head, beak, tail, and feet with crayon. Or use cutouts from colored paper or cloth.

A BUTTON PURSE

An attractive purse may be made with buttons. Sew and knot the buttons into a network approximately 8½ x 5½ inches in size. Use a strong thread, or a tightly twisted cotton yarn for meshing the buttons into a net. Draw the thread through the buttons and knot it at the crossings. This keeps the buttons in place and adds to the attractiveness of the purse.

For a lining select a piece of firmly woven cloth, and cut it into a rectangle slightly larger than the purse. Make the lining about 9 x 6 inches to allow for seams on all sides. Baste the button network to the lining. Fold the purse crosswise. Turn in the edges of the lining and sew the network and lining together along the seams. Add a zipper at the top of the purse.

BUTTONS FOR COSTUMES

Buttons for costumes are fascinating and fun to make. They may be made from a variety of stiff materials, such as an old broomstick or heavy cardboard.

BROOMSTICK BUTTONS

Saw an old broomstick crosswise into slices. Slice off as many buttons as you need. Drill two small holes in the center of each button or glue a cord to the back for a fastener and sandpaper smooth. Paint or decorate the buttons with sealing wax in a design suitable for the occasion.

CLOWN BUTTONS

Heavy cardboard, covered and padded with red cloth, makes good buttons for clown costumes. Cut a cardboard circle about 2 inches in diameter and punch a small hole in the center. Now

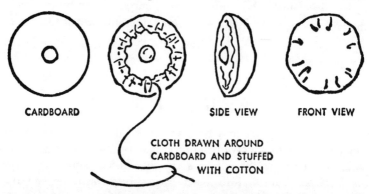

CARDBOARD   SIDE VIEW   FRONT VIEW

CLOTH DRAWN AROUND
CARDBOARD AND STUFFED
WITH COTTON

fix a fastener for the button. Take a piece of cord 1 to 1½ inches long. Tie a knot in one end and thread the other end through the hole in the button and sew to the costume. Or pull the padding through the hole and use it as a fastener. From red cloth cut a circle larger than the cardboard circle, and run a stout thread around the edge. Pad the top of the cardboard button with cotton batting. Place the red circle over the padding and cardboard and pull the ends of the thread taut and tie.

A BUTTON-TRIMMED FLOWER VASE

Select an attractively shaped bottle and trim the bottle with a network of buttons. The buttons may be either uniform in size and color or assorted in sizes and colors and with two or four eyeholes. Use a stout thread, or a tightly twisted cotton cord for meshing the buttons. Sew and knot the buttons into a net to fit the lower half of the bottle. Begin at the base of the bottle and work up. Draw the thread or cord through the buttons and knot it at the button eye on the right side of the network for effect. To keep it from slipping off, paste the button network to the bottle with glue or mending cement, the kind used for mending china. Then lacquer or shellac to give it a finished look.

A CALENDAR MOUNT

FOR THE ELEMENTARY GRADES

An attractive mount or card for mounting a calendar may be made from a discarded phonograph record. Cover the record with a gay fabric such as chintz or cotton. Fold or place the material double and use the record for a pattern. Cut the circular covers large enough to allow for a seam all the way around. Place the record between the two pieces of fabric. Sew a ruffle on the edge of the covering. To do a neat job, place the ruffle in the seam; that is, between the two pieces of fabric.

Paste or stitch a small calendar on the front of the mount. Make a small loop and sew it to the back of the mount to serve as a fastener for hanging the calendar on the wall.

CANDIED APPLES

A RECIPE

To make candied apples, you need these materials:

1 cup dark molasses   1 tablespoon vinegar
½ cup sugar   ¼ teaspoon salt

Mix the ingredients thoroughly. Bring the mixture to a boil and stir constantly until it is brittle. To test for brittleness, put a few drops in cold water. Then add 1 tablespoon of butter or margarine. This will candy about 10 apples.

Spear an apple with a sucker stick and ladle the candy mixture over it. Place the candied apples on wax paper until they are cool. They are now ready to be served.

A CANDLEHOLDER

A holder for a candle may be made with modeling clay. Use a cream or a milk carton for a mold. A ½-pint size carton is about the right size. If you are using a quart-size carton, however, cut it down to a height of 3 inches. Whatever size you decide upon, use two cartons for a pair of holders, since it is not practical to re-use a mold. Fill the mold with wet modeling clay. While the clay is still pliable, make a socket, or hole, for supporting the candle by pressing the end of a candle into the clay. When the clay is thoroughly dry, break away the cardboard carton and paint the candleholder with calcimine paint.

A CANDY JAR

An ice-cream carton or one of Dad's discarded tobacco tins makes an excellent candy jar. Decorate the jar with paint or papier-mâché or crepe paper. For instructions for decorating objects by winding with crepe paper, see page 85.

A CANISTER SET

Select cans that are graduated in size, that are clean, free from rust, and that have good-fitting tops. Tin cans and glass jars are excellent. You will need four for a set; that is, for tea, coffee, sugar, and flour. The containers may be lacquered, enameled, or painted. Perhaps you prefer to cover them with braided raffia glued on braid by braid or to wind them with twisted rope of crepe paper (page 85). Other suggestions are pictures cut from magazines and glued on.

Effective labels may be made by firmly twisting crepe paper and then by forming handwriting to spell out the contents.

A CARDBOARD CLOCK

A cardboard clock for each child in the schoolroom has a number of uses. It enables the child to gain practice in telling time. He may, for example, set his clock when he enters the schoolroom, when he leaves for lunch, and when he begins a lesson or activity. By looking at the child's clock, the teacher can tell how long it took him to complete a lesson.

To make a clock, cut a cardboard circle 6 inches in diameter. To indicate the hours, write the numerals with black crayon. Cut the hour and minute hands from cardboard. Color the hands black and fasten them in place with a roundhead (brass paper fastener). Roundheads are sometimes called "brads."

CASEIN GLUE

To make casein glue, heat ½ glass of skimmed milk in an enamel saucepan to a temperature of 90 degrees Fahrenheit. Remove it from the stove and add ⅓ cup of vinegar. As you stir in the vinegar, curds will appear. Remove the curds by straining the mixture through cheesecloth. Wash the curds carefully in cold water and let them dry. The curds are the casein.

To make the glue, put in twice as much water as you have curds. Mix thoroughly until the ingredients are blended. Dissolve 1 tablespoon of washing soda (sodium carbonate) in a glass of warm water, and add it to the casein solution. Stir the mixture until it gains the consistency of glue.

Casein glue may be used for the construction projects described in this book. It is also known as cold water glue.

CATCHING AND CARING FOR LIZARDS

Perhaps some of the boys and girls may like to keep a lizard as a pet for a few days. Chameleons also make good pets. But children should not try to keep a lizard or any reptile or animal unless they can provide it with the kind of food and shelter that it needs and then only for a few days.

There are many different kinds of lizards and at least one or two varieties may be found in their natural habitat in nearly any region in the United States.

Although they are wary, lizards often can be caught with a grass lasso. To make a lasso, tie a slip knot in one end of a long blade of grass. Sneak up cautiously on the lizard, and slip the noose over its head. Accustomed to the feel of grass, the lizard is caught unawares. But do not try to catch a lizard by its tail because it may fool you. It may break off its tail and escape. If it does break off its tail, the lizard will soon grow a new one.

Keep the lizard in an empty aquarium. Put sand in the bottom, and keep the aquarium covered with a screen.

CATCH THE CAT

A GAME FOR THE PRIMARY GRADES

In Catch the Cat some one is chosen to be the cat. All the players except the cat are blindfolded. The cat carries a bell which rings continuously as it circulates among the blindfolded players, dodging this one and jumping away from that one. The player who finally catches the cat becomes the next cat. Inexpensive blindfolds may be made by folding butcher paper into bands.

CATEGORIES

AN INDOOR SEAT GAME

Here is a game that children enjoy. Categories is a word game, and the difficulty of the words may be determined by the players themselves. Let the grade level and general background of the players be your guide.

To play the game each player prepares a rectangular plat similar to the one on this page. Make the plat 5 rectangles high and 5 wide. With the aid of the teacher, the players decide on a 5-letter word to use as a title. Avoid a word in which two

	C	A	M	E	L
animals	coyote	antelope	monkey	elephant	lion
countries	Colombia	Austria	Mexico	England	Liberia
trees	cedar	ash	maple	elm	locust
famous people	Caesar	Adams	Madison	Edison	Lincoln
parts of the body	chest	arm	mouth	eye	leg

letters are the same and avoid letters, such as *q, y,* and *z.* The title of the model given on this page is "Camel," and *the rectangles were filled out as a timesaver for the teacher.*

Then for each row across, the children volunteer titles. The titles must name large categories or classifications, such as animals, birds, rivers, motion picture stars, cities, mountains, livelihoods, countries, presidents, states, the counties in your state. Each player writes the category at the left side of the plat.

Each player fills in the rectangles in his plat. For the first row in the example given on page 39, the player thinks of the name of an animal beginning with the letter at the top of the row. If the 5-letter word, for example, is "camel" and the first category is "animals," the player needs an animal beginning with *c*. If he decides on "coyote," the player writes the word in the first rectangle. For the second rectangle, the player thinks of an animal beginning with *a*. He continues to fill in the first row. The category for the second row across is "countries," and he fills in this row. The categories for the third, fourth, and fifth rows are "trees," "famous people," and "parts of the body."

When they have filled in the rectangles, or as many as they can, the players read their answers aloud. Appoint someone to keep the score on the board. If three or more players have the same answer for a rectangle, each scores 1 point. If only two have the same answer, each scores 3 points. If he comes up with a unique answer, a player scores 5 points. The player making the highest score wins.

CELLOPHANE PICTURE SLIDES

A fairly satisfactory slide from which a picture may be projected by a magic lantern or by a projector can be made from cellophane. Cut the cellophane into squares and bind the edges with cellophane tape. The overall size of the slides that most projectors take is 2 x 2 inches. A large magic lantern accommodates a 4 x 1¼-inch slide.

Draw the pictures with India ink. Try to get cellophane with a mat surface because ink will not adhere readily to a smooth surface. Colored cellophane, or colored ink, produces pictures in color.

In typing captions on the slides, place the carbon paper face down on the cellophane.

A plain wall surface, or a bed sheet, makes a good screen.

CELLOPHANE PLACE MATS

FOR A GIFT

Colorful place mats may be made by weaving strips of cellophane. Plan to combine uncolored cellophane with perhaps two or three colors. Use the uncolored for the lengthwise strip and the colored for across. If you use three colors across, for example, repeat the colors in the same order every time.

Plan to make the mat 16 x 11½ inches. Cut the cellophane into strips 1½ inches wide, and fold lengthwise into ¾-inch strips to strengthen them. After you have woven the mat, stitch around the edges to prevent fraying. Make enough mats for a set of four, six, or any number that you want.

CEMENT MORTAR

Cement mortar is needed for some of the construction projects described in this book. To make it, take one part of cement and mix with two parts of sand. Add enough water to make the mixture pliable. Sand helps to keep the cement from cracking.

CHAIN CHARADES

A GUESSING GAME

This game is a favorite with boys and girls. Begin by dividing the class into two teams or by letting them choose sides. Then Team 1 leaves the room while Team 2 selects an incident that may be pantomimed easily. They may choose incidents, such as firemen rescuing a woman from a burning building, a man finding a burglar in his bedroom, a woman learning to drive an automobile, a boy taking his puppy for a walk on a leash.

One player from Team 1 is invited to return. An actor from Team 2 pantomimes the incident. The returned player watches intently and tries to guess the incident that is being pantomimed. Team 2 does not tell him whether he is right or wrong. A second player from Team 1 is called in, and the first player now re-acts the incident as he saw it. The second player tries to come up with an answer, but he, too, is not told whether he is correct. This procedure continues until all the players on Team 1 have had a turn. Then Team 2 repeats the original performance, which may not be recognizable by the performance of the last actor.

The teams reverse the order of play and the game continues.

CHAIN MAIL

An item of costuming that is in frequent demand for "just a simple little play" is chain mail for the knight. The effect of chain mail may be achieved with mop cloth. Get the kind that has a heavy weave, large knots, and deep ridges. Textile wholesalers usually carry it. Dye the mop cloth dark gray. For further embellishment touch the tops of the knots with silvered aluminum paint.

Mop cloth usually comes in tube form. It is a handy and effective material for soldiers' armor. The costume may be worn with a cord around the waist.

CHARADES

Charades that call for the pantomiming of syllables in words are usually too difficult for pupils in the elementary grades. There are, however, simpler forms of charades. Nursery rhymes, fairy tales, myths, and proverbs, for example, are almost inexhaustible sources for this type of guessing game.

Divide the group into two sides or teams. Each team takes its turn at acting out a charade. Team 1 leaves the room. The home group, Team 2, prepares the charade. Then Team 1 is recalled and its players try to guess the charade. Now Team 1 leaves the room while No. 2 prepares a charade.

A team may exhibit originality and organization in pantomiming maxims, such as: "Great oaks from little acorns grow"; "He laughs best who laughs last"; "Blest be the tie that binds."

Stimulated by team spirit, children forget themselves and gain naturalness in acting.

CHARM STRINGS

A CHRISTMAS DECORATION

In bygone times people made charm strings to chase away evil spirits. The strings were hung on doors at Christmas time. They were made of materials that were supposed to bring good luck, such as evergreens, pine cones, juniper boughs, burrs, pods, holly, bird feathers, sleigh bells, and ribbons.

A modern charm string may be made of the same kind of materials. The materials may be used in their lovely natural colors; or, if you wish to add glitter, paint or gild them. In whatever form you use it, the charm string is a beautiful decoration for the Christmas holiday season.

CHECKERBOARD

Children often enjoy making their own checkerboards. Start by cutting a 14 x 14-inch square from heavy cardboard. This size allows for a 1-inch border on all four sides and for a playing area 12 x 12 inches. After allowing for the border, mark off 8 squares across and 8 down. Each space will be $1\frac{1}{2}$ inches square.

Color alternate squares black with India ink or crayon. Start with the first row in the upper left-hand corner and go across. Allow the first square to remain uncolored.

Color squares 2, 4, 6, 8 in row 1
Color squares 1, 3, 5, 7 in row 2

Continue to color alternate squares until you have colored 32 squares. The board is now ready for play.

CHECKERS

Checkers may be made from a number of materials described below. Twenty-four men or checkers are needed for the game, 12 white and 12 red. Make a few spares for good measure.

1. Checkers may be made from a discarded *broomstick*. Saw the stick crosswise into slices. Sandpaper the checkers and then paint 12 of them red. The other 12 may be shellacked.

2. They may be made from *milk bottle tops*. Scrape off the wax and paint 12 of them red, or color them with crayon. The other 12 may be used as they are.

3. They may be made from *English walnut shells* by cracking 12 walnuts into unbroken halves. Paint 12 of them red. After

the paint is dry, shellac the red shells and also the other 12 in their natural color.

4. They may be made from *buttonmolds*. Paint 12 of them red and shellac the other 12.

5. They may be made from *soda pop bottle caps*. Paint 12 of them red. Clean the other 12 and use them as they are.

CHINESE CHECKERBOARD

In recent years the game of Chinese checkers has become popular in the United States. Like checkers it is a board game, but the board has not been standardized so you will come upon various sizes. The board described here has 73 holes and 36 marbles. Others have as many as 121 holes and 60 marbles.

To make a Chinese checkerboard select a heavy cardboard 18 x 18 inches square. Plan to make the playing area 16 x 16 inches, which allows for a border of 1 inch on all four sides. Draw a 6-pointed star that will fit the 16 x 16-inch space. If you study the picture, you will see that a 6-pointed star is made of two equilateral triangles that interlock.

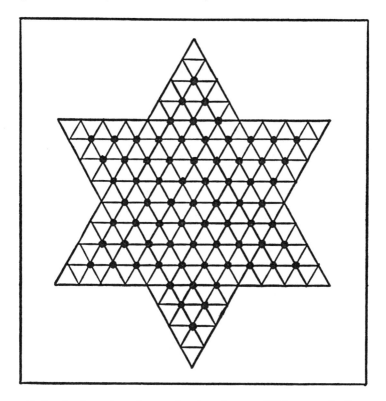

Rule the board as shown in the picture. With a penknife or razor blade, cut 73 round holes at the intersections of the lines. Cut the holes small enough so that they will support a marble.

You will need 36 marbles in six colors: 6 yellow, 6 white, 6 green, 6 blue, 6 red, and 6 black. The object of the game is to move your marbles from one point of the star to the opposite one before your adversary can move his marbles. The game may be played with two, four, or six players.

CHICKEN AND THE HAWK

AN OUTDOOR GAME FOR ANY NUMBER OF PLAYERS

In this game one of the players is chosen to be the hawk. The other players are chickens who pretend that they are eating corn in the chickenyard. The hawk decides secretly on a chick that he wants to catch and then swoops down on it. The chickens rapidly circle and try to hide the chick that they think the hawk is after.

If the chickens guess correctly, the hawk flies away to try again a moment later. If they have guessed wrong, the hawk calls the name of the chick that he is after. The chickens try quickly to circle the chick. If he catches the chick, the hawk carries it away.

The hawk continues to catch as many chickens as he can until everyone is caught. The last one caught becomes the next hawk.

A CHRISTMAS BELL

An attractive bell may be made from colored paper. From paper about the thickness of shelf paper cut a strip that is approximately 1½ yards long and 3½ inches high. Wallpaper also is suitable. Fold the paper back and forth like an accordion as in the figure at the left. Make each fold 2½ inches deep.

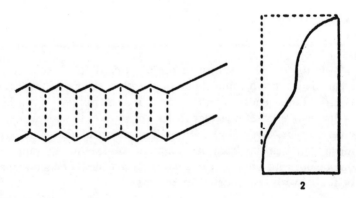

2

Draw and cut a pattern of half a bell from any kind of paper. Place the pattern on the tightly folded paper and cut out the

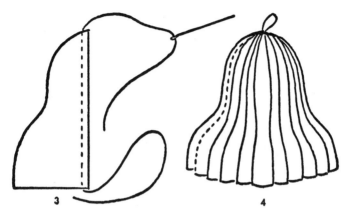

half bell as in the second figure. Cut along the black line which forms the outline of the bell. Then sew through the other side, which is also composed of many folds (Fig. 3). Now draw the sides of the bell around to form a circle. Sew the two ends together. Allow a thread long enough to make a loop for hanging the bell on the tree. The bell will look like the one in the picture at the right.

CHRISTMAS CANDLES

Save the stub ends of candles. When you have a goodly number, a dozen or so, melt the pieces. Put them in a saucepan and heat over a very low flame or on a hot radiator until the wax is melted.

To make a short, square candle use a low half-and-half milk carton or a similar container for a mold. If you wish to make a tall, square candle, use a quart size milk carton. Pour the melted wax into the carton. For a wick, dip a string in hot wax and hold it vertically in the center of the mold while pouring in the wax. When the wax is cold, in about twenty-four hours, break away the cardboard carton.

CHRISTMAS CARD ENVELOPES

From a sheet of light colored construction paper, cut an envelope similar to the pattern illustrated. The size and shape of the envelope, of course, needs to be adapted to that of the card. Make the envelope a trifle larger than the card.

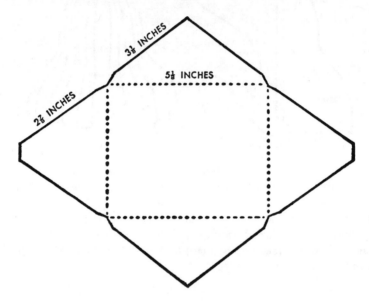

To make an envelope 5⅛ x 3⅛ inches use a sheet of paper 11 x 8½ inches. Follow the dimensions given on the pattern. The dotted lines indicate the position of the folds. Fold the right and left sides toward the center. Then fold the bottom flap toward the center. Glue the edges together. Fold the top toward the center. Then fold back to apply the glue and let dry before folding back again.

CHRISTMAS CARDS

The manner of making Christmas cards and the kinds of cards that may be made are limited only by people's ingenuity. In this

48

project we shall limit the making of cards to the types of designs that lend themselves well to the three methods of printing or reproducing designs, explained elsewhere in this book.

The methods are (1) block printing (linoleum-block printing, page 153 and potato-block printing, page 212); (2) blueprinting flowers and leaves, page 24; and (3) spatter printing described on page 252.

Block printing.—For linoleum-block printing, plan a design with a minimum of detail, such as a candle, a stylized Christmas tree, bells, a church steeple, or an angel. Potato-block printing lends itself well to a small allover design, as a sprig of holly or a holly leaf or two. An allover pattern may be stamped many times on the front of the card, depending upon the size that you are making. Be careful to allow a goodly amount of space around each stamping. Use a stamp pad with red ink for holly berries and green for leaves.

Blueprinting.—Embellish Christmas cards with pictures of holly, poinsettia, mistletoe. If you wish to get away from the conventional, use other flowers and leaves that you like (see page 24).

Spatter printing.—Stick to designs with a minimum of detail, such as those suggested for block printing. Spatter printing may be used on many kinds of paper.

A CHRISTMAS LANTERN

A lantern may be made from a round oatmeal carton or from a shoe box used perpendicularly. Cut off the top and bottom of the carton or box. Cut patterns of filigree; that is, ornamental openwork in the sides of the lantern. Try cutting diamond-shaped openings, circles, squares, perhaps a candy cane, a bell, any design that appeals to you. To enhance the lighting effect, paste colored tissue paper or cellophane over the openings on the inside of the lantern. Paint the outside green or a pastel color. If you use a pastel color, you will need to give the oatmeal carton at least two coats in order to paint out the dark colors.

To complete the festive lantern, fit it over an electric light.

CHRISTMAS TREE ORNAMENTS

The possibilities for making Christmas tree ornaments and decorations are limitless and everyone has a few favorite tricks of his own.

In this project a number of materials are listed. Suggestions are given for making ornaments from these materials. Some of the materials are close at hand in many communities while others can usually be secured without too much difficulty.

ACORNS

In the fall gather a small quantity of acorns. Be careful not to rob the squirrels. Gild, silver, or paint the acorns. Make a small loop from a thin strip of Scotch tape. Fasten the loop to the top of the acorn and thread it with a string for a fastener.

COLORED PAPER

The possibilities for making ornaments from colored paper are many. You may make paper chains, bells (pages 46–47), gingerbread men (page 124), rainbow pictures (page 226).

COTTON

Roll cotton into snowballs. If the snowball needs to be rounded, shape the cotton here and there and fasten it with needle and thread. Fluff the cotton a bit. Then daub glue on the cotton ball and sprinkle with sequins or confetti.

In addition to fashioning snowballs, you may also cut bells and stars from cotton and apply the sequins in the same manner.

CRANBERRIES

With a stout needle, string cranberries on a string substantial enough to carry the weight of the berries. Make the string as long or short as you like.

Cranberries strung on fine wire may be shaped into figurines like those made from berries and twigs on page 19.

LIGHT BULBS

Burned-out light bulbs make handsome ornaments. Lacquer or cover them with colored sawdust or confetti. Coat the glass bulb with glue and sprinkle with confetti or sawdust. To color sawdust, mix it with wet tempera or calcimine paint and put the mixture on a newspaper to dry. Fasten a fine wire around the neck of the bulb and hang the ornament on the tree.

PINE CONES

Small pine cones may be hung on the Christmas tree separately or in chains. If you wish, you may gild, silver, or paint them. Larger cones may be trimmed to look like miniature Christmas trees. You may wish to use the cones in their natural color. Trim them with cotton, tinsel, tiny colored paper chains, or yarn.

POPCORN

With a needle and strong thread, make a string of popcorn as long as you like.

RINGS

Attractive chains can be made from fruit jar rubbers or from rings cut from an old inner tube. If you decide to make rings from an inner tube, make them about the size of fruit jar rings. Lacquer, silver, or gild the rings, and make a chain by tying them together with thread.

TINFOIL

Save scraps of tinfoil and silver colored paper. Smooth out the tinfoil and keep it in a box until you are ready to use it. From cardboard, cut bells, stars, candy canes, Christmas stockings, angels, clowns, bears, giraffes, monkeys. Cover the cardboard on both sides with tinfoil or silver paper, pasting as you proceed. Thread a short string through the top, and the glittering ornament is ready to be hung on the tree.

CIGAR BOX VIOLIN

To make a violin from a cigar box, you need these materials:

  1 wooden cigar box 6 x 8½ x 2½ inches
  1 piece of soft pine board 12 x 2½ x ¾ inches
  1 small piece of wood 2½ x 1 x ¼ inches for the "bridge"
  4 wooden pegs cut from sucker sticks
  4 violin strings. These may be horsehair, fine wire, or
  catgut violin strings

Use the cigar box for the "chest" of the violin; the long pine board for the "neck"; and the small piece of board for the "bridge." Drill 4 small holes in one end of the narrow board large enough to accommodate the wooden pegs made from sucker sticks. Arrange the holes in two rows, placing the second row to one side of the first to allow for fastening the violin strings.

Place the cigar box in front of you on a table with the open side of the cover toward you; that is, with the hinge of the cover away from you. Open the cover and drill four small holes in one end of the cigar box at position B. Nail the pine board "neck" to the other end of the cigar box. Place the board or "neck" so that it is slightly below the level of the box. Drive the nails through the box into the end of the board from the inside.

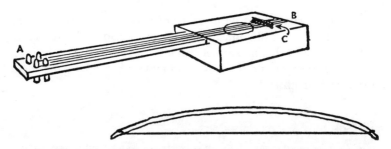

Glue down the top of the box securely. Cut a round opening in the top as in the illustration. This is the sound hole. Cut a "bridge" 2½ x 1 x ¼ inches and glue it to the cigar box at C. Tie the violin strings in the holes at B and to the pegs at A.

Make a bow, suitable in size from a flexible branch or strip of wood. String it with horse hair or fine wire.

CITRUS FRUIT PIG

FOR THE PRIMARY GRADES

A clever little pig may be made with an orange, a small lemon, raisins, six toothpicks, and several Brazil nuts. Use the orange for the body and the lemon for the head. Let the pointed end of the lemon form the snout. Fasten the head to the body with toothpicks. To make the ears, cut two strips in the lemon rind and peel back. Do not cut off the strips but form them into ears. Stick four toothpicks through raisins to form the legs. Anchor the legs at an angle so that

the pig can stand on all fours. Make the feet from Brazil nuts. Cut out the hoofs for a cloven-footed effect. Cut the orange rind and peel back a very narrow strip for the tail.

A CLASS MEMORY BOOK

FOR THE ELEMENTARY GRADES

A memory book of class and school events sustains children's interest over a period of time, and supplies the class with a record of its elementary school days. Events and occasions worthy of being included in a book of this type are classroom plays, athletic contests in which members of the class participate, mothers' teas, music recitals and choruses, picnics, and field trips. Children's individual contributions may include art work, snapshots, letters, creative writing perhaps in the form of reports on class activities and special events.

For a memory book make a large loose-leaf scrapbook. Bind the memory book by lacing with shoestrings or strong cord. This type of book permits the removal of sheets so that several people may work on the project at the same time.

A CLASSROOM ELECTION

FOR THE UPPER GRADES

Class activities provide excellent opportunities for expressions of opinion. The teacher and pupils may need to discuss plans, projects, and programs for the school year. They may want to concern themselves with matters, such as classroom management, class excursions, parties, committee work, playground activities, and raising money for school and community drives. To arrive at a decision about these matters calls for discussion and finally for an expression of opinion from everyone. So why not have a classroom election based upon issues and party affiliations?

During the course of the school year groups or parties spring up to start and carry on a program or project. One group, for instance, may favor greater pupil participation in classroom management and call itself the Self Government party. Another group may sponsor a thrift program and name itself the Save-for-Christmas party. A group, interested in improving playground activities, may be the Sportsman party.

Like the great political parties, each group party may hold a convention to nominate candidates, to draw up a platform, and to make preparations to have its candidates elected. The candidates and their supporters may try to influence the voters by making speeches and personal appearances. Finally, a board is appointed to conduct the election by secret ballot, and the voters go to the polling place to cast their ballots. A coat closet with a curtain across the doorway may serve as a polling booth. Then after the polls have closed, the election board counts the ballots and announces the results.

THE CLASSROOM LIBRARY

The sources from which the elementary grades receive library books and the number of books which they receive vary greatly from community to community. In some towns and cities large enough to have a public library, the library board and the school board work hand in hand to provide books for the elementary grades. In other school systems, the school board supplies and houses books in a central school library where teachers may go to check out books for their classroom needs. Many public libraries offer special services to teachers. Teachers, for example, are given access to picture files and the privilege of checking out large numbers of pictures and books.

In communities that have meager collections of books or none at all, systems of interlibrary loans often aid the teacher in obtaining the materials she needs. Information about loan collections may usually be secured from your state library commission. Bookmobiles are extending into more and more rural areas. When all other resources fail, the class may decide upon some activity such as a puppet show or bazaar to raise money to buy books.

Whatever may be the manner in which books are secured and whatever may be the number, be it 12 or 1200, the teacher and pupils of the elementary school very often must devise ways of housing and circulating books. If this is the situation, try to locate the library in a corner of the room or perhaps in a space between windows. Suggestions for making book cases and for circulating books that children may carry out co-operatively are given below.

For low, open shelves nail together several orange crates or apple boxes. Sandpaper the rough edges and apply a coat of lacquer or calcimine paint. Books may be shelved in groups such as science (nature study), story books, history, lives of people. Label the shelves to aid the reader in locating books. Use cardboard for lettering the labels and attach to shelves.

Let the class choose a "librarian," a person who is neat and a capable worker. His duties are to check books out and in, to report missing and badly worn books, and to assume responsibility for the orderliness of the library. A system of library cards and book pockets may also be worked out if the library has enough books. The librarian may need an assistant.

If instruction in the care of books has not been given earlier, now is an excellent opportunity to do so. Select a committee to mend books. You, as teacher, may need to give instruction on how to repair torn pages, loose leaves, and loose hinges.

Pupils may wish to give their library some publicity. They may prepare posters, book borders (page 24), or join the "Professors' Club," page 213.

THE CLASS SOCIAL HOUR

Set aside a short period of time—perhaps a recess—at regular intervals for a social period. Try to make the period a natural, friendly sort of thing, an occasion when children enjoy bringing in their friends from other rooms.

A boy or girl, for example, may enjoy introducing his guest to some of his friends and in chatting with them. To get the conversation started he may say, "John's hobby is the same as yours, Jack. He builds miniature racing cars. Tell him about the model that you are making." Mary may say, "Elizabeth has a Scotty which does amazing tricks." Usually the ice is broken and they're off! The children may enjoy taking their guests around to some of the class displays.

In addition to these voluntary, friendly gestures, there are activities that lend themselves to group participation. The class may extend an invitation to another room to attend a program, a play, an exhibit, an excursion, or a picnic.

A CLASS SYMPOSIUM

FOR THE INTERMEDIATE AND UPPER GRADES

Once or twice a week the class may get together for an informal discussion period. To prepare for the meeting, boys and girls gather articles and pictures from newspapers and magazines. They bring poems, short stories, or other items that may be of special interest to them.

The class president takes charge of the meeting and leads the discussion. The teacher is a member of the "audience," perhaps in the rear of the classroom.

CLAY ANIMALS

FOR THE PRIMARY GRADES

Children enjoy making clay animals from modeling clay. You will need some clay and several animal-shaped cooky cutters. Perhaps the children can induce their mothers to let them bring cooky cutters to school.

Roll the clay in the same way as you would pie crust. Roll it into a smooth sheet about ¼ inch thick, and cut out the animals with the cooky cutters. While the clay is still pliable, flatten the animals' feet a bit so that you can stand up the animals. When the clay is dry, paint and then shellac.

CLAY BOOKENDS

Because of its weight and bulk, modeling clay is a good material to use for making bookends. It lends itself well to molding shapes and forms, such as animals, large balls, cubes, or thick

right angles. Plan to make the base at least 6 x 6 inches and the upright part, if it is an animal, about 8 inches high. To keep the bookend from marring the furniture, glue felt to the bottom of the base and to the back of the upright. Finish with calcimine paint, varnish, or shellac. (For bookends made from wood, such as orange crates, see pages 25–26.)

A CLOTHESPIN APRON

FOR A GIFT

A practical clothespin apron may be made from materials such as denim, burlap, sugar or flour sacking. You will need ⅔ of a yard of material. Cut a piece lengthwise 24 inches (⅔ yard) long and 15 inches wide. Fold back 8 inches of the material to make the pockets as in the illustration. Turn the raw edges at the sides about a quarter inch and hem. Stitch down the middle of the folded part to make the pockets.

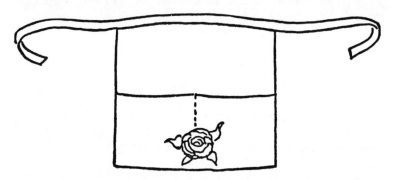

For the band and apron strings prepare a strip 3 inches wide from the material that you cut off the side. You probably will need two 24-inch strips. Sew the strips together and fold down the middle lengthwise. This makes a band 48 inches long and 1½ inches wide before the seams come off. Sew the band to the apron, fitting a small amount of fullness to the band. Trim the apron any way that you like. Embroidering a rose with yarn in appropriate colors is effective.

CLOTHESPIN DOLLS

To make clothespin dolls—both girl and boy dolls—you need a clothespin and a pipe cleaner for each, a bit of yarn, a scrap of crepe paper or starched cotton print, India ink, and yellow wax.

Paint the face of the girl doll on the clothespin. Use yellow wax to make the hair. Soften the wax and spread it over the top of the clothespin. If you like, make the hair from yarn instead. Wind the middle of the pipe cleaner around the neck of the clothespin and let the two ends form the arms.

Make the skirt from a strip of crepe paper or starched cloth, gather and sew to a band. The crepe paper or material should be stiff enough to support the doll. Cut a triangle from crepe paper or cloth for a shawl.

Paint the face for the boy doll and fashion the hair in the same way as you did for the girl. To make the trousers, wrap the prongs of the clothespin with crepe paper. Support the doll by pressing its feet into a platform of wax.

CLOTHES SPRINKLING BOTTLE

FOR A GIFT

An attractive bottle for sprinkling clothes may be made from a vinegar or catchup bottle. To make the sprinkler, drive holes in the bottle top with a small nail. Paint a design on the bottle with lacquer or nail polish.

COASTERS

FOR A GIFT

The possibilities for making coasters to protect a table from moisture are varied, and additional suggestions will occur to everyone. Felt trimmed with yarn, sheet cork painted with nail polish or lacquer, and inner tubing are only a few of the suitable materials. Coasters may be made any desired size or shape. The usual shape, however, is circular. Whatever may be the shape, allow an area about three inches in diameter on which to set the tumbler. Coasters are more useful when made in sets.

CODE PUZZLES

Code puzzles offer a challenge to students who finish their work ahead of the others and who always are ready for more work.

1. Code Puzzle
YY U R, YY U B
I C U R YY 4 me

Boys and girls take delight in inventing their own codes or secret messages. The teacher may give them some hints about the codes described here and encourage them to experiment.

2. Number Code Puzzle
3–15–13–5 6–15–18 4–9–14–14–5–18

Each letter of the alphabet has been replaced by the number which indicates its sequence in the alphabet, as 1 stands for *a*, 2 for *b*, 3 for *c*, etc.

3. Alphabet Code Puzzle
d p n f g p s e j o o f s

In this case, each letter in the original message has been replaced by the next letter in the alphabet. Thus, *d* stands for *c*, *p* for *o*, *n* for *m*, etc.

Answers to Code Puzzles
1. Too wise you are, too wise you be
   I see you are too wise for me.
2. Come for dinner
3. Come for dinner

CODE RHYTHM GAMES

Games based upon code rhythms are perennial favorites with children. The dots and dashes, the longs and shorts of telegraph codes, for example, are based on rhythm and hold a fascination for the uninitiated.

To play a rhythm game divide the class into two teams and clap out a rhythm, such as "Pop Goes the Weasel," "Yankee

Doodle," "Old Black Joe," "America." The players on each team take turns in imitating the rhythm. If he succeeds in giving an accurate imitation, the first clapper on Team 1 scores a point for his team. If he fails, the first clapper on Team 2 takes up the challenge. If he succeeds, the clapper scores a point for his team. If he does not, the play goes back to the second clapper on Team 1. If the rhythm is lost before any one imitates it successfully, the teacher may repeat it; or, to sustain interest, she may clap out a new one after a rhythm has been missed once by each team. The teacher is the judge of the rhythms, and the team scoring the greater number of points wins.

Tapping, humming, or drum beats may be substituted for clapping. Basic rhythms may be repeated frequently. Gage the complexity of the rhythm upon the grade level of the children and upon the skill that they have developed in rhythm games.

COLONIAL GAMES AND SONGS

Many of our songs and singing games have come down from colonial times. Some had been brought to the Thirteen Colonies by Europeans immigrating to America. These songs and games may be used for various occasions during the course of the school year. For example, what more appropriate material can be found to enliven an observance of Washington's birthday? Or in connection with a unit on colonial life? Or "just for singing"? Many song and music books for the elementary grades contain a number of these songs and singing games.

"Hail Columbia," a patriotic song, by Joseph Hopkinson
"Itiskit, Itaskit," a singing game
"Jennie Jenkins," a song
"London Bridge," an old singing game
"Looby Loo," a singing game
"Old Man in the Woods," a singing game sometimes known as "Old Grumble." The singers pantomime the lyrics.
"Pop Goes the Weasel!" a folk song and game
"Ring-around-a-Rosy," a singing game
"Yankee Doodle," a song

A COLONIAL HAT

A hat for the colonial period may be made from a rectangular piece of paper 32 x 22½ inches. Use construction or butcher paper. To get the knack of it, practice folding a hat with a sheet of newspaper. It is just the right size. Instructions for folding are given below.

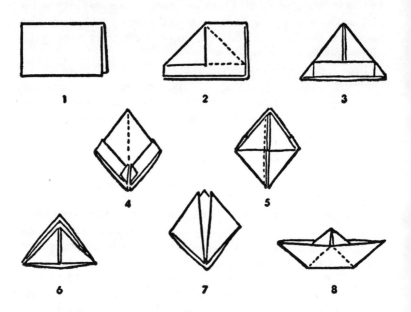

1. Fold the paper crosswise.
2. Fold the two folded ends so that they meet in the center.
3. Fold the two bottom strips upward, one on either side.
4. Tuck the overhanging flaps under each other and draw the two bottom corners of the hat together, refolding it to make a square.
5. Bring one bottom point up to the top of the hat.
6. Do the same with the other bottom point.
7. Again take the two bottom points of the hat and bring them together, refolding to make a square.
8. Grasp the top of the hat lightly and slide back the outside layer and there is your hat, which looks slightly like a boat.

A COLOR WHEEL THAT SPINS

Color relationships can be demonstrated by a spinning color wheel like the one illustrated. From cardboard cut out a circle approximately 4 inches in diameter. Color it red, yellow, and blue as indicated by the letters *Y*, *B*, and *R*. These are the primary colors. Punch two small holes in the center of the circle as in a button. Thread the circle with twine about a yard long and tie the ends together. Roll the twine and then pull it. As you pull it, the twine winds and unwinds in a purring rhythm and turns the color chart at the same time.

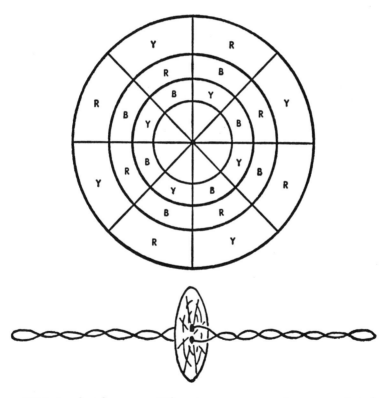

This is what happens: When two or more colors are painted side by side on a color wheel and when the wheel is spun, the colors blend to make a different color.

A COOKY JAR

A cooky jar may be made from an oatmeal box or other round container. Cover the box with small-figured wallpaper or with printed calico or chintz. You may prefer to decorate with calcimine paint or red and white crepe paper. For instructions for decorating objects with crepe paper, see page 85.

CORNCOB INDIANS

To make Indians, you will need corncobs, some cornhusks, and colored yarn or string. If the corncobs and husks are still quite green, let them dry. Harvested ears of corn are best. Husk the ears by stripping off the external covering and shell the corn off the cob by hand.

Use a corncob for the body of each Indian that you make. Fashion the trousers, blanket, and headdress from the cornhusks as in the illustration. Paint in the face and costume details.

Make the foundation for the papoose cradleboard from a piece of cardboard. Cover the cradleboard part with a cornhusk and thread the yarn or string crisscross as in the picture. Paint the head of the papoose.

CORNHUSK CREATIONS

If you live in an area where cornhusks are easily obtainable, you have an inexpensive substitute for raffia, a material used for baskets, hats, table mats, and dolls. Most farms and restaurants will supply classrooms with corncobs and husks in quantity when corn is in season.

Husk the corn by stripping off the external covering. Dry the husks and store. Then when needed soak them in water until soft, and wrap in a towel to take up the excess moisture. Cut or tear the husks into long narrow strips and weave while they are still pliant. If you wait until the husks are dry, they will be too brittle.

Cornhusks may be used for weaving such articles as small baskets, dolls' hats, table mats, carpets for doll houses, and for making Indian dolls (see opposite page).

A CORNSTALK FIDDLE

Select a cornstalk with pliant fibers and cut it off just beyond two adjacent joints. With a sharp penknife cut four parallel slits lengthwise along the fibers of the stalk from joint to joint. Cut each slit approximately $\frac{1}{8}$ inch deep and allow $\frac{1}{8}$ inch between slits. Slip the knife blade gently under each slit and raise the fibrous material to form a string. There will be three strings instead of the usual four.

Carve a tiny bridge from balsam wood. Insert the bridge under the strings near one end of the cornstalk. Use a small cornstalk for the bow. You can play a squeaky tune on this tiny fiddle.

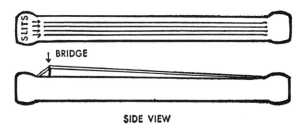

SIDE VIEW

CORRUGATED PAPER MINIATURES

Here is an excellent use for the corrugated paper that you have been saving. Use it for making miniature jungle huts, Spanish tile roofs, colonial cabins, stockades, and picket fences. It is also an excellent imitation of a plowed field. Corrugated paper is normally used as a protective wrapper and as a lining for cardboard cartons.

JUNGLE HUT

To make a jungle hut, fashion a cylinder from corrugated paper so that the corrugations run vertically to resemble bamboo. Add a cone-shaped cardboard roof. Cut an opening in the hut for a door, or bend the cardboard back to form flaps for an entryway. The flaps may be ornamented with drawings.

SPANISH TILE ROOF

Cut a rectangle from corrugated paper the size of the roof, and fold in the middle to form a pitched roof. Arrange the paper so that the corrugations run vertically; that is, from the ridge of the roof to the eaves. Paint the roof red.

COLONIAL LOG CABIN AND STOCKADE

Corrugated paper forms an excellent imitation of logs in making a pioneer's cabin and stockade. Use the corrugations horizontally for the log cabin. Use the paper vertically, however, for the stockade, since it is a line of posts placed closely together that forms the barrier. Cut loopholes in the stockade for lookouts.

PICKET FENCE

Cut a strip of paper the height of the fence that you are making. Use the corrugations vertically to represent wooden pickets. Cut the top into a series of points or pickets. A quick, easy way to achieve this effect is to use pinking shears. A picket fence is useful in constructing a model miniature community.

PLOWED FIELD

Place the corrugated paper flatly to make plowed prairie land. If you wish to show rolling fields, mold a rolling terrain from papier-mâché and cover it with the corrugated paper. Paint the plowed fields the color of soil.

COSTUME DOLLS OF LINCOLN'S GENERATION

A PROJECT FOR LINCOLN'S BIRTHDAY

The clothes worn by the people of Lincoln's generation may be recreated by dressing dolls in the costumes of that period. Clothespins may be used for dolls, crepe paper for clothes, and poster paints or colored ink for drawing in the details. (See also "Clothespin Dolls," pages 58 and 59.)

A Lincoln and Mary Todd in miniature, generals of the War between the States, and belles of the South may form a part of the colorful assembly.

COSTUME JEWELRY

The possibilities for making costume jewelry are many, and everyone has a few ideas of his own. In this project directions are given for five varieties made from (1) paper, (2) macaroni, (3) gumdrops, (4) rubber washers, and (5) paste.

PAPER BEAD NECKLACE

To make a bead, cut construction paper into a strip 6 inches long and 1 inch wide at one end and taper off to a point as in the picture on the next page. Starting with the wide end, roll the strip on a kitchen match or toothpick and paste the paper down as you proceed. Pull out the match or toothpick to leave a hole through which to string the bead.

Before you settle on the size of the bead, experiment with the thickness of the paper and the length of the strip. In addition to construction paper, try out a thin paper. Select a brightly colored

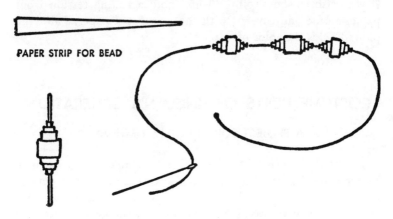

PAPER STRIP FOR BEAD

page from a magazine, and cut a strip about 12 inches long and ½ inch at the wide end of the paper.

Make as many beads as you need for a necklace and tie a bow, with narrow ribbon.

MACARONI BEADS

Interesting beads may be made from macaroni since it comes in a variety of shapes and sizes. Grocery stores carrying Italian food excel in interesting macaroni. Some comes in shapes ready to be used for beads. Other kinds must be heated in water until the macaroni is soft enough to be pierced with a needle. Color the macaroni beads any color you like by dipping them into a vegetable dye. Spread the beads on a newspaper to dry and then string the beads for a necklace or bracelet.

GUMDROP NECKLACE

Gumdrops of all shapes and sizes may be cut and pinched into realistic baubles. To make a "pearl" necklace fit for a queen, select small, round, light colored gumdrops. With a large needle and strong thread, string them into a "string of pearls."

Assorted long and short gumdrops may be made into a string resembling an Indian's tooth necklace. A cone-shaped gumdrop may be used for a flashy ring. Thread a string through the lower part of the gumdrop with a needle and tie around the finger on which you wish to wear the ring. Bracelets, of course, may be made to match the necklaces and rings.

Do not plan to wear gumdrop jewelry during hot weather.

RUBBER WASHERS

Attractive chains, girdles, necklaces, and bracelets may be made of washers cut from inner tubing. Adapt the size of the washers to the size of the article that you want to make. Graduated sizes, for example, are attractive for necklaces. Paint the washers by dipping them into lacquer and hanging them up to dry.

To link the washers into a necklace, cut every other washer and link it into an uncut washer. Mend the break with rubber cement. Fasten the necklace with a narrow ribbon.

PASTE JEWELRY

Costume jewelry—beads, hatpins, bracelets—may be made with dough. To make the paste you need these ingredients:

¾ cup of flour
½ cup of cornstarch
½ cup of salt

Mix the ingredients in a bowl. Add warm water gradually until the mixture can be kneaded into a stiff dough. Dust with dry flour to reduce stickiness. Roll the dough thin, cut off a long strip, and with your hands roll into a long round strip. Cut the strip into bead-size segments. These may be used in this shape or they may be rolled into balls. Pierce the bead with a toothpick and allow to dry. Pull out the toothpick to leave a hole through which to string the bead. Finish the bead by painting with nail polish or lacquer.

If you are making a hatpin, form the dough into a ball and spear on one end of a long pin. Paint the ball with nail polish or lacquer, and enhance with a tiny design, if you wish.

COSTUMES FOR WOODLAND FAIRIES

Fairyland elves and pixies live in the forests and spend much of their time dancing and resting in trees. Their costumes may be made from the leaves of large-leaved plants. Leaves suitable for this type of costume are elephant's-ears, cannas, figs, and pond lilies. Since many of these plants are not available in most regions, nor in sufficient quantities, cut the leaves from green crepe paper. Get a shade of green that is called forest green.

For a foundation garment on which to sew the leaves, use a bathing suit, sports shirt and shorts, or a slip with a built-up shoulder. A simple dress will serve equally well.

COSTUMING WITH CHEESECLOTH

Cheesecloth is a material that is sometimes used for costuming "just a simple little classroom play." It is often used for Halloween costumes and for fairies and angels. It is especially suitable for accessories, such as sashes, headdresses, fichus.

Some play costumers, however, do not recommend cheesecloth for entire costumes, since it is not very satisfactory and therefore expensive.

COTTAGE CHEESE

Cottage cheese, or Dutch cheese as it is sometimes called, is the dried curd of sour milk. To start it, allow milk to sour in a covered jar. Place it in a warm (not hot) place until the whey, or liquid part of the milk, separates from the curd. Another way to sour milk is to heat a small quantity—1 quart perhaps—of old milk slowly and watch it curdle. Here, too, the whey separates from the curd.

Pour all of it, the curds and whey, into a cheesecloth. Press the curds to squeeze out the whey. Pour cold water through to wash away more whey. The remaining curds form cottage cheese.

The germs, or lactic acid bacteria, which make the milk curdle work best in warm milk. In addition to affording a lesson in science, the cottage cheese, when seasoned with salt and pepper, makes an enjoyable classroom treat. Serve it with crackers.

CRAYON AND PENCIL HOLDER

A porcupine-shaped holder for crayons and pencils is a handy device to help keep a desk in order. Fashion a porcupine from modeling clay. Make the porcupine small enough to fit into a

child's desk. While the clay is still wet, make a number of holes large enough to accommodate crayons and several smaller ones for pencils. The crayons and pencils form the porcupine's quills or spines. Paint the holder and after it is dry, shellac it.

CRAYON BOX REFILLS

Individual crayon boxes can be kept in good order by keeping a general supply box for crayons on hand in the schoolroom. Stray crayons that children find on the floor and odds and ends that anyone has on hand at the time of starting a new box may be added to the general supply box. Whenever he lacks a color, a child helps himself to a crayon. This procedure encourages trustworthiness and a wholesome respect for the rights of others. A general crayon box is a convenience.

A CRAYON FINISH

Pictures drawn with crayon and areas colored with crayon may be given a glossy finish by rubbing the drawing briskly with a cloth. Bear down heavily upon the rubbing surface.

CREATING AN ATMOSPHERE FOR GHOST STORIES

To help create an eerie atmosphere for Halloween ghost stories, prepare a sputtering candle by cutting its wick. Sink the point of a manicure scissors into the candle at several points near the top and cut the wick. To disguise the holes, fill them with hot wax.

If it is feasible, draw the shades to darken the room enough for candlelight. Light the candle, keeping it near you but safely out of the children's reach. Begin with a spooky tale and build it up until the children are wide eyed with wonder. Suddenly the candle sputters and goes out. Relight it and ask another child, perhaps one who knows the trick, to continue with the tale.

The candle sputters and goes out again. The children wonder if ghosts are blowing it out. Each time the candle is relighted ask someone else to continue with the story which, by this time, is proceeding in a spooky, Halloween tradition.

CREATING A PARTIAL VACUUM

A partial vacuum can be made by performing this experiment. You will need a glass bowl, a glass tumbler, a jar lid, and a candle about 2 inches long.

Soften the bottom end of the candle over a low flame. A lighted match will do the trick. Place the soft end of the candle on the jar lid. The candle will stay in an upright position as soon as the wax cools. Set the candle in the glass bowl and pour in enough water until most of the candle is submerged. Allow about $\frac{1}{2}$ inch of the candle to remain above the surface of the water.

Light the candle, invert the tumbler, and lower it over the candle into the water. The flame will burn up the oxygen from the air in the tumbler. This creates a partial vacuum. The water in the bowl will rise inside the tumbler because air presses down on the water in the bowl and forces it to rise in the tumbler. The water may even rise high enough to put out the flame.

CREATING DESIGNS WITH PAPER SCRAPS

The odds and ends of colored paper that are left over from construction work and handicraft projects may be put to a useful purpose. Put the scraps in a pile and let everyone help himself. Equip each worker with a sheet of white paper $8\frac{1}{2}$ x 11 inches, scissors, and a pat of paste. Encourage children to visualize a design in the size and shape of the paper. A long, narrow strip, for example, may resemble a tree trunk. Another narrow, ribbon-like strip may resemble a winding river or a road. If it has a wide part, the scrap may remind one of a long-tailed bird. An angular scrap may suggest a pelican snapping at a fish; a lumpish one may form a gnome or dwarf. A constellation of stars or a patch of spring flowers may be made with small odds and ends.

Then, with a bit of cutting and manipulating, encourage the child to perfect the design and mount it on white paper.

CREATIVE DRAMATICS

Dramatic activities are more natural and spontaneous if children make up suitable dialogue and act out the play in a free, easy manner. The class should have the story or play well in mind whether it be an original story by the class or one presented by the teacher.

The term "creative dramatics" is known to students of the drama as *commedia dell' arte*. It had its origin in medieval Italian comedy. The plot was written, but the dialogue and details were improvised by the actors.

CREPE PAPER FEATHER

From cardboard cut a feather the desired shape and size. From crepe paper that has been folded double, cut two feathers ½ inch larger all around than the cardboard. Paste the crepe paper to the cardboard. Use the paste sparingly to do a neat job. Fringe the edges of the crepe paper to give a feathery effect.

**FEATHER WITH CARDBOARD
CENTER AND CREPE PAPER EDGE**

FEATHER WITH FRINGED EDGE

CROSSWORD PUZZLES

The play element in the Language Arts may take the form of crossword puzzles. Puzzles are helpful in building vocabulary, in improving spelling, and in encouraging the use of the dictionary. Acquaint the class with the crossword puzzle by drawing one on the blackboard. Use colored chalk to add interest. Then work through the puzzle with the class.

To use the puzzles on the pages that follow, make a blank copy of the puzzle and of the numbers in the squares on the blackboard. Ask the pupils to copy the puzzle and the numbers in the squares on paper. Write the clues to the puzzle on the board. *The puzzle squares were filled out as a timesaver for the teacher.* Pupils may work individually or in teams. As they become more experienced, pupils will need less help from the teacher.

Teachers will find that they can enrich subject fields—English, social studies, science, arithmetic—by making up puzzles that suit the subject matter. Pupils, especially the more advanced, will find that they have talent in this direction.

CROSSWORD PUZZLE NO. 1

ACROSS

3. A small vegetable that grows in the ground and that is loved by monkeys

DOWN

1. A flying machine
2. A place where pigs live

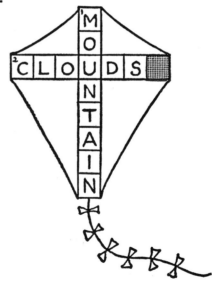

CROSSWORD PUZZLE NO. 2

ACROSS

2. They float higher than a kite

DOWN

1. A very high place from which to fly a kite

CROSSWORD PUZZLE NO. 3

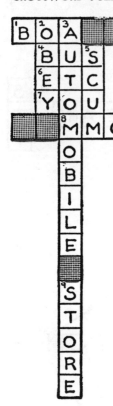

ACROSS

1. A large snake
4. A vehicle with many seats
6. And so forth (abbr.)
7. Yourself
8. Two thousand one hundred (Roman numerals)

DOWN

2. To mind
3. A car
5. Dirt that floats on the top of a pond
9. A place in which to go shopping

CROSSWORD PUZZLE NO. 4

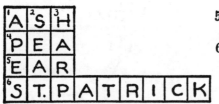

ACROSS

1. What Dad dumps out of his pipe
4. A little green vegetable

ACROSS—*continued*

5. The part of the body used for hearing
6. An Irish saint on whose birthday we wear green

DOWN

1. Large monkeys
2. Something to sit on
3. A musical instrument famous in Ireland

76

CROSSWORD PUZZLE NO. 5

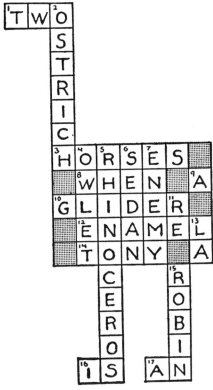

ACROSS

1. The number of pints in a quart
3. Animals we ride on
8. At what time
10. An airplane without an engine
12. A kind of paint
14. Nickname for Anthony
16. Exists
17. Substitute for *a* when placed before a word beginning with *a, e, i, o,* or *u*

DOWN

2. A big bird
4. A baby owl
5. A large animal with a horn on its nose
6. An automobile with four doors
7. Foe
9. First letter in the alphabet
11. Regarding (abbr.)
13. Los Angeles (abbr.)
15. A bird that comes in the springtime

CROSSWORD PUZZLE NO. 6

ACROSS

3. Pairs
7. Untie
9. What men do with a razor
10. Tidy
12. An animal that can see at night
13. The opposite of yes
14. An ocean
20. Substitute for *a* when followed by a word that begins with *a, e, i, o,* or *u*
21. The rising and falling of the sea
22. As far as
23. Japanese money
24. Opposite of "this"

DOWN

1. An ocean
2. Something very pleasant to hear
4. A ridge of water
5. A large sea
6. Southeast (abbr.)
8. New Hampshire (abbr.)
11. As far as
14. Pennsylvania (abbr.)
15. A small insect that lives in the ground
16. Something that is neither he nor she
17. What men catch in the sea
18. Notion
19. One penny

CROSSWORD PUZZLE NO. 7

ACROSS

1. Master of ceremonies (abbr.)
4. As far as
6. Not hot
7. By
8. Pleasant
11. Thus

DOWN

1. Mountain (abbr.)
2. An animal that howls at night on the prairie or desert
3. What the desert is covered with
5. What shines on the desert nearly every day
6. A spiny plant that grows on the desert
10. A boy child

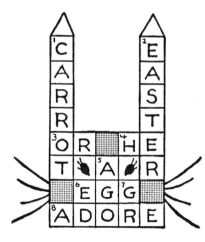

CROSSWORD PUZZLE NO. 8

ACROSS

3. Otherwise
4. Pronoun for man
6. The Easter bunny's gift
8. Love

DOWN

1. A vegetable that rabbits like
2. The season for eggs
5. Past
6. Nickname for Edward
7. Greek (abbr.)

CROSSWORD PUZZLE NO. 9

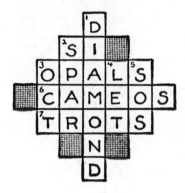

ACROSS

2. The Spanish word for "yes"
3. A gem of various colors (pl.)
6. Stones carved into pictures and worn as rings
7. The way a horse gently runs

DOWN

1. A precious stone
2. A pole used on a ship
3. October (abbr.)
4. Permit
5. A signal sent by a ship in trouble

CROSSWORD PUZZLE NO. 10

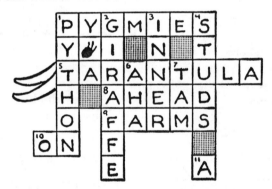

ACROSS

1. Small African natives
5. A large hairy spider
8. In front of
9. Places where food is raised
10. On top of
11. First letter of the alphabet

DOWN

1. A large snake
2. An animal with a long neck
3. Within
4. Large nailheads used for ornament as on a belt
6. An expression meaning, "I thought so!"
7. A flat cap like a beret

80

CROSSWORD PUZZLE NO. 11

ACROSS

2. The kind of house in which Lincoln grew up
3. A seat for one person

DOWN

1. A seat for several people
2. A bed or a seat

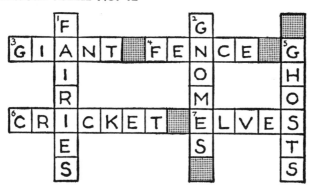

CROSSWORD PUZZLE NO. 12

ACROSS

3. A man of great size
4. Something built to keep cows from running away
6. An insect that chirps in the dark
7. Fairies

DOWN

1. Small folk from the land of make believe
2. Fairies that live under the ground
5. Spooks

CROSSWORD PUZZLE NO. 13

ACROSS

2. Pronoun for girl
3. Cake frosting
4. A present
5. Street or saint (abbr.)
6. By
7. Songs sung at Christmas time
8. Things that ring
9. Father Christmas

DOWN

1. The best day of the year
10. As far as

CROSSWORD PUZZLE NO. 14

ACROSS

1. A device that indicates time
3. A watering place in the desert
7. Short periods of time

DOWN

1. A kind of clock named for a bird
2. Quick
4. Forenoon (abbr.)
5. Southeast (abbr.)
6. Within

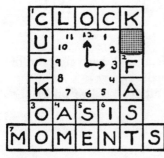

82

CYMBALS

A pair of cymbals that produce a sharp sound when clashed together may be made from two old tin lids or from pie tins. If you use pie tins, make a handle for the back of each tin. Punch two holes near the center of the tin and about as far apart as the width of the hand. Thread the ends of a shoestring through the holes. Leave enough slack so that the hand can be slipped through and tie the ends together on the inside.

A DANCING SNAKE

To make a snake that dances, you need a sheet of typewriter or construction paper, a pencil, an empty spool, and a pin. From the paper cut a circle approximately 6 inches in diameter. Cut the circle into a coil as shown at the right. Paint it the color of a snake. Stick the pencil point into the spool. Stick a pin through the center of the coil and into the eraser on the end of the pencil. Set the spool on a hot radiator and watch the snake coil around the pencil. This is caused by rising warm air.

DEAD LEAVES AND BREEZES

A GAME FOR THE PRIMARY GRADES

To play Dead Leaves and Breezes, the players form into a circle and become "breezes." Two players are chosen to be "leaves." They play dead in the center of the circle. The breezes steal up and touch the leaves cautiously. The leaves come to life and chase around to tag as many breezes as they can. The breezes that are caught become leaves and the game ends as soon as all the breezes have been caught.

DECORATING BOXES

Boxes for jewelry, handkerchiefs, lingerie, and hosiery may be made from cardboard boxes and containers of all shapes and sizes. They may be covered and lined with chintz, starched cotton, lace, or quilted material. Other suitable coverings are small-figured wallpaper, gummed paper, and decals. If you use a figured material or paper on the outside, use a plain color for the lining and vice versa.

DECORATING CLOSET SPACE

FOR THE ELEMENTARY GRADES

The bareness of school cloakrooms and supply closets may be brightened by decorating the walls. Secure permission from the proper authority to do this. Tack up heavy wrapping paper on the cloakroom or closet walls and let the children decorate with designs of their own ingenuity.

DECORATING EASTER EGGS

In decorating Easter eggs, select a harmless dye, such as a vegetable dye. Directions come with most standard brands and usually call for dissolving a dye tablet in hot water and dipping the eggs in the dye bath.

COLORED SAWDUST

Decorating Easter eggs with colored sawdust makes an attractive gift. To a vegetable dye bath, add sawdust and let it remain in the bath long enough to absorb the coloring. Remove the sawdust from the dye bath with a spoon or tea strainer and spread it on a newspaper to dry. Dabble a coat of glue on the eggs and roll them in the sawdust.

Dabble a thin coat of glue on the eggs and roll the eggs in confetti. The gay bits of paper make attractive Easter eggs.

DECORATING WITH CREPE PAPER ROPE

Have you ever tried decorating objects, such as a perfume bottle or flower bowl, with coils of crepe paper rope? To make this attractive decoration, cut the crepe paper into long strips 1 inch wide, and roll the strips into a tight rope.

To make a lining on which to glue the paper rope, wrap the base of the bottle or vase with a flat layer of crepe paper. Wrap

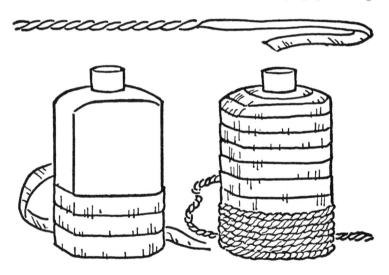

the bottom, too. This will help to hold the lining in place. Fasten the crepe-paper lining temporarily with rubber bands or string.

Begin at the side bottom to wind the paper rope. Wind around and around, pasting the rope to the lining as you proceed. When you have finished winding, allow the paste to dry. Then shellac. Almost any shaped bottle or vase may be decorated in this way.

DECORATING POTTERY WITH LEAF PRINTS

If you are interested in making pottery—ash trays, bowls and vases—you may decorate them with leaf prints. Select a small, well-formed leaf of any tree that is at hand, such as an elm, maple, oak, willow, chestnut, birch, or a delicate fern frond.

After the bowl has been molded but while it is still pliant, press the leaf or frond into the wet clay. Then remove it carefully. Practically any bowl may be decorated in this way. A low, saucer-shaped bowl will take the design on the inside; a vase may be decorated on the outside. When the clay is thoroughly dry, paint the bowl and then apply a coat of shellac.

DECORATING WITH SEALING WAX

Sealing wax gives a nice finish to articles, such as necklaces, bookends, and buttons. To make these articles, look in the Index of this book under the name of the item.

There are two ways of applying sealing wax as a decorative medium. These methods are described below.

1. Melt one end of a stick of wax over a low flame. Dribble the wax over the area to be decorated. Apply as thin a coat of wax as possible. Then apply another coat of another color over the first one. Heat the waxed surface slightly by holding the object that you are decorating upside down over a low flame until a porcelain-like smoothness is achieved. Do not hold the object over the flame long enough so that the wax drips.

2. Chop up a small amount of sealing wax—about one stick—and dissolve in methyl (denatured) alcohol about twenty-four hours. Apply with a brush, as you would apply lacquer. When it is dry, rub the wax with a fine glass paper and then polish with pumice flour. If you wish to add glitter to the decoration, sprinkle with bits of broken Christmas tree ornaments.

Denatured alcohol, glass paper, and pumice flour are obtainable at paint counters and stores. Glass paper is paper coated with glue and sprinkled with powdered glass. It is used as a polish. Pumice flour is a gritty polish used for refinishing furniture.

DEFINITIONS

A LANGUAGE GAME FOR THE UPPER GRADES

Divide the class into two teams. Give each team a list of words to define. Choose a suitable number from a spelling list. The teams prepare their definitions in writing within a limited time. Team 1 reads its definitions aloud. It scores a point for each definition clear enough so that Team 2 recognizes the word that is being defined. Then Team 2 reads its definitions to Team 1. The team scoring the larger number of points wins.

"Definitions" is an interesting game. At the same time the game helps to develop exactness in stating definitions.

DESIGNS BASED ON LETTER COMBINATIONS

Allover patterns made with letter combinations are especially effective for areas and surfaces that you may want to decorate with a bold design. The patterns on the next page, for example, are made by combining the letters K T and S P. Sometimes the school initials may combine effectively, much to the delight of the boys and girls. Other effective combinations may be worked out after a bit of experimentation.

A folding screen, for example, may be made into a handsome article of schoolroom furniture by giving it the letter-design treatment. Materials, such as burlap, flour or sugar sacking, canvas, butcher paper, or cheesecloth, are suitable for covering a screen.

Cut the material to fit the panels of the screen, allowing for a ¼-inch turn-under on all four sides. With thumbtacks fasten the material to an old table top or to the floor. Rule the material into squares, adapting the size of the squares to the area to be decorated. If, for example, the screen panels are very large, you may wish to make 1-foot squares. The design also will be a factor in deciding on the size of the square.

Use calcimine paint or pencil crayon for putting the design on the material. The children enjoy coloring the squares and carrying on the other details of the project. Either paste or tack the decorated material to the screen. Wallpaper paste, sold in powder form at most paint and hardware stores, is easy to apply.

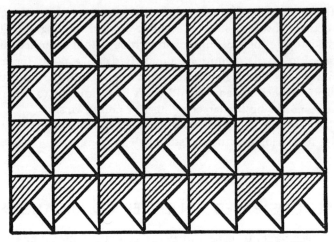

The design is formed by combining the letters K and T.

The letter P forms the basis for this design which is connected with a series of modified S's.

DESIGNS BASED ON NUMBER COMBINATIONS

In addition to the letter designs discussed in the previous project, number combinations also lend themselves equally well to allover patterns. These patterns are not only suitable for large areas but they are also adaptable to small articles, such as book covers, notebook and scrapbook covers, and gift wrapping paper.

The design on this page is made by combining 4's and 7's in one square and by making an ornamental design resembling the figure 8 in the adjoining one. If you are decorating wrapping paper, for example, use butcher paper and rule it off in fairly small squares. Use India ink, crayon, colored pencils, or water colors to execute the design.

DEVELOPING ORIGINAL COMPOSITIONS

Creative work whether in music, language, or dance rhythms lends itself to close co-ordination. Children may take a familiar nursery rhyme and compose a tune for it. The tune may in turn serve as a starting point for a dance or for an original poem that the teacher and pupils work out together.

As they gain confidence and experience in creative work, children are eager to undertake additional projects.

A DICTIONARY PROJECT

FOR THE PRIMARY GRADES

One of the best introductions to learning how to locate a word in its alphabetical order in the dictionary is to have everyone compile his own dictionary. Provide each child with a chalk box and cards. Make the cards

from medium-weight cardboard to fit the box. Decorate the boxes any way you wish. Small-figured material or wallpaper makes an attractive exterior. Use a plain color for the lining or vice versa.

Compiling a dictionary on any school level is a long-term project. On the primary level begin by having the pupil ask about a word that is troubling him. Then write the word on a card for him. After each word write the meaning. The pupil then files the card alphabetically, thus gaining skill in spelling and alphabetizing. At this level alphabetize according to the first letter only. Do not attempt to alphabetize beyond the first letter.

If you wish to do a professional job, make cards that show the alphabetical changes. Make a card the same size as the others but with a tab sticking up above the others. Make a tab card for each letter of the alphabet and print the letter on it. Place the cards in the chalk box in alphabetical order and file each dictionary entry behind the alphabet card. This affords fun for children who are learning the alphabet.

A DICTIONARY PROJECT

FOR THE ELEMENTARY GRADES

For Grades IV, V, and VI continue with the dictionary project that the children began in the primary grades. Continue to use the card system, since you can add new words so easily.

Continue to add words that trouble children. At first you still may need to write the words for the children to be sure that the words are spelled correctly and written neatly. Later encourage children to take over these tasks under your supervision.

Teach the children to alphabetize beyond the first and second letters in a word. Since maintaining proper alphabetical sequence beyond the first letter is a difficult skill, give practice in mastering each step before proceeding to the next. Alphabetizing is important in using telephone directories, indexes, dictionaries, and general encyclopedias.

As soon as the children are ready for more advanced work, teach them how to maintain alphabetic sequence in words such as St. Louis or St. Paul. Even though these names are abbreviated, alphabetize them in the dictionary as though they were spelled out: Saint Louis, Saint Paul. Thus St. Paul (Saint Paul) would come before Salt Lake City, for example. The third letter *i* in Saint precedes the third letter *l* in Salt.

If you wish to bring the project to a close, have the pupils make a dictionary in book form. Have the pupils copy the words from the cards into a notebook. Have the pupils proofread the spelling and alphabetical sequence of words on the cards before they transfer their dictionary into a notebook.

THE DIVING IMP

To show air pressure, fill a gallon bottle nearly full of water as in the picture. Weight a cork with a nail so that the cork barely floats. Experiment with the size of the nail until you find one the right weight. Drive it into the bottom of the cork part way. You may need to pour out some of the water or pour more in. Then draw a face on the cork to represent an imp.

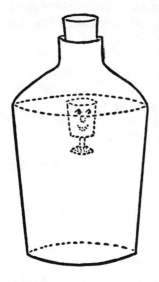

Use a second cork as a stopper. Putting in the stopper compresses the air above the water, and the air, in turn, presses down harder on the water and floating cork. The water will not compress easily but the cork will be forced down by air pressure. The cork now is heavier than water and sinks to the bottom. Raise the stopper, and as if by magic the imp will rise to the surface of the water instantly.

DOLL HOUSE FURNITURE

THREE CARDBOARD CREATIONS

Here are examples of an almost limitless variety of doll house furniture and accessories that can be made from cardboard and cardboard boxes.

A CHAIR

For a doll's chair you need a small box of thin cardboard with a flap cover. A teabox $4\frac{1}{2}$ x $5\frac{3}{4}$ x $2\frac{1}{2}$ inches is recommended. If the teabox is attractive, use it as it is. If it is not, cover it with an attractive paper. Be sure to glue it down well all over.

To make the chair, glue the flap of the cover shut. With a ruler draw rectangles *A, B, C,* and *D* on sides 1 and 2. Do likewise on the other two sides. Cut out the rectangles on all four sides. Mark the dotted line for rectangle *E*. Do *not* cut on this line,

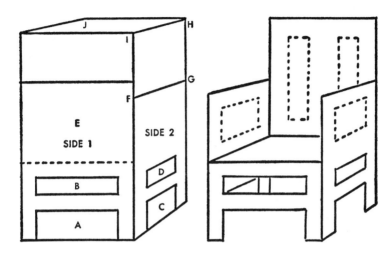

but cut the other three sides of rectangle *E*. To make the seat of the chair, bend the cardboard along dotted line *E*. Cut along the line *F* to *G;* turn and cut from *G* to *H;* turn and cut from *H* to *I;* turn and cut from *I* to *F*. Do the same for the opposite side. The line *JH* forms the top of the back of the chair.

The ornamentation may be elaborated upon by cutting out additional rectangles in the arms and back as suggested by the dotted lines in the sides and back of the chair at the right.

DOLL BUGGY

To make a doll buggy you need a round oatmeal box, a round, pasteboard salt box, 2 sucker sticks, 4 thumbtacks, a few round-heads (brass paper fasteners), a sheet of cardboard about 10 x 10 inches.

Cut the salt box in half lengthwise. Use one-half of the box for the bottom of the buggy. For the top, cut off approximately one-third of the bottom end of the oatmeal box. From the sheet of cardboard cut four wheels approximately 2½ inches in diameter.

93

Cut a handle for the buggy. Follow the dimensions given in the pattern below. Punch four holes in the body of the buggy near the bottom where the wheels belong. Insert the sucker sticks for axles. Fasten each wheel to the end of the sucker stick with a thumbtack. Glue the buggy top in position. Put it either on the inside or on the outside of the body of the buggy. If glue does not work too well, use roundheads. Bend back the cardboard handle at the ends to form the tabs for fastening to the buggy top. Fasten with glue or roundheads and the buggy is ready.

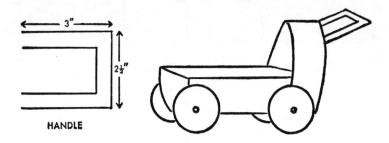

HANDLE

A WHEELBARROW

You will need a dry-cereal box 9 inches long by 6¾ inches wide by 2½ inches thick, a mammoth sucker stick 6½ inches long, a sheet of cardboard 8½ x 11 inches, 2 thumbtacks, and roundheads (brass paper fasteners).

To make the floor, sides, and handles of the wheelbarrow, put the cereal box in front of you with the open end to your right. With a ruler draw a slanting line *AB* on the side towards you as in the diagram. Then a straight line *BC* as in the pattern at the left on the next page. Do the same on the opposite side of the box, too. Label the lines as in the pattern.

Cut along the slanting line *AB*; now cut on the straight line *BC*. The line *C* to *D* is the open end. Cut along *D* to *E*. Do the same on the opposite side. Now cut from *E* on one side to *E* on the other side, straight across the floor of the wheelbarrow. This removes a section of the bottom of the box. Now cut from *A* on one side to *A* on the other. This removes the top of the box.

Now we are ready for the legs and wheels. Cut two strips of cardboard 1 x 3½ inches in width and length for the legs. Fasten them into position with glue or with brass paper fasteners (round-heads). Cut two cardboard circles 3 inches in diameter for the wheels. This is a two-wheel barrow rather than the usual one-wheeler. Punch two holes near the front and bottom of the body for the axle. Insert the sucker-stick axle. Fasten the wheels to the ends of the axle with thumbtacks.

A stronger wheelbarrow may be made from a chalk box. Use buttonmolds for wheels and fasten the wheels with small nails.

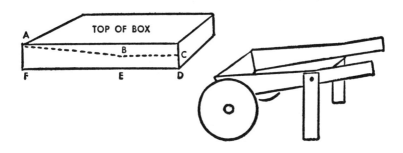

DOMINOES

FOR THE PRIMARY AND ELEMENTARY GRADES

Children will enjoy the game of dominoes more, if they make the domino blocks. A set consists of twenty-eight small, flat oblong pieces. A line divides one side, or the face, of the domino evenly. Each half either is blank or it has from one to six spots. The arrangement of the dots is such that the teacher will need to have a set on hand to serve as a model.

Dominoes may be made from wood, carved from soap, or cut from rubber inner tubing. If you make the pieces from wood or inner tubing, paint the dots with lacquer or nail polish. If you are making them from soap, use sealing wax.

The most common form of the game is played by matching the dots on the dominoes. The game provides experience in number work for children in the primary grades. Older children, however, also enjoy making the dominoes and playing the game.

A DOORSTOP

A doorstop should be heavy enough to stop the motion of a door. A stop can be made by covering a brick with oilcloth, or by painting a can and filling it with sand. Still another can be made from a goodly sized gourd. Cut the gourd in half, scrape out the seeds, fill it with dry sand, and glue the halves together. Shellac the gourd to give it a shiny finish.

DRAWING IMAGINARY BIRDS AND ANIMALS

When they are given an opportunity to draw imaginary birds and animals, children's imaginations are likely to run rampant. They, for example, thoroughly enjoy drawing exotic birds, beasts, dragons, and dinosaurs. To stimulate them to their best efforts, ask the children to close their eyes and to visualize the story that you tell them. Dramatize the story so that it forms a word picture of the subject that you wish them to draw. One or two examples usually are enough to send the group off artistically.

DRAWING MADE EASY

FOR THE ELEMENTARY GRADES

The progressive sketches on the next page show that some objects which seem complicated to draw are really easy if taken step by step. The drawing of a face, for instance, is not difficult if one begins with an oval as in Step 1. Add the eyes as in 2; the eyebrows, nose, and mouth as in 3; and the hair as in 4.

In drawing a bird, for example, the oval is placed at a different angle. The head is added in 2, and the tail, wings, and feet in 3. The chair, rose, and butterfly likewise are drawn in easy steps. Progressive sketches may be worked out for other objects.

1 2 3 4

1 2 3

1 2 3

1 2 3

1 2 3

97

DYEING

Attractive costumes may be made from flour sacks, cotton bags, and other inexpensive, light-colored materials. Dyeing the materials enhances their attractiveness and is useful in getting the right shade and color.

NATURAL OR VEGETABLE DYES

Commercial dyes are usually inexpensive, but excellent colors may be secured from plants growing in the yard and garden. Use roots of the common nettle or leaves of the elderberry bush for magenta, onions for a rich saffron, camomile daisies for yellow, and mustard for chartreuse. A small amount of salt, vinegar, cream of tartar, or acetic acid are good fixative agents. Boil the root, leaves, or plant until the color has gone into the water. Strain the dye through a piece of the cloth that is to be dyed, if you prefer. Wash the cloth. Then boil the cloth in the dye. Rinse thoroughly in cold water.

When they experiment with natural or vegetable dyes, boys and girls gain experience in a handicraft that was (and is) important in a pioneer community.

BATIK DYEING

Batik is a method of producing designs in color originally done by the people of the Dutch East Indies. The patches or parts of the fabric that are not to take the dye are protected by a coat of wax. Heat paraffin or beeswax and brush the cloth with the wax to form the design desired. Lift the cloth off the table from time to time to make sure that the wax has soaked through to the reverse side.

Prepare the dye and dip in the cloth, but do not permit it to remain long enough to melt the wax from the cloth. Rinse in cold, clean water. Lay a newspaper on the ironing board and put the cloth on the paper. Then lay another newspaper on top of the cloth. Press with a warm iron. The wax will leave the cloth and soak into the newspaper. Remove the remainder of the wax by washing the cloth in a cleaning solvent.

The design is secured by bunching and tying folds of the material. Tie the cloth tightly where you do not want the dye to take hold. Submerge in the dye, then rinse and untie the cloth. It will show softly blended waves of color.

It is wise to experiment first with paper napkins. When he becomes experienced in tying and untying, the dyer can work with several colors. He can submerge, for example, the tied material first in a blue dye. Then he can untie the fabric, dip it in yellow so that the tied area is yellow, and the remainder a yellow green. Interesting patterns may be created in this way.

See also "Removing Color," page 231.

EASTER CHICKS

To make an Easter chick, twist two pipe cleaners together and shape them into a little chicken. Use one cleaner as a foundation for the body and the other for the legs. Make the legs substantial enough to support the body. Bend the end of the wires into feet so that the chick can stand. Pad the body with cotton batting.

Fasten the cotton inconspicuously with thread or glue. Dust the chick with dry calcimine paint. Make a bill from orange colored paper or from white paper colored orange with crayon.

Make as many chicks as you need to complete your flock.

AN EASTER EGG TREE

The egg tree is an Easter custom of the Pennsylvania Dutch who are descendants of the early German settlers in Pennsylvania. Select a small tree that is bare or semibare and decorate it with colorful Easter eggs in Christmas-tree fashion.

To prepare an egg for an ornament, show the children how to blow out an egg. Put something soft like a Turkish towel or rumpled tissue paper on a table. Then place the egg, small end up, on the towel. It is easier to balance the egg on a soft surface. Drive a needle through the shell at the top of the egg, and wiggle the needle around to make a hole about the size of a pea. Make another hole in the other end. Now blow the egg out into a dish. Ask the children to blow out the eggs at home and to bring the shells to school to prepare them for the Easter egg tree.

Before you decorate the eggs, make fasteners with thread and toothpicks. Break a toothpick in half and tie a thread about 6 inches long to one of the halves. Lower it through the hole in the egg. Pull the thread and the stick will fall into an horizontal position and will not pull out.

There are numerous ways to decorate the eggs. Three examples are described here. To make the ornament at the top left, select a brown-shelled egg preferably, since it makes an especially pretty background. Dabble glue in a circle around the egg as in the picture and sprinkle with tiny multicolored candies, the kind used in decorated cake frostings. Make as many circles as the egg can accommodate effectively.

To decorate the egg in the second picture, cut out the parts of the flower from colored crepe paper and glue them to the shell.

To make the pirate at the right, begin with the skull cap. Cut a 3½-inch square from a piece of red and white or blue cotton cloth. A piece from an old bandanna handkerchief is ideal. A faded cap adds to the effectiveness of the costume. Fashion the cap to fit the pirate's head, glue it in place and tie the ends in a knot in back. Make the eye flap of black paper and glue on at the top only. With India ink draw the band to which the flap is attached. Also draw the good eye, the mouth, and whiskers. Mold the nose, ears, and pipe bowl with chewing gum. Use a toothpick for the pipe-stem and poke a hole in the eggshell. For earrings use gummed cloth reinforcements, the kind used in loose-leafed notebooks.

AN EASTER GREETING

Tiny Easter greeting cards or small candy eggs may be hidden inside empty egg shells. To prepare a shell, break the egg carefully and remove the white and yolk. Let the inside of the shell dry. Then put the greeting or candy in the shell and glue the two halves together or fasten with Scotch tape. Decorate the egg shell in any way that you wish. Make a small tag to read, "Look inside," and attach it to the egg with a thread or Scotch tape.

AN EASTER RABBIT AND CART

To make a rabbit and cart, you will need 5 twigs, a small matchbox, either an empty thread spool or two buttonmolds, a paper grass nest, an Easter egg, some twine, thread, cotton batting, a bit of cardboard, glue, calcimine paint, and a small brush.

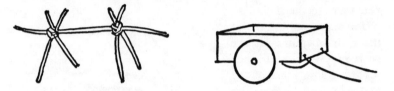

To make the rabbit, fasten the twigs together with twine so that they form the body and legs of the rabbit. (See the illustration at the left, above.) Fashion the head, including the ears and body, from cotton batting and tack to the twigs with thread. Paint the eyes, nose, mouth, whiskers by dabbing on color.

To make the cart, slide off the top of a small matchbox. Use the inside box for the body of the cart. Cut a small arc in the bottom to fit the spool which forms the wheels and axle. If,

instead of a spool, you are using wooden buttonmolds, use a kitchen match for the axle. Punch a hole near the front and bottom of the box on each side. Insert the match and fasten the wheels to the ends of the axle with thumbtacks. Make a harness from string or yarn. If you wish to have a black leather harness, dip the string in black ink, or use black yarn.

Fix a grass nest in the cart and put an Easter egg in it.

AN EGGSHELL GARDEN

A garden planted in eggshell halves is a fascinating project. Encourage the boys and girls to bring eggshell halves and egg cartons to school. It is not necessary, of course, that two halves of the same egg are brought. All that is required is that each eggshell half be intact.

Decorate the egg cartons with paint or cover them with colored paper. Place the half shells in the egg carton. Fill the shells with good soil, and plant a seed or two in the soil. Label each shell with the name of its gardener.

Each gardener, of course, will tend his own. Several gardens placed in sunny spots about the school are attractive and interesting to watch grow during the winter months.

EGG STAND-UP CHARACTERS

A variety of animated personalities may be made with hardboiled eggs. Select eggs with a brown shell to simulate a sun tan, or dye white eggs with a vegetable or with an Easter egg dye. Directions and patterns for making three egg stand-up characters —an Indian, Old Timer, and Sister Sally—follow below and on the next two pages. The characters may be grouped in a set for a room decoration. They may be made for gifts to be taken home.

INDIAN

To make the Indian, use either a brown egg or dye one a coppery brown. Fashion the hair from crepe paper and paste to the thick end of the egg. Smooth out the paper as much as you can to give a straight effect to the hair. Cut the paper into long narrow strips for braiding the hair. Make two braids and tie them near the ends with black thread.

From colored construction paper, cut a headband and feathers as in the illustration on the next page. To add variety, color some of the feathers with crayon. Cut the feathers individually from paper of various colors and then paste on the headband.

To make the features, cut a nose from brown paper. Use the pattern below. Fold on the dotted lines and paste in position along the folded edges. Draw the other features with a colored pencil, and add a few dashes for war paint.

Using the pattern below for a guide, cut the base or stand from lightweight cardboard. Bring the ends together, paste or fasten with roundheads. Modeling clay also makes a good base. While the clay is still soft, press the small end of the egg into the clay to make a suitable depression. Color the clay with calcimine paint.

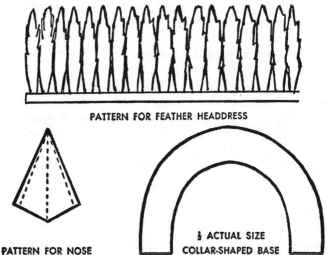

PATTERN FOR FEATHER HEADDRESS

PATTERN FOR NOSE

½ ACTUAL SIZE
COLLAR-SHAPED BASE

OLD TIMER

Use either a brown egg or color a white one a deep tan. Fashion the ears and nose from chewing gum and stick them in place. Draw the eyes and mouth with colored pencil. Shape the glasses from fine wire and hook them over the ears. Using the drawing of the Old Timer on the next page as a guide, cut the beard from crepe paper. Select white, brown, or copper colored paper.

To make the hat, cut a brim from lightweight cardboard or construction paper. For the crown, use a round top from a small paprika can or similar container. Glue the crown to the brim. Crumple some tissue or crepe paper to make a few wisps of hair. Match the color to that of the beard. Tuck the hair under the edge of the hat and glue in place. Use the pattern on page 104 for the base. Cut the pattern twice as large; that is, 4 inches across instead of 2 as in the picture. Cut the collar about $7/8$ inch wide. With crayon draw checks to represent the shirt.

SISTER SALLY

Use a white egg shell for the girl. For the base follow the pattern on page 104. Remember to make the pattern twice as large.

Make Sister Sally's hat from colored construction paper. Turn up the brim to give a rolled effect. Allow for an open crown. Fashion the hair from canary-yellow yarn. Cut enough yarn in 10-inch lengths to give her a "healthy" head of hair. Braid and tie with hair ribbons. Dabble glue on the inner circle of the hat and glue the hair in place. Draw the features with crayon. Use red for the lips, blue for the eyes, and yellow for the eyebrows.

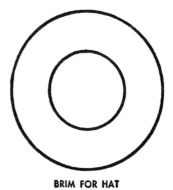

BRIM FOR HAT

ELECTRICITY

A GAME FOR THE INTERMEDIATE GRADES

This game gives practice in distinguishing left from right. The players form a circle and join hands. The teacher takes her station in the center of the circle and chooses one of the players to start a "shock." A player produces a shock by squeezing his neighbor's hand when the teacher calls out a direction. If she calls "To the right!" the shock producer squeezes his right hand. His neighbor likewise passes the shock on with his right hand. The shock continues to the right until the teacher calls "To the left!" When this happens, the last player to receive the shock squeezes with his left hand to send the shock in that direction. The teacher may alternate with right and left calls several times in rapid succession to keep the players on their toes.

As soon as the players have gained some skill in distinguishing right from left, the game may be put on a competitive basis and "short circuits" and "fuses" may be added. When he makes a mistake, a player becomes a "short circuit" and goes into the center with the teacher. He helps her to discover the next short circuit and then returns to the circle as a "new fuse."

This game is called Electricity because the shocks travel around the circle like an electric current.

ENCOURAGING GOOD HEALTH HABITS

FOR THE PRIMARY GRADES

Good health habits may be encouraged by building a "house of health." On drawing or butcher paper draw the outline of a large house. Make the house large enough so that you have room for as many window spaces as there are children in the class. Make the windows large enough to accommodate a small snapshot. But, in the place of windows, put in shutters that open and close. To make a shutter, cut along *EF*. Then cut along the lines *AB* and *CD*. Fold back the shutters along *AC* and *BD*.

Ask the children to bring snapshots or small photographs of themselves. Paste them behind the shutters. The picture should be larger than the window. If it is not, mount it on paper somewhat larger than the window. In either case paste the picture behind the shutter with Scotch tape.

Then, when he comes to school neatly dressed, the child will find his shutter open and his picture in the house of health. To achieve the well-groomed look, his teeth must be brushed, his hair combed, and he must have that well-rested "look." If he does not meet these requirements, the child stays behind closed shutters.

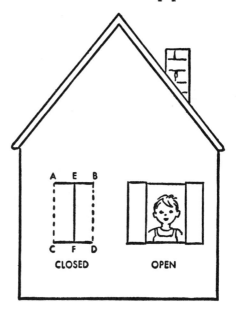

ENCOURAGING GOOD THOUGHTS

If they are given encouragement, children are as ready with compliments as they are with abuse or tattling. One way to develop mutual appreciation is to set aside a box for good reports and compliments. A shoe box or any box of similar size will serve the purpose.

Children enjoy writing a good thought about others in the group on a slip of paper and depositing it in the box. The report may say, "Barbara picked up my pencil for me." "Gerald said 'thank you' when I gave him the ball." "Jack is a fast runner."

At the end of the week the reports may be read by the class president or secretary at a meeting of the group. Children look forward eagerly to this meeting.

ERMINE FOR COSTUMING

To give the effect of ermine, sew black crepe paper tails on cotton batting. To give the tails body, double the crepe paper and cut into long strips ½ inch wide. Twist the strips into rolls. As it loosens, the roll gives the effect of a fur tail. Cut the tails into 1½ inch lengths and sew to the cotton batting. Space the tails evenly to form an allover pattern.

Ermine is a symbol of royalty. It is used in costuming kings and judges in some countries.

ESTIMATING MEASUREMENTS AND WEIGHTS

Situations arise from time to time that call for skill in estimating lengths, distances, heights, weights, quantities. Children enjoy practice in learning these skills. Have them go to the board to draw their conception of lengths such as 6 inches, 9 inches, 12 inches, 1 yard. Then ask them to draw perpendicular lines for 6 inches, 9 inches, 12 inches, 1 yard. Have them check their answers with a yardstick.

Ask the class to guess the number of beans in a bottle, the number of people in a school auditorium, the weight of a book, a grocery box, the height of their friends, and of the room. Skill in estimating enables children to visualize measurements that occur in their arithmetic problems.

These experiences may be carried out as games. Sides may be chosen and teams may compete for accuracy in estimating weights and measures.

EXPERIMENTS WITH AIR PRESSURE

1. To demonstrate that air occupies space, fill a bowl half full of water. Invert a glass tumbler and put it in the bowl gently. The air in the tumbler will force down the water level in the tumbler below that of the surrounding surface.

2. To show the pressure of air, suck water into a straw. Hold your thumb over the top of the straw. The water will remain in the straw because the pressure of the air pushes up on the water from below. Remove your thumb, and the air rushes in from above and pushes the water out at the other end. At sea level the air presses down at the rate of 15 pounds per square inch.

3. To cause air pressure to push a soft-boiled egg into a milk bottle, peel the shell from the egg. Light a small piece of paper and push it into the bottle. Lay the egg over the top of the bottle. The burning paper heats and expands the air in the bottle, and forces some of it out. As the fire dies, the oxygen in the air inside the bottle has been burned up and the air cools and contracts. The egg is drawn into the bottle because a partial vacuum has been created. The pressure of the air is greater on the egg on the outside of the bottle than from the inside.

A FATHER'S DAY GREETING

An attractive greeting card for Father's Day may be made from a scrap of small-figured wallpaper. Cut a piece two feet square. Place the paper on a table with the figured side toward you as in picture below. Letter "Happy Father's Day" in the open spaces of the design and sign your name. The dots show you where the folds will be after the card is completed. Do not put the dots in.

To fold the card above so that it will deliver its message in the right order, begin with figure 4 at the bottom of this page and work backwards. Fold the square on page 109 from top to bottom to get the rectangular shaped card in 4. Then follow by folding as in 3, 2, and 1. The possibilities for making greeting cards for dads are many. A suggestion or two usually is enough to start the class off.

To fold the card so that it will deliver its message in the right order, begin with the 2-foot square on page 109. Place the square in front of you flat on a table. Take hold of the top edge of the square and fold from top to bottom. You will have the rectangular-shaped card as in 4, page 110. The fold will be at the top and the plain side of the paper now will be on the outside. Decorate with drawing and lettering.

Fold the paper from left to right as in 3. Each time after you have folded the paper, decorate the card with drawing and lettering, as there will be no folds to interfere with your work.

Fold again from top to bottom as in 2; then again from left to right as in 1. The card now will be about six inches square. Then as it is unfolded, the card will deliver the message and pictures in the right order.

FELT BELTS

Attractive belts may be made from old felt hats. For a foundation use an old belt of any material including leather that is soft enough to be pierced with a needle. Remove the buckle.

OVERLAPPING CIRCLE DESIGN

From felt cut circles the size of a silver dollar. Cut as many circles as you need to make the belt by overlapping the edges as

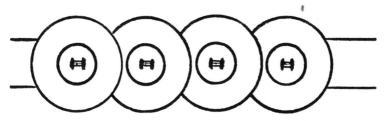

in the illustration. Arrange the circles on the foundation belt. Place a button the size of a dime in the center of each felt circle and sew through the felt and foundation. Sew two or three strong hooks and eyes to the ends of the belt to hold it in place.

LEAF DESIGN BELT

An interesting belt may be made with a leaf design. Choose a leaf of a tree or plant that is close at hand, one that is about

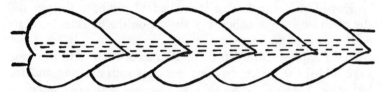

2 inches long and 1½ inches wide. Use it for a pattern in cutting the design from felt. Place the felt leaves on a belt foundation by overlapping the ends as in the picture and stitch in place with four rows of stitching. Use a running stitch and heavy gold or silver thread or colored yarn.

FELT LAPEL PINS

Attractive lapel pins like those illustrated on these two pages may be made from old felt hats.

ROSE LAPEL PIN

To make the petals for the rose, cut four circles the size of a 50-cent piece. Cut two leaves from green felt. Arrange the

petals and leaves as in the picture. Stitch the petals and leaves firmly in place. Sew on an attractive button for the center of the rose and a safety pin to the back for a fastener. For rose petals select different felt, either yellow, pink, red, or white—whichever is your favorite color. Rose lapel pins make lovely gifts for occasions, such as birthdays, Mother's Day, and Christmas.

CRESCENT MOON LAPEL PIN

Make a pattern for a crescent moon like the one on the left. Lay the pattern on yellow or orange felt and cut it out. Sew on a black button for an eye and a small safety pin on the back for a fastener. This makes an unusual gift for any occasion.

HEART-SHAPED LAPEL PIN

From felt cut a heart 2 inches across at the widest part. Cut an arrow 2½ inches long from a different color felt. Cut two slits through which to pull the arrow. Sew a small safety pin to the back for a fastener and you have completed an attractive pin.

A FIFE

A fife is a simple form of flute. It is used chiefly to accompany a drum. If you wish to have a fife-and-drum corps, you will find instructions for making a drum on page 137.

A fife 14¼ inches long may be made from a straight hollow reed such as a pumpkin vine or a bamboo fishing pole. To make a fife from a pumpkin vine, cut the vine at the place where there is a block; that is, a leaf. Cut it just ahead of the block. The other end should be open. Do likewise with bamboo. If, however, you cannot use a natural block, use beeswax, modeling clay, or chewing gum to block the opening.

To make the mouth hole, 2 inches from the blocked end, cut an oval slit ½ inch long and ⅜ inch across. Beginning 2 inches from the other end, drill or cut six holes along the length of the flute 1 inch apart and slightly less than ⅜ inch in diameter. Tunes may be played by blowing into the mouth hole and by

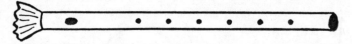

covering the holes with the correct finger combinations. The player does not blow directly into the hole, but he blows at an angle as if he were blowing a tune into an empty milk bottle. Playing a fife takes practice. An inexperienced player may find that he does better when part of the hole is closed, forming half a circle or slit. Use Scotch tape to partly cover the hole.

FIGURING DISTANCES ON A MAP

FOR THE UPPER ELEMENTARY GRADES

This activity leads up to the basic skill of reading distances on a map (pages 227–28). To show how distances are represented on a map, start with the floor of the classroom. Suppose that you want to make a map of the floor. You decide on a scale. A scale shows how much the floor has been reduced to get it on the map. Suppose that the classroom floor is 30 x 40 feet and that you decide on a scale of 1 inch = 1 foot. Thus the distance has been reduced 12 times. Draw the rectangle on the floor with chalk.

You would need a sheet of paper 30 x 40 inches to represent the floor on the map. You decide that the sheet would be too large to handle conveniently; so you reduce the scale of the map by ½. The scale is now ½ inch = 1 foot. Then your map will be 15 x 20 inches. Draw it on the floor beside the first map. Write the scale at the bottom of the map (Scale: ½ inch = 1 foot). The distance has been reduced 24 times.

You take a look at the second map and decide that it is still too large to put on a sheet of paper. So you reduce the scale again by $\frac{1}{2}$. The scale now is $\frac{1}{4}$ inch = 1 foot. Your map will be $7\frac{1}{2}$ x 10 inches. Write the scale at the bottom (Scale: $\frac{1}{4}$ inch = 1 foot). Thus the distance has been reduced 48 times and you can handle this reduction conveniently on paper.

Now mapmakers have the same problem of representing distances on the earth's surface on a map as you did in drawing a map of the floor. Since distances on the earth are many, many times greater, the mapmakers need to reduce distances many, many times more. If you look at the key to a map, which is usually in one of the lower corners, it may read, "1 inch = 15 miles" or "1 inch = 37 miles."

FILING PICTURES AND CLIPPINGS

Encourage children to collect pictures and clippings of materials suitable for the various holidays and seasons of the year. These materials will come in handy for classroom decorations and for use as visual aids.

Arrange the material according to the month in which it is most likely to be used, and the months will fall naturally into the seasons. September, October, and November will comprise the fall; December, January, and February, winter; March, April, and May, spring; June, July, and August, summer.

Make cardboard folders to hold the material; or use 10 x 13-inch Manila envelopes. With the open end of the envelope to your right, slit open the side which is now at the top. This type of folder, with two open sides only, will also take oversized materials. Prepare an envelope for each month.

Older boys and girls may keep their own files. This gives them valuable training in organizing and filing materials.

FINGER PAINTING

Finger painting is an art experience that is especially suitable for children. It is an art medium which supplies physical activity and develops muscular co-ordination. Instead of a brush the artist uses his fingers, fingernails, the palm of his hand, forearm, and even his elbow.

Make provision for protecting children's clothing. Dad's old shirt worn backwards serves as an excellent protector.

To make finger paint, boil household starch to the consistency of pea soup. Mix calcimine or any other dry paint with warm water and add this to the starch. A glossy paper works best, and apply the paint fairly thick in large sweeping motions. Blend one color into another. When the paint has dried, press the paper on the back with a *warm* iron.

FINGER PLAYS

Finger plays, or "handsies," are poems that are dramatized with the hands. They are a perennial delight to small children. Two examples are given below. The class, however, will enjoy creating its own finger plays.

THE PUPPY

Here is a puppy
Long ears and short nose
Wagging his tail
Wherever he goes.

THE COWBOY

Cowboy, tip your hat politely

As your horse trots by so lightly,

Twirl your lasso, brave and high

As the angry steer runs by,

Rope and take him to his **pen,**

Cowboy, tip your hat again.

FIREPROOFING CLOTH

In producing plays in the classroom and assembly, costumes, curtains, and cloth backdrops often constitute a fire hazard. To reduce this source of risk, you may fireproof cloth by dipping it in a solution. Mix 1 cup of borax and ¾ cup of boric acid in 1 gallon of boiling water and allow to cool. Then soak the cloth in the solution, wring out, and hang up to dry.

FLAGS

The flags of many states and nations have colorful origins which children enjoy delving into. Flags are easy to make and afford the children a lot of pleasure.

A flag, of course, may be made any size, depending upon its use. The proportions and shapes vary greatly, but the majority are rectangular. Our own national flag, the Stars and Stripes, for example, is nearly twice as long as it is wide.

If you wish to make a tiny flag, make one 4 x 2½ inches, or a somewhat larger one 5 x 3 inches, and fasten it to a staff made from a sucker stick. For a flag 15 x 8 inches, use an 18-inch staff. For school parades make flags somewhat larger. Begin by drawing the design on paper. Then copy it on a closely woven fabric such as flour or sugar sacking. Use crayon for coloring since this gives it a glossy finish. Press the crayon coloring with a warm iron to insure a more permanent finish.

Small flags without staffs make a colorful, eye-catching wall frieze. For an ambitious long-term project the flags of the states in the Union, or the flags of the countries of the United Nations, is an interesting undertaking.

FLOUR PASTE

To make flour paste for some of the projects in this book, mix flour with water. Begin by adding a small quantity of water to

1 cupful of flour. Stir and add more water slowly until you have a creamy consistency.

A paste shortage will never occur if you keep flour on hand. Keep it in clean paste jars and store the jars in the supply closet.

FLOWER PLAQUES

A decorative wall plaque may be made from a discarded phonograph record. Paint the record a pastel color with calcimine or tempera paint. Paste or paint a floral picture on it. Trim the edge with ruching, lace, or crepe paper made into a ruche. Designs made from sealing wax or gesso paste (page 122) are attractive. For a hanger, make a loop from a cord and glue to the back of the record. Sealing wax also will hold the cord firmly.

FLOWER SEED EXCHANGE

FOR THE INTERMEDIATE GRADES

Encourage boys and girls to gather flower seeds, both wild and garden varieties. Have the children bring the seeds to school, make small cellophane envelopes, label the envelopes, and put in the seeds. Tie the envelopes with colored string or ribbon and adorn with a perky bow.

Promote this activity during the opening weeks of school while seeds are maturing. Later in the school year, during early spring, for example, the children will enjoy holding a seed exchange. The flower seeds may be put on display on a table and the children select those they want to plant. Perhaps they prefer to make a drawing game of the occasion. Have them tie strings about a yard long to the packages, and put them in a box. The children take turns at drawing. This may be made a holiday occasion. However, if no suitable time is available, the exchange can be worked in during a rainy recess. In any event the children take the seeds home and plant them in their gardens.

A FLY SWATTER

A practical fly swatter may be made from an old inner tube or from wire screening. Cut off a piece 5½ x 3½ inches. If you are using inner tubing, perforate several holes in the center near one end and lace to the handle. Use a paper punch for making the perforations and fine wire for fastening the swatter to the handle.

If you are using wire screening, bind the edges with a narrow strip of inner tubing. Use rubber cement for gluing the binding to the fly swatter. Another good finish is to bend back the edges of the the screening and bind with yarn. Use a close overcasting stitch or a buttonhole stitch.

FOOT SCRAPER

To make a handy foot scraper, assemble a goodly number of soda pop bottle caps. Remove the corks from the tops. Prepare a thick board, such as the end of an orange crate. Place the bottle caps on the board in rows open side up. Nail the caps in place. Put the foot scraper outside near the door and it is ready.

GEOGRAPHY BASEBALL

The purpose of geography baseball is to develop a knowledge of place names and to locate them on the map. To play the game, let the classroom represent the baseball diamond. Choose one corner of the room for home base. Counterclockwise from home base assign first base, second base, and third base to the remaining three corners.

Near home base hang a map of the continent, the country, or the state that you wish to use for locating places. If the map is in a case that cannot be moved easily, arrange the baseball diamond so that home base is near the map case.

Any number of players may play geography baseball. Organize the teams in any convenient way. Appoint a captain, for example, for each team and let the captains choose up sides quickly; or put the boys on one side and the girls on the other. The teams may be called Team A and Team B, or the children may wish to name the teams for their favorite baseball club. The teacher may serve as pitcher and scorekeeper.

To start geography baseball, Team A comes to bat. The first batter takes his place at home plate. The teacher may say, "Locate Buffalo." If he succeeds in locating the place in fifteen seconds, the batter goes to first base. If he does not, the teacher says, "You're out." The player takes his seat and the next batter on Team A comes to bat. If two batters succeed in getting on base, the first batter, now called a runner, advances from first to second base. When all the bases are filled and a fourth batter is about to get on base, all the runners advance, and the runner on third base comes "home" to score.

Team A bats until three players are out. It is quite possible that the side is out or "retired" without anyone getting on base. This happens if the first three batters miss the question.

Team B takes its turn at bat. When both teams have been at bat once, the first inning has been completed. If you have perhaps fifteen minutes for the game, call the game at the end of a full inning in order to give both teams an equal chance. The team with the higher score wins. The game may end in a tie.

A GEOGRAPHY RACE

FOR THE ELEMENTARY GRADES

A geography race can be fun if you can supply each player with a copy of the same map. Encourage the children to collect maps over a period of time. These may often be secured from gas stations, chambers of commerce, or travel bureaus.

Divide the group into two or more teams. Call out a location. The first player to find the place on his map scores a point for his team. The first team to score five points wins.

GESSO PASTE

Gesso paste is a plasterlike substance, resembling a delicate modeling clay. It is very satisfactory for decorating articles, such as workbaskets, candlesticks, jewel boxes, canisters, and picture frames.

To make gesso paste, mix 1 teaspoon of seccotine and 1 tablespoon of gum arabic with as much whiting as can be absorbed. Knead until the paste becomes pliable. Seccotine is a glue, and it may be obtained by that name at art and handicraft stores. It is a French import. Du Pont's Duco Cement may be substituted. Gum arabic is a solution used for stiffening fabrics and generally is obtainable at drugstores.

To decorate with gesso paste, be sure that the article is clean. Apply the paste with a funnel in small amounts so that the ornamentation does not dry too rapidly and crack. A small funnel similar to that used in squeezing frosting designs on cakes can be made from cellophane.

A GET-ACQUAINTED TOUR

FOR THE PRIMARY AND LOWER ELEMENTARY GRADES

Try to plan for a guided tour of the physical plant of the school early in the school year. A tour of this type acquaints children with places such as the offices of the school administrators, the library, the auditorium, the gymnasium, the lavatories, the boiler room, the location of exits, fire escapes, and play areas. Introduce them to the custodian of the building, the school doctor, nurse, principal, clerks, and other school personnel. Even in a small school system, a tour is advisable and beneficial.

Later in the semester, plan a tour through the community of which the school is a part. Acquaint the children with safety equipment, regulations, and hazards, such as traffic signals, water hydrants, and railroad crossings and warning signals. Libraries, playgrounds, and other points of interest in the neighborhood may be pointed out and explained.

GIFT WRAPPING PAPER

The suggestions given below for decorating wrapping paper are suitable for class projects.

DECORATING NEWSPAPERS

Use newspapers for wrapping paper and ornament them with large, bold designs. Borders and allover patterns done in color with a broad crayon pencil point or paint brush lend themselves

to this type of work. Avoid a fine pointed pencil or brush. Choose a section of the newspaper that is not broken up with large headlines, and use the lines of type and the columns for a guide in drawing the design. Choose a geometric type of design.

STAMPED DESIGNS

Wrapping paper may be easily decorated by stamping freehand allover designs. Use a plain paper, and a stamp pad for inking. Stamp pads come in various colors. For stamping use your finger or fingers, the eraser end of a pencil, a wooden buttonmold, a rubber washer, or a cork stopper.

An interesting pattern may be made by using three fingers. Place the second, third, and fourth fingers together with the tip of the forefinger under and between the other two.

FINGER PAINTING

Designs made by finger painting are interesting. For this art medium, see pages 115–16. This is an activity for young children.

GINGERBREAD BOYS

Gingerbread boys and animals are a traditional part of the fun at holiday time. They make gay party decorations and Christmas tree ornaments. Instead of being made of dough, the gingerbread boys described here are made from brown construction or wrapping paper. To make a symmetrical figure, fold the paper and draw one half of the figure as at the left. Cut out the figure, open the paper and there is the pattern for a gingerbread boy.

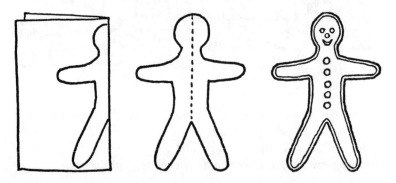

Prepare enough duplicate patterns so that each child has one. From wrapping paper and cardboard, have him cut three duplicates of the pattern, two from the wrapping paper and one from cardboard. Put the cardboard in the middle for stiffening, and paste the brown cutouts to the cardboard. To represent pink frosting, make the face and buttons from pink yarn. Trim the edges by pasting on pink yarn.

GOBLINS

A GAME FOR THE PRIMARY GRADES

A leader is chosen by the group or the teacher may serve in this capacity. The leader asks one of the players to close his eyes and then motions to another to leave the room. As he disappears, the group assumes that the player has been stolen by mischievous goblins. The second player opens his eyes, looks around to see who is missing. If he guesses correctly, or if he does not after a reasonable length of time, the player stolen by the goblins returns to the group and becomes the next player to close his eyes.

GOSSIP

AN INDOOR GAME

Without leaving their seats, the players rapidly pass a message from one to the other. The teacher may start the message by whispering to a player or she may ask one of the players to begin. The first player whispers the message to his neighbor and he in turn passes it on. Thus the message passes rapidly down one row and up another, or around a circle.

The last player tells the group what he *thinks* he heard. The first player repeats the original message usually to the amusement of all. Then play is resumed with a new message.

A GOURD BANJO

To make a banjo from a gourd, select one with a long stem. Do not cut off the stem. Cut the gourd lengthwise just above the stem so that the part you cut off is less than half the gourd. Use the larger half for the banjo. Clean out the pith and seeds and lacquer or varnish the gourd. Stretch a wet chamois over the opening and lace around the gourd with heavy string, narrow ribbon, or leather thongs. Space the lacings as indicated in the illustration and in a manner to hold the chamois firmly in place. From thin wood, cut a bridge 2½ x 1¼ inches, and glue it to the chamois near one end of the banjo. Cut four small notches near the neck end. Stick a nail in the other end of the gourd about 1½ inches down from the edge. Tie four banjo strings or thin wires to the nail. Separate the strings and tack securely to the chamois. Draw the strings over the bridge and through the notches in the neck. Tie all four strings around the stem firmly. Raising the strings over the bridge makes them transmit vibrations to the sound box. This banjo, the fife (page 113), the cigar box violin (page 52), the marimba (page 164) can be added to the music corner.

A GOURD BIRDHOUSE

To make a birdhouse from a gourd, cut a round hole in the center. Clean out the pith and seeds. Varnish, paint, or shellac the gourd. Fasten the birdhouse to a tree with a wire or strong string as in the picture. The house is ready for bird tenants to move in.

To attract birds, in addition to providing shelter, keep a supply of water on hand.

GOURD BOOKENDS

Select two sizable and well-shaped gourds for a pair of bookends. Cut off the tops of the gourds far enough down so that you can hollow out the insides. Fill the gourds with sand. Glue the tops back in place. Shellac the gourd bookends and allow to dry.

A GOURD BOWL

A bowl to hold Dad's pipe, tobacco, matches, cigarettes, or cigars can be made from a gourd. Select a gourd that is dry. Cut off the top, and clean out the inside. To make it fireproof, line the bowl with a thin coat of clay. After it is dry, paint the outside, allow it to dry, and then shellac.

GOURD CONTAINERS

Round gourds make good baskets and containers. You may use them for sewing baskets or button boxes. The dipper gourd—a gourd used by the early pioneers as a dipper, water bottle, or spoon—is an interesting shape for a vase. Conceal a small bottle or glass inside to hold the water.

To prepare the gourd, make certain that it is thoroughly dry. Cut off the top and scrape out the pith and seeds. Shellac the gourd and allow to dry thoroughly.

GUESSING BY TOUCH

AN INDOOR GAME

Here is a game that develops the sense of touch and affords practice in drawing and spelling. Ask the class to collect a variety of objects beginning with the same letter, as

banana	bat	basket
book	blotter	bell
ball	belt	block
box	bean shooter	boat

Divide the class into two teams or let them choose sides and a captain for each team. The captains take turns in calling upon a player from their teams to go to the front of the room, to be blindfolded, and to identify one of the objects handed him by the teacher. When he thinks that he has identified the object, the player returns it, removes the blindfold, draws a picture, and spells out the name on the blackboard.

A picture and correct spelling give the player's team a point.

HALLOWEEN JACK-O'-LANTERNS

In addition to the traditional pumpkin lanterns, attractive jack-o'-lanterns may be made from cardboard shoe boxes, oatmeal cartons, and paint pails. Cut out the eyes, nose, and mouth for the jack-o'-lantern. On the inside of the lantern paste colored tissue paper over openings made for the features. Fit the lantern over an electric light bulb and a soft glow will be cast through the tissue paper.

A HALLOWEEN NOISEMAKER

To make this noisemaker, drive a hole through the bottom of a tin can with a hammer and nail. Tie a string about 3 feet long to the nail, and thread the string through the bottom of the can, placing the nail flat in the can. Resin the string and tie several knots near the free end. Hold the string taut and rub the thumb over the knots. The resulting noise is like radio static.

HALLOWEEN PUMPKIN DECORATIONS

Here is a good use for discarded phonograph records. Paint the records orange color on both sides and use black for the Halloween face. Paint a face on both sides. Hang the Halloween "pumpkins" from the ceiling with a strong string fastened through the hole in the record. They make an effective decoration.

If you prefer not to hang them, paint one side only, and set the "pumpkins" about here and there on plate racks.

A HALLOWEEN TRICK

A NOISEMAKER

Here is a Halloween noisemaker that is a good imitation of the sound of a curtain being torn. You will need an empty spool, about a yard of string, a lead pencil, or a stick of similar size.

Notch the edges of the spool. Tie one end of the string to the spool and wind the string around it. Stick a pencil, or a stick of similar size, into the end of the spool to serve as a handle. The noisemaker is now ready. To use it, hold the spool against the outside of a window and pull the string suddenly. The noise is that of a tearing curtain.

HALLOWEEN WINDOWS

The soaping of windows by Halloween pranksters has exasperated many a businessman. To counteract this annoyance, an increasing number of communities are making efforts to direct the energies of boys and girls into constructive channels.

Businessmen, for example, offer the windows of their business places for decoration. School administrators and teachers are usually eager to accept the challenge, and teachers and children set about to plan suitable art work. Children become intrigued in Halloween art, in sketches of witches, spooks, jack-o'-lanterns, corn shocks. The children choose the best ones and a committee of school artists reproduces the decorations on the windows of stores and other business places.

For painting on glass mix equal parts of Bon Ami and alabastine with dry tempera paint. (Alabastine is another name for glass paint or whiting. It comes in powder form and is obtainable at hardware or paint stores.) Add enough water to make a creamy paste. The paint, of course, supplies the color.

Merchants and businessmen, boys and girls are enthusiastic about this new method of "soaping," and, in some instances, prizes are given and "honorable mentions" are bestowed for the most effective windows.

HANDKERCHIEF APRON

You will need three handkerchiefs for this apron. Cut one handkerchief on the diagonal to make two triangles and another

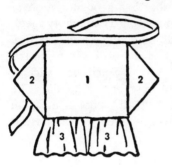

one across the center to make two rectangles. Use the uncut one for the center of the apron for the part marked "1" in the illustration. Sew the two triangles marked "2" in position. Shirr or gather the two rectangles to the bottom of the first handkerchief (3 in the picture). Sew a ribbon to the top for apron strings.

A HAT RACK AND UMBRELLA HOLDER

FOR A GIFT

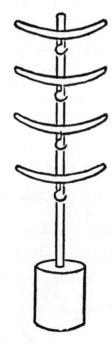

For a convenient, inexpensive hat rack and umbrella holder, you will need these materials:

A broomstick
4 wooden clothes hangers
4 screws
1 empty two-gallon paint can
5 lbs. plaster of Paris
A drill with a bit that will bore a hole smaller than the screws.

Screw the clothes hangers to the broomstick upside down to form the spreading arms of the hat rack. Select screws that are neither too large nor too small. Nails are not very satisfactory as they are apt to split the broomstick. Drill starter holes in the broomstick to start the screws, and also in the clothes hangers if it is necessary.

To make a weighted base, moisten the plaster of Paris with water and mix to form a paste. Fill the paint can about three-fourths full with wet plaster of Paris so that the top of the can will help to support the umbrellas. With a broomstick or similar object, press holes into the wet plaster of Paris and work the holes large enough to accommodate umbrellas of various sizes.

Push the broomstick supporting the hat rack into the center of the mixture. Hold or fasten it in position until the plaster of Paris sets firmly. When the plaster is dry, paint the hat rack and umbrella holder and then wax.

HEIGHT AND WEIGHT PROGRESS CHARTS

Children enjoy watching the progress they make in height and weight. Mark off on paper a column for each pupil so that he can write his name, the date, his height and weight.

Draw a perpendicular 6-foot rule on a strip of butcher paper. Show feet and inches on the ruler. Pin up the ruler and record sheet in a corner of the room or on other available space. Let the children measure each other by standing against the ruler. If there is a scales in the building, take the group to have them weighed.

Repeat the process about every four or six months. The children will be delighted if they can show progress.

HIDING THE ERASER

AN INDOOR GAME FOR THE PRIMARY GRADES

To start Hiding the Eraser, ask one row of players to leave the room. Ask someone in the room to "hide" the eraser in plain sight. The players return to the room to look for the eraser. As soon as a player sees it, he says nothing and slips quietly into his seat. The others do likewise. The first player in his seat is given the privilege of hiding the eraser the next time.

THE HIGH FLIERS

A SPELLING CLUB

As an inducement for pupils to improve their spelling, encourage them to join the High Fliers. To be eligible for this club, the pupil must be able to keep his bird up in a tree; and, to keep his bird up, he must make a good score in spelling.

Prepare a roost for the birds by painting a large tree on art paper. Cut it out and hang it on the bulletin board. Then each speller cuts a bird from colored construction paper, writes his name on the bird, and pins it on the tree. If he makes a high score in spelling for the week, the speller's bird remains in the tree. If he does not, his bird comes down in the hope that he will be a High Flier the next week. The teacher may cut out a tree from a large piece of old felt. Green or brown felt is suitable. Then the children cut out birds from variously colored scraps of felt. The birds will "roost" in the tree without additional support, because one piece of felt adheres to another.

Select a box in which to keep the "bird" during a week the speller does not make a high score. Then when he does score, the speller can go to the box, get his bird, and place it on the tree.

HILLS FOR A SAND TABLE

CONSTRUCTION WORK

A quick, economical way to make hills on a sand table is to turn a cardboard box or boxes upside down to form the foundation for the hills. Cover the top and sides of the box with rumpled newspapers. Dip more papers in a watery paste so that they will stick together. When the hills are dry, color with calcimine or tempera paints. Color them green or earth color, depending upon the season and the effect that you wish to achieve.

To get the effect of steep, high, round or flat-topped hills, use boxes, such as oatmeal and standard cereal boxes, shoe and stationery boxes.

132

HOPSCOTCH AND SQUAT HOPSCOTCH

Hopscotch is a game played on a kind of court, which often varies in shape and complexity from region to region and country to country. The court may be marked with a stick on a dirt playground or with chalk on a hard outdoor or indoor playing area. Make each compartment 2 feet square.

The word "hopscotch" practically explains the game. It means *to leap* (hop) *a line* (scotch). To play the game, players take turns in tossing a puck, which may be a small block of wood or pebble, into Square 1. The first player hops on one foot across the line into Square 1, kicks the puck back across the line, and hops back to the starting position. This time he tosses the puck into Square 2. He hops through Square 1, into Square 2, kicks the puck, and hops back via the route he came.

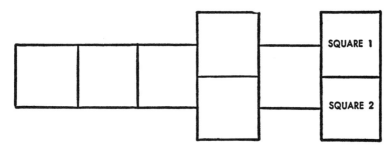

The play continues from square to square until a player misses. He misses by stepping on a line, by losing his balance, or by getting the puck into the wrong square. He loses his turn and waits until the others have played. He wins if he moves successfully through all the squares.

SQUAT HOPSCOTCH

Squat hopscotch is played like the game described above except that the players squat on their heels and place their hands on their hips, instead of hopping on one foot. This is more difficult, and it is suitable for those who have outgrown the easier form of hopscotch.

133

HOUSE NUMBERS

Attractive house numbers can be made with a board and enough pop bottle caps to form the numbers. Select a thin board about 12 x 4 inches. Sketch the number on the board with pencil. Make the pencil numbers wide to give room for the tops. Then follow the pattern by nailing the caps to the board smooth side up. Paint the board a neutral color and the numbers a bright contrasting color to make them stand out.

ILLUSTRATING BOOKLETS

Children often enjoy illustrating booklets. This type of activity may be worked up in connection with the story hour. Take a sheet of butcher paper 15 x 20 inches. Fold it twice to make a 4-page booklet. Slit the pages at the top and bind the booklet with yarn.

Read or tell a story to the class. Then encourage each child to illustrate an incident from the story. Crayon lends itself well to butcher paper. Older children will enjoy writing text to go with the pictures.

The books may then be arranged into an attractive display, or into a book border as in the illustration on page 24.

IMPROVING ENUNCIATION

An activity in lip reading interests most boys and girls and improves their enunciation. A lip reader catches the words of a speaker by watching the movements of his mouth and facial expressions without hearing his voice.

Demonstrate how carefully words must be formed with the lips and mouth without speaking aloud but so that the speaker may be understood. At first the children try to understand what the teacher is saying. Then the children take turns speaking silently to their classmates.

INDIAN COSTUMES

The costumes described in this project are for Indians in general. They are not those of a particular tribe. Encourage boys and girls to bring burlap sacks that have been laundered and pressed. These usually are obtainable at feed stores.

INDIAN WOMAN'S COSTUME

To make a squaw's dress, use the bottom of the sack for the top. Using the pattern on the left as a guide, cut a pattern from paper in the size desired. Then cut out the dress from the material and sew up the side seams. Fringe the bottom of the skirt and the sleeves. Make the fringe for the skirt about 2 inches deep and 1 inch for the sleeves. Use calcimine paint to decorate the dress with Indian designs (see page 136).

Long strips of beads wound around the neck five or six times may be worn with the costume. See page 68 for macaroni beads.

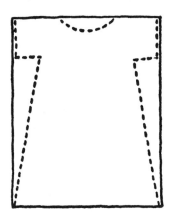 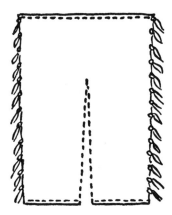

INDIAN BRAVE'S COSTUME

Make a two-piece costume for an Indian brave consisting of tunic and trousers. Use the same pattern as for the squaw's dress but cut off the garment at the hips. Cut out a pair of long trousers, using the pattern at the right as a guide. Sew up the inside seams. Plan for a fringe up the outer sides of the trouser legs.

Cut two strips as long as the trousers and 2½ inches wide. Make the fringe 2 inches and sew to the outer sides of the trouser legs.

Children enjoy making their own Indian costume under the teacher's supervision and taking it home to enjoy as a costume after it has passed its usefulness at school.

INDIAN DESIGNS

The designs of the Indians were symbolic, and they were created from the forms of nature that were close at hand. Every line, circle, and zigzag stood for something. The designs in the top row beginning at the left, for example, represented whirling logs in a river, the thunderbird was thought to cause lightning and thunder, a stepped pyramid indicated a mountain, and a zigzag arrow a snake or lightning. In the middle row are falling rain and a single cloud above the earth. The three lower designs represent a group of rain clouds, a single storm cloud, and the earth divided into north, east, south, and west.

The patterns in Indian art and crafts varied from tribe to tribe and from region to region. No attempt is made to identify the designs given above with any particular group of Indians.

INDIAN DRUMS

To make an Indian drum, you will need a strong, round container approximately 10 inches in diameter and 14 inches deep, such as a nail keg, a wooden cheese box, a casein glue keg, or a large fruit juice can (often obtainable from the school cafeteria or local restaurant). A tall container—one that is no more than 6 inches in diameter—makes an excellent drum, too. You also will need strong string or leather thongs, a stout needle with a large eye, and two strong sticks for drum sticks.

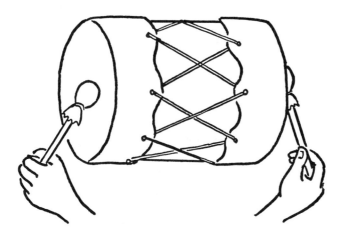

If you have a container that is the right height, remove the top and bottom. If you do not have, cut one down that can be used for the body of the drum. If you wish, decorate the drum with an Indian design. Avoid putting the design near the rim of the drum since this will be covered.

Cut two circles of chamois large enough to cover the ends of the drum. Allow for a generous overlap. Wet the chamois and stretch it tightly across the ends. Lace the chamois together with stout string or leather thongs as indicated in the picture. If you are using a cardboard container for the body of the drum, apply a coat or two of lacquer or shellac and allow to dry thoroughly before stretching the wet chamois over the cardboard.

To make the drum sticks, pad the ends heavily with wadded cloth. Cover the padding with cloth and tie to the drum stick.

INDIANS PEEPING OUT OF A PUMPKIN

A TABLE DECORATION

To make this intriguing table decoration, you need a pumpkin large enough to accommodate two or three corn-ear Indians, two or three unhusked ears of corn, and as many apples. Cut off the top of the pumpkin and hollow it out as for a jack-o'-lantern.

To make an Indian, make a hole in the base of an ear of corn by driving in a nail 1½ inches deep. Pull out the nail and insert a toothpick. Spear an apple on the other end of the toothpick for the Indian's head. Make the hair from black crepe paper, the nose with a gumdrop, the eyes with white beans, and carve the mouth with a paring knife. Arrange the Indians in the pumpkin so that they are peeping over the rim.

INDIAN TEPEE

Tepees, used for shelter by most Plains Indians, have an allure for children. To make a tepee big enough for children to stand up in, you need about 7 or 8 bamboo fishing poles and 6 burlap sacks. The Indians, of course, used buffalo hides. The poles should be at least 6 feet long.

To make the framework for this conical tent, lace the poles together firmly about 8 inches from the top with wire or heavy string. Spread the poles apart at the other end so that they form a circle.

Slit the burlap sacks apart on one side and across the bottom to make rectangular pieces. Then sew the rectangles together to form a large sheet. Cover the frame with the burlap, and fold back the corners at the top to allow for ventilation and for the escape of smoke. With heavy string, sew or tack the covering to the poles near the top and bottom to keep it from slipping. Lace together the edges of the covering down the front. Allow for an entrance down the front by folding back the flaps.

Decorate the tepee in an Indian design with calcimine paint. This may be done before or after the cover is put in place.

AN INDIVIDUAL FILE

Children have need for a place to keep samples of their written work, such as lessons for the week, test papers, or any work that they are particularly proud of. Spindles may serve as individual files.

To provide spindles for a class, drive long nails about ten inches apart through laths. Use the projecting nails for spindles. Fasten the laths to the wall at a height convenient for the children and safely above their heads. The laths may be arranged in rows. Assign the spindles to the children, giving the spindles in the top row to the taller children.

INK BLOT DESIGNS

Designs made with ink blots are often very pleasing and surprising to children. Fold a sheet of ruled or typewriter paper once or twice if you wish to make two or four pages. Open the paper and drop several small drops of ink near the fold. Fold the paper again gently and press along the folds and then smooth outward to the edge. Open the paper to see what has happened.

INVISIBLE INK

Boys and girls always have been fascinated by writing with invisible ink. It may be used for a Halloween treasure hunt in preparing maps and clues leading to hidden treasure (page 275).

Another use for "magic" ink is invisible drawing. A picture of a classmate, or perhaps of one's favorite pet, drawn with invisible ink usually gets out of hand and affords merriment and laughter when the drawing is made visible.

Lemon juice is an excellent invisible ink. Use a clean steel pen and write on white paper. When the paper is pressed with a warm iron or held over a hot radiator, the ink turns brown, seemingly by magic.

JACKETS FOR DRINKING GLASSES

FOR A GIFT

Attractive jackets for drinking glasses may be made with crepe paper rope. To make the rope, cut crepe paper into long strips 1 inch wide, and roll the strips into a tight rope.

To make the jacket, begin by fashioning a lining. Cut a circle from wax paper to fit the bottom of the glass. Then cut a rectangle from wax paper and make a cylinder to fit around the sides of the glass about half way up. The purpose of the wax paper lining is to protect the glass from glue that you will use in making the jacket. Make another lining in the same way from crepe paper. Put the two linings together by placing the wax paper lining inside the crepe paper one. Set the glass in the jacket linings and fasten the linings to the glass temporarily with rubber bands.

Now you are ready to wind with crepe paper rope. Glue one end of the rope to the center bottom. Wind the bottom, gluing the coils to the crepe lining as you proceed. Work out to the sides and half way up the glass. Allow the glue to dry thoroughly. Then remove the glass. Shellac the crepe paper rope jacket and allow to dry. Make as many jackets as you need for a set. They are welcome gifts especially during the hot weather period.

JACK-IN-THE-BOX

To make a jack-in-the-box, cut two strips from butcher paper about 2½ to 3 feet long and ½ inch wide. Lay the ends of the paper at right angles to each other and fold one strip over the other to form a spring.

Draw the head of a clown on a paper circle about 1 inch in diameter. Cut it out and paste it to one end of the spring. Paste the other end to the inside of a match folder. Close the folder and press it down hard for a few moments. Raise the cover and the jack-in-the-box pops out.

JAPANESE CARP KITE

In some of the eastern countries—China, Japan, Korea, the Malay Peninsula—kiteflying is an old custom. There kite holidays make kiteflying a national pastime. In Japan, where the carp is a symbol of strength and courage, men and boys fly elaborate carp-shaped kites. This is true especially on Boys' Day when carp kites are seen everywhere. The kites are made from beautiful, sheer materials, such as rice paper and thin silk, and decorated in delicate colors and designs.

If you wish to try your hand at making a carp kite, use a variety of strong tissue or other thin paper. Double the paper and cut a fish approximately 4 feet long and 18 inches wide. Paint the eyes and fish scales in bright colors. Make the fins and an elaborate tail from long crepe-paper streamers. Then glue the edges together to make a fish-shaped paper bag.

For the fish's mouth, use a large ring or small hoop about 6 inches in diameter. One hoop of a pair of embroidery hoops is ideal. Fasten a string in two places to form a loop as in the picture. Fasten one end of a 15-foot string to the loop and the other end to an 8-foot bamboo pole. The pole will serve as a handle for maneuvering the kite.

A JEWEL BOX

A sparkling jewel box may be made from a cardboard, tin, or wooden box. Choose a box that is of appropriate size, and cover it with papier-mâché. To add to the "jewel touch," stud the top and sides of the box with beads, sequins, or bits of broken Christmas tree ornaments while the papier-mâché is still wet. If the "jewels" used for decorating do not have enough body to become embedded in the papier-mâché, coat one side of a bead, sequin, or bit of ornament with glue and then press into place. To make papier-mâché, see page 195.

JIGSAW PUZZLE MAP

Maps make ideal jigsaw puzzles. Use commercial maps, maps from discarded geography books or atlases, or use schoolmade maps. Mount the maps on heavy cardboard. Shellac and when dry cut them into small, jigsaw pieces. Mix the pieces and the puzzle is ready to be put together.

JIGSAW PUZZLES

Jigsaw puzzles in endless numbers can be made from the colored pictures that are reproduced in magazines. As soon as a magazine has lost its current usefulness, clip the pictures that you want to use for puzzles. Glue the picture on cardboard or thin softwood. Shellac to preserve the surface. When it is dry, cut the mounted picture into small pieces with scissors, penknife, jig saw, or coping saw.

KEEP AWAY

AN ARITHMETIC GAME

To play Keep Away, children form into a circle. Four or five players volunteer to go into the "mush pot," which is in the center of the circle. The teacher chooses a problem from a recent arithmetic lesson that involves the skill in which she wishes to review the class. She calls upon a player in the circle and he tries to give the correct answer before anyone in the mush pot does. If he succeeds, the teacher calls upon another player. Should anyone in the mush pot come up with the correct answer first, he and the player called upon exchange places. The point of the game is for players to keep out of the mush pot.

KEEPING TRACK OF A TREE

An interesting project for a class is to watch and to record the seasonal changes of trees. Encourage each pupil to select a tree near school or his home and to draw a picture of the tree once a month. In early September the tree may still have most of its summer foliage. Be sure to watch for seeds, nuts, or acorns. By October the leaves may have turned bright yellow and perhaps some of them have fallen to the ground. By November the tree probably will have lost all of its leaves.

During the winter months, cut a small twig from the tree to study its buds and leaf scars. The buds are there even during the coldest weather.

In spring, do not let the tree steal a march on you. Watch for the buds and flowers as trees have flowers just like other plants. On some trees, the flowers appear before the leaves and are so tiny that you will need a magnifying glass to see them.

The monthly pictures should be kept so that you will have a pictorial record of the tree.

KEY RING ORNAMENTS

An ornament or tab is a convenient device to have on your key ring as an aid in finding your keys. The ornament may be a figurine of a bird, a pixie, or anything that appeals to you.

Make the figurine from thin wood. Draw the outline of the figure on paper, cut it out and use it for a pattern by tracing it on the wood. Sandpaper, paint, and shellac it. Drill or whittle a hole large enough to insert a key ring or chain.

Key ring ornaments may also be made from felt, inner tubing, or pipe cleaners. Pipe cleaners may be manipulated into a figurine and trimmed with yarn.

KITES

A project that involves kitemaking is always popular with boys (and girls, too) and furnishes valuable experience in handicraft pursuits. Kites vary in complexity from plane surface and box kites to elaborate dragon- and fish-shaped kites flown by boys in oriental countries. (See Japanese Carp Kite on page 141.)

The kite described here is the bow kite which is made with two sticks crossed at right angles and with one of the sticks drawn in to form a bow. Select two strips of balsam or any lightweight wood, one 2 feet long and the other 3 feet and each about 1 inch wide. Notch both ends of each stick and wind the stick near the notches with strong, light-weight string to keep the stick from splitting. Lay the shorter stick across the longer at right angles about 8 inches from one end. Tack the sticks together and then wind with string at the intersection as in the illustration.

Draw the crossbeam into a bow by stretching a stout string tightly from end to end through the notches. Stretch another string through all four notches or stickends to form the perimeter or outline of the kite.

To cover the kite, cut butcher paper or wrapping paper in the shape of the kite, allowing for an overlap of $1/2$ inch on all sides. Paste the covering on the bow side. Turn the overlap over the string edge and paste down to make a firm border.

Tie one end of a 40-inch string to the long stick about 4 inches from the top. Punch a small hole in the paper and thread the string through. Tie the other end to the long stick about 4 inches from the bottom. Again punch a small hole to put the string through and then tie. Give the string a little slack on the paper side. This slack string on a kite is called a "bridle." Tie one end of a ball of string to the bridle. Make a tail about 18 inches long

144

by tying short strips of rags to a string. Fasten the tail to the end of the kite. The kite is ready to fly.

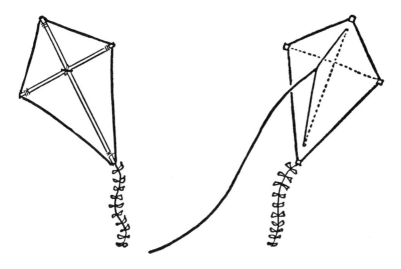

WARNING: Never use a wire for a kite string if you fly a kite anywhere near an electric power line or during an electrical storm. Boys have been electrocuted when their kite strings touched electric wires. Be sure to keep away from electric wires.

LABELS FOR TREES

FOR THE PRIMARY AND INTERMEDIATE GRADES

When they learn the name of a tree or shrub in the school-yard, children enjoy identifying it for others. They may make a label of wood or metal and letter the name with a small paint brush. If tin is used for the label, punch in the letters with a hammer and nail. Tie the label around the tree or shrub. Drill or punch a hole in each end of the label. Thread a string through the holes and tie around the tree. Do not nail the label to the tree, and do not use a wire instead of a string. A wire could harm the growth of the tree.

LAPEL ORNAMENTS

Lapel ornaments are acceptable gifts at all seasons of the year, for birthdays, Christmas, Easter, Mother's Day, or for "just a gift." (For Felt Lapel Pins, see pages 112–13.)

FALL AND WINTER ORNAMENTS

Lapel ornaments are about as seasonal as hats, and attractive ones in fall and winter colors may be begun soon after school opens in the fall. If the region abounds in pod-, cone-, and acorn-bearing trees, such as eucalyptus, cypress, and oak, children are indeed fortunate. Encourage them to gather these tree "seeds." Burrs gathered from weeds are ornamental, too.

FEATHER ORNAMENT

Collect small, downy feathers and dip them in calcimine or tempera paint. Let them dry and then fluff them out. With fine wire, fasten the feathers to a small twig, and wire a safety pin to the back side for a fastener. The ornament is ready to wear.

RIBBON AND BUTTON ORNAMENT

Buttons and odds and ends of ribbon may be made into flowers for a different type of lapel ornament. Select a ribbon about ½ to 1 inch wide. To make a petal, fold the ribbon into a loop.

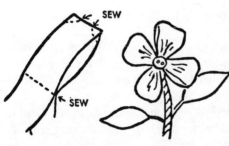

Sew across the top corners, turn the petal right side out, and gather at the bottom. All four petals may be made from the same piece of ribbon, but twist the ribbon so that two petals are at right angles to the other two. Stitch the petals in the center to hold them in place, then add the button. Make as many flowers as you wish from the same ribbon.

146

Make the stems from twigs or wire. If you are using wire, wind it with green ribbon or crepe paper. Attach a safety pin for a fastener. Beautiful ornaments may be worked out with ribbon.

LAUNDRY BAG

FOR A GIFT

Suitable for a laundry bag are materials such as burlap, denim sugar, or flour sacking. You will need 1½ yards of material about 27-inches wide. The width of the material will be the width of the laundry bag. Fold the cloth double and sew up the sides. Hem the top to form a casing for a drawstring and then pull a string or cord through. Write or letter the word "Laundry" across the bag. Handwriting adds a personal touch. Then embroider the word with yarn.

A LEAF COLLECTION

To help boys and girls identify trees and plants in the neighborhood or community, encourage them to gather leaves from plants and trees and to work out a system of labeling.

The leaves may be pressed, mounted, and arranged into a scrapbook collection, or they may be mounted on cardboard and used for a frieze. Instead of pressing, you may want to make blueprint pictures of the leaves as described on page 24. Children may also enjoy drawing them and mounting them on cardboard for a border Be sure always to letter the name of the leaf.

A LEAF PLAQUE

o make a plaque from a leaf, select a leaf with well-defined ins and an interesting shape. Cut out a base for the plaque from soft wood. Let the size of the leaf determine the size of the plaque. However, 4½ x 6 inches is a convenient size. Sandpaper the wood smooth.

Lay the leaf face down on a soft pile of newspapers and spread ink on it. Apply the ink with a roller, which may be obtained at a store carrying art or stationer's supplies. Lay the leaf inked side down on the plaque and cover it with a sheet of thin paper. To transfer the ink to the wood, rub the surface evenly and firmly with your fingers. Remove the paper and the leaf and retouch the design with pen and ink or use a small brush. Paint the leaf with water colors.

To bring the pattern into relief, cut away the parts of the surface of the plaque that are not necessary for the leaf design. Also allow for a plain border of suitable width. Use a chisel and a spike or any pointed tool for carving away the background.

Finish the plaque with a coat of shellac, and the plaque is ready to be hung on the wall.

LETTER HOLDER

To make an attractive letter holder or rack, use a chalk box. Cut off the top and ends. Shorten the front side by cutting it down about 2 inches. Use the sides and bottom of the chalk box for the sides and bottom of the holder. Reinforce the sides by driving small nails into the side pieces from the bottom.

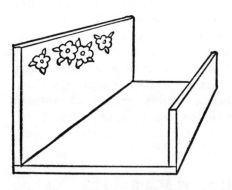

Paint the holder any color you like and decorate it with a picture. If you are not clever at drawing or painting, cut a picture from a magazine and paste it on the holder. If you prefer a design in an allover pattern, adapt one of the designs described on pages 87–89.

148

LETTERS TO A CLASSMATE

Anyone absent from school for any length of time will be cheered by letters and greetings from his classmates. An opportunity is provided for a practical lesson in letter writing and for keeping the absentee up to date on school affairs.

LETTERING

To keep the bulletin board up to date, you will need to change the "headlines" frequently. To meet this situation, prepare letters early in the school year and keep them on hand for ready use. The letters should be simple, bold, and easy to read. Design them with this in mind. Use dark letters on a light bulletin board and light letters on a dark background.

Make the letters from construction paper. Cut the paper into long strips. Let the width of the strip be determined by the height of the letters. If, for example, you need letters 1 inch high, cut the strip that width and fold the strip into 1-inch squares in accordion fashion. Then draw a letter in each square. The letters *M* and *W* will fill the squares completely, but an *I* will take up little of the width of its square.

Cut the letters apart on the fold and cut out the outline of the letters. Make duplicates for the more commonly used letters, such as *A, E, T, S*. Put them in a box until you need them. Use pins for tacking up the letters, as pins are less damaging and not as conspicuous as thumbtacks.

On this page and the next is an alphabet. If the letters are the right size, you may want to trace them. Be careful to trace lightly in order not to damage the book in any way.

EFGH
IJKL
MNOP
QRST
UVWX
YZ?

LIBRARY PASTE

A good library paste can be made from the starch of a sweet potato. Peel and grate a large sweet potato. Wrap the gratings in cheesecloth and dip into a bowl of cold water. Squeeze the starch, a milky-looking substance, into the water. Allow the starch to settle several hours. Then pour off the clear water, and wash the starch with fresh water. Allow the starch to settle again. Pour off the clear water a second time, and allow the starch to dry.

Mix the starch with water to a pasty consistency. Be careful not to add too much water.

LIGHT-BULB FIGURINES

A parade of comical characters may be made with burned-out light bulbs and dressing them in crepe paper and lace paper doilies. Two kinds—a soprano and basso—are described in this project, but children may enjoy continuing the parade to include an entire choir or the chorus of a musical show. A project like this has possibilities and children will come up with suggestions.

THE SOPRANO

Choose a frosted light bulb of 60 or 75 watts. From white cardboard, cut an oval that is about 5 inches in diameter at the wide part. Decorate the border with musical notes or leave it plain to resemble a spot light. Cut a hole in the center of the oval large enough to slip the screw end of the bulb through. Mold a base from modeling clay and press the screw end of the bulb into the wet clay to hold it upright.

Dress the prima donna in a white bodice and long, full lace skirt. Fashion the bodice from crepe paper and cut a swath from a paper doily for the skirt. Allow for a 1/4-inch overlap at the waistline and glue the overlap to the bulb. Use a narrow colored ribbon for a sash and a strip of doily scallops for the collar.

To make the hair, dust cotton batting with dry calcimine paint and glue the wig in place. Draw in the features with India ink or with a wax pencil, obtainable at an art or stationery store. Make the music sheet ahead of the hands. Cut a rectangle from paper 1 x 1½ inches and fold it crosswise. Decorate the covers to resemble those of sheet music. Now cut the hands from adhesive tape and stick them in place so that they appear to be holding the music. Anchor the music with Scotch tape.

THE BASSO

To make the basso, turn a frosted light bulb upside down, turn it so that the screw end is at the top. Make a 5-inch oval cardboard with a hole in the center large enough to press the end of the bulb through and into a base of wet modeling clay.

Dress the basso in a white choir robe. Let the frosted bulb represent the robe and draw lines to give an open front effect. Make the collar and tie from adhesive tape. Color the tie with crayon before cutting it out. Cut the features from adhesive tape that has been colored black or any color that you like. For the mortar board, cut a 2-inch square from black construction paper and a hole in the center just big enough for the small end of the bulb to fit through. Anchor the mortar board with Scotch tape. Cut thread into 3-inch lengths for the tassel and fasten it in place with black adhesive tape.

Fashion the music and hands as you did for the soprano. Cut the feet from black adhesive tape and paste them in place.

LINOLEUM-BLOCK PRINTING

To print from a block, you cut away the parts of the surface of a block that you do not want to print. To block print from linoleum, cut a piece of unembossed linoleum to fit a smooth rectangular or square block of wood any size from 1 to 8 inches. Use battleship linoleum because of its thickness. Glue the bottom side of the linoleum to the block of wood. Paste on the linoleum paper cut out of the design that you wish to print. The cutout serves as a guide to the carver. With a penknife, or with block-print cutting tools, cut away the unnecessary parts of the design to a depth of about $\frac{1}{16}$ of an inch. Apply oil paints or special block-printing paints to the raised areas. The paints and the cutting tools can be obtained in most stores that carry art supplies.

Lay the material or paper to be block printed on a flat surface. Place the block print face down on the material, and press with a block-print roller or with a kitchen rolling pin. Remove the block print and allow the material to dry.

Cloth, paper, and cardboard lend themselves well to printing from linoleum blocks. Articles that may be printed follow:

A LITERARY AND HISTORICAL MAP

A map showing the location of some of the literary and historical landmarks in your state is fun to assemble and even more fun to draw. Spend some time in gathering the information and in planning the map. Then draw an outline map of your state on lightweight cardboard or drawing paper. Mark the sites by drawing a small picture or a flag. If you use a flag to designate the site, arrange a key in the lower right- or left-hand corner giving the date, place, and event.

Here are a few suggestions for a map, taking California as an example. Other events may be substituted or added.

About 4000 years old . . .	General Sherman, the largest of the giant sequoias in Sequoia National Park
1542 San Diego	Cabrillo discovers San Diego
1559 Drake's Bay	Sir Francis Drake sails into Drake's Bay
1602 Monterey Bay . . .	Vizcaino rediscovers Monterey Bay
1769 San Diego	Father Junípero Serra founds mission
1776 San Francisco . . .	Presidio built and still standing
1781 Los Angeles	Los Angeles founded
——— Hemet	Home of Ramona, the title and heroine of a novel by Helen Hunt Jackson
1839 Sacramento	Sutter founds colony
1848 Coloma	Gold discovered at Sutter's mill
1851 Point Loma	Old Spanish lighthouse, honoring Cabrillo
1864 Angel's Camp . . .	Mark Twain mines gold
1888 Los Angeles	First trainload of oranges leaves for eastern market

THE LITTLE MOUSE THAT COULDN'T SEE

A GAME FOR THE PRIMARY GRADES

The players form a circle. Someone is chosen to be the Little Mouse who is blindfolded and stands in the center of the circle. On a signal to begin, the players join hands and walk slowly to the right. Meanwhile the mouse gropes her way to the perimeter of the circle to stop and to identify one of the players. If she succeeds in three guesses, the mouse and player exchange places. The new Little Mouse is blindfolded and moves into the center of the circle, and play begins again.

LIVE DOLLS THAT PERFORM

This is an activity in which boys and girls become live dolls and perform on a "table" from behind a screen. They may act out short stories or episodes from longer stories. To dress the doll actors, draw the costumes large enough so that the actors can stick their heads and hands through the necks and sleeves of the costumes.

On a large sheet of wrapping paper or on an old bed sheet that is large enough to be used for a screen, draw costumes for the

characters that you wish to portray. Do not draw the heads and hands of the characters. Draw the costumes two or three feet tall and show them standing on a table as in the illustration. Cut holes for the head and hands and use crayon for coloring paper costumes and calcimine for cloth.

Adjust the height of the screen so that the actors can reach the costumes when standing on the floor. Tack the screen in a doorway, or hang it from a rope drawn across a corner of the room, or tack it to a rod cut down perhaps from an old fishing pole. To support the rod horizontally, set two orange crates lengthwise on each side. Put one on top of the other and place several heavy books inside the crates to hold them in place.

LIVE MODELS

FOR THE PRIMARY AND INTERMEDIATE GRADES

Working with live models greatly improves the ability of boys and girls to draw. Let several boys and girls volunteer to serve as models. Ask them to come to the front of the class. Point out the proportions of the human figure: the size of the head, the length of the arms, the position of the waist, the knees, the elbows, and the width of the shoulders. Children will make useful observations that will lead to more creative work. This type of activity aids in developing children's power of observation.

LIVING WORDS

A SPELLING GAME FOR THE PRIMARY GRADES

Here is a spelling game that children thoroughly enjoy. Prepare two flash cards for each letter of the alphabet. Separate the cards into two sets of alphabet cards. Use one as a working set and keep the other in reserve.

Give a card to everyone in the class. Then begin by pronouncing a word from the spelling lesson. The children, holding the right letters, take their cards, step quietly to the front of the class, and arrange themselves in the order that spells the word correctly.

Before game time, however, the teacher needs to scan the spelling list for words containing double letters, such as ball, doll, door, kitten, look, tree, and to assign doubles from the reserve alphabet cards. If there are more than twenty-six children in the class, assign the double letters to the extras. If there are fewer, do not distribute the less frequently used letters. If there are only eight or ten children, for example, give each speller two or more letters. Should it so happen that a speller needs to stand in two places at the same time, he can loan one of his letters to a neighbor letter in the word. The neighbor holds his own card and the additional one, too.

LOCATING CITIES

A GEOGRAPHY GAME

To prepare for this instructive game, cut out the states from a road map or from a discarded geography book or atlas. Mount each state on a separate piece of heavy cardboard or thin piece of wood. Shellac and allow to dry. From another map cut the names of cities throughout the United States. Mount the name of each city on a separate strip of cardboard. Shellac and allow to dry. Put the strips in a box.

To play the game, give each player a map of a state. The leader draws the city from the box, calling the name aloud. The players try to find the corresponding city on their maps. The first one to do so, claims the strip. The first player to claim five cities wins.

If you wish, divide the class into two teams and the first team to get ten cities wins.

LOCAL V.I.P.'s

It is well occasionally to invite people from outside the school to talk to the class. Talks by officers and employees of the local governmental units, for example, stimulate pupils' interest in their community.

Men and women, such as the policeman, the public librarian, the postman, the fire chief, the public health nurse, and the sanitary inspector, are usually willing to visit the classroom and give talks about their work. If you live in a rural community invite the county nurse, the county agricultural agent, or the president of the township board to address the class.

The personal contact of the pupils with the people who make the community "tick" arouses a livelier interest in community problems and achievements and a better understanding of the importance of the services that the officials and employers render. Pupils may be made to realize that they are citizens now and that they do not have to wait until voting age to begin practicing a fine type of citizenship.

A LOCUST SINGER

During the spring and summer months, the parks and forests are filled with the song of the locusts. But the locust like its cousins, the grasshopper and cricket, does not actually sing. It makes a shrill, persistent noise by rubbing its hind legs together. Another variety "sings" by rubbing its legs against its wings.

In studying the grasshopper family, the teacher may want to imitate the "song" of the locust by preparing a mechanical device. Notch a large sucker stick near the top and rub resin into the notch. Punch a hole through the bottom of a small paprika or pepper can with a nail. Resin a horsehair and tie one end to the stick at the notch. Thread the other end through the hole in the can, and tie it to a pin or small nail, which will serve as an anchor. Swing the can by using the stick as a handle, and the "locusts will be singing" even though it may be midwinter. The sound is the result of friction just as it is when the locust rubs its hind legs together.

LOG CABIN

FOR THE UPPER ELEMENTARY GRADES

One of the first tasks of the early settlers upon their arrival in America was the building of a cabin in the forests that overwhelmed them everywhere. It is thought that the first log cabins were built by the Swedes in their settlement on the Delaware River, since they came from a land of forests. In time the typical home of the pioneer was the log cabin.

A log cabin project presents an opportunity for older boys and girls to construct a replica made to scale. A cabin that duplicates one built by the American pioneers, for instance, may be put to use in a social studies unit on colonial life or the westward movement. The early settlers built many varieties of log cabins ranging from crude shelters without floors and windows to substantial and comfortable dwellings with attic floor, windows, and slab doors hung on leather hinges.

158

The cabin of the pioneer was usually rectangular. A common size was 20 x 16 feet. Another popular size was 24 x 18 feet. Four logs were placed on the ground to form the rectangular foundation. The logs for the walls were notched about 9 inches from both ends and laid horizontally one at a time all the way around. The interfitting of the logs at the corners held them in place.

The simplest type of roof was a continuation of the walls. The two opposite sides sloped until they met at the ridge of the roof.

Now the cabin was ready to be chinked. The cracks between the logs were filled with clay. Windows were often covered with the dried stomach lining and intestines of large animals. These were translucent though not transparent. Doors were sometimes made of animal skins. The fireplace and chimney were made of logs and plastered with clay.

To make a replica of a cabin, decide on a convenient size. Let us take the 20 x 16-foot cabin. If you decide to make it $\frac{1}{20}$ as large as the original, the replica will be 12 x $9\frac{3}{4}$ inches. For "logs," use cornstalks, bamboo, or the dry stalks of plants, such as cattails, sugar cane, or western milkweed. To make the smaller size cabin (12 x 9¾ inches), cut enough logs 12 inches long to build the side walls and the roof. Cut 9 ¾-inch logs for the ends of the cabin and 4-inch logs to go at the sides of the doorway. Taper off the logs for the gable walls. Use smaller logs for the gables. Chink the cracks between the logs with modeling clay. No window is shown in the model, but it may be made in the same way as the door.

LOG CABIN "QUICKIE"

If you do not have time to build a log cabin as described on pages 158–59, an effective one may be made quickly with corrugated paper. Study the dimensions given in the preceding project, and decide upon a convenient size.

Cut the corrugated paper for the roof and long walls. This may be cut in one piece if you wish. Then cut the walls for the ends and gables, and allow openings for the door and windows. Use the corrugated side of the paper for the outside of the cabin. Join the corners of this "prefabricated" cabin with Scotch tape. Build a fireplace chimney at one end.

If you wish to make the roof with the corrugations running up and down instead of lengthwise as in the preceding project, cut the roof to fit the cabin, allowing for short eaves on all four sides. To make the ridge of the roof, fold the paper in the middle and place the roof in position. Fasten it with Scotch tape.

LOG CANDLEHOLDER

An interesting candleholder can be made from a small log or sizable branch cut into a log twelve inches long. Plan to use the log horizontally. Flatten it on the bottom to keep it from rolling. Drill three holes in the top side of the log for anchoring the candles. Begin by marking the place for the holes with a piece of chalk and ruler. Place the first hole 2 inches from the left end, the second 6 inches from the left, and the third 10 inches from the left. This arrangement, of course, places a candle two inches from each end of the log and the third one in the middle. Drill the holes large enough to anchor the candles firmly, stick in the candles, and the holder is ready for service. An artificial log may be molded from clay or papier-mâché.

LOG FLOWER HOLDER

An attractive flower holder may be made from a small log about 4 or 5 inches in diameter and 12 inches long. To keep it from rolling, flatten the log by splitting off a segment. Then hollow out a water trough with a hammer and chisel, and line the trough with a thin coating of cement. (Directions for mixing cement mortar are given on page 41.) Allow the cement to dry thoroughly and the holder is ready to be used. This is an article that boys enjoy making and giving as a gift.

LOTTO

A NUMBER GAME FOR THE PRIMARY GRADES

Lotto is a game played with cards bearing numbers, and the first player to cover five in a row wins. A simplified version is described here.

For each player, prepare in advance five blank cardboard markers $\frac{1}{2}$-inch square. On separate slips of paper write numbers from 1 to 20. Keep the markers and the slips of paper until you are ready to play the game. To make lotto cards, give each pupil a small sheet of paper and ask him to put it on the desk in front of him with the long side toward him. Have him rule off twenty $\frac{1}{2}$-inch squares in a pattern similar to the one in the picture on the next page. Write in numbers from 1 to 20 in scrambled order.

To play the game, put the slips of paper in a hat and the teacher draws out one number at a time. She calls the number aloud, and each player covers the identical number on his card

	6		18		11		8		5
	2	17		19		1		13	
4		12		16		10		15	
	7	14		20		3		9	

with a marker. The first player to cover five numbers in a row quickly raises his hand and calls, "Lotto."

LOTTO

AN ARITHMETIC GAME FOR THE INTERMEDIATE GRADES

A version of lotto adapted to the abilities of older boys and girls is similar to the one described in the previous project. On separate slips of paper write numbers from 1 to 20. You do not, however, need markers for this version of the game and the lotto cards are different.

On a small piece of writing paper, the players prepare cards bearing ½-inch squares. They fill in problems in addition, subtraction, multiplication, and division similar to the model on this page. Each player makes up his own problems. The problems must be such that the answers range from one to twenty.

7	14	3	18	9
+5	−8	×6	÷3	+6

The slips bearing numbers from 1 to 20 are deposited in a hat. The teacher draws a number and calls it aloud. If the answer to one of their problems is called, the players write the answer in the square below the problem. Not all players, of course, write every time that a number is called. The first player to fill all five squares raises his hand and calls, "Lotto." He is the winner.

162

MAGIC FLOWERS

AN EXPERIMENT

An impressive experiment may be performed with flowers, sulphur, and a glass tumbler. The purpose of this experiment is to show the reaction of sulphur fumes on the color of flowers. Be careful, however, not to burn sulphur in a house where there are pets nor near silverware or jewelry.

Put ½ teaspoon of powdered sulphur on a noninflammable surface, as an old saucer or a lid from a tin can. Light the sulphur with a match. Turn an old glass tumbler upside down and put it over the burning sulphur, but let in enough air to keep the sulphur burning.

When the sulphur has just about stopped burning, pick up the tumbler now filled with fumes, and quickly put it over a flower. The fumes from the sulphur will take out the color from the flower because sulphur fumes act as a bleaching agent.

WARNING: Boys and girls must keep a safe distance from the fire, and must not lean over the sulphur fumes.

In addition to removing color, white flowers can be given color. Put a small amount of commercial dye in water and put the stem of the flower in the water for an hour or so. The flower will take the color of the dye. White carnations, for example, may be colored green for St. Patrick's Day. Daisies are also good flowers with which to experiment.

MAKING A CHURN AND BUTTER

FOR THE PRIMARY GRADES

A class studying dairies may choose to make a small churn by using a quart glass jar. Select a jar with a screw top but one that is not porcelain lined.

Pour about a pint of cream into the jar. Use cream that is several days old. Shake the cream gently until small lumps of butter form. The children enjoy taking turns at the churn.

If, however, you want to churn with a stirrer, or paddle, whittle one from a piece of wood. Cut a hole through the screw top just large enough for the handle of the paddle. Churn by stirring with the paddle until small lumps of butter form. In a larger churn the stirrer is called a dasher, and it is worked up and down.

Put the butter into a bowl and work it into a lump with the paddle, squeezing out the remaining buttermilk. If you wish add a pinch of salt. Continue to knead the butter with the paddle until it forms a smooth lump. Then serve the butter on crackers as a special treat for the buttermakers.

MAKING A MAGNET

FOR THE UPPER GRADES

If placed gently upon the surface of water, a sewing needle will float. An easy way to lay it on water is to place the needle on a small piece of thin paper and float the paper. When it becomes soaked, the paper will sink, and the needle will remain on the surface of the water.

Point out to the class that the needle takes no special direction. Then make a magnet of the needle. Take the needle out of the water and stroke it about twenty-five times with one end of a magnet. Stroke the needle evenly and in the *same* direction. The needle will become magnetized and therefore a magnet.

Lay the needle on the water a second time. You will notice that one end of the needle now points north just as a magnet.

A MARIMBA

The marimba described here is an 8-note or one octave instrument. It may be made from redwood, rosewood, or maple obtainable at most lumber yards.

The base for the keys is 18 inches long on one side and the ends are 10 and 6½ inches respectively. The fourth side slants as in the illustration. Glue the frame together at the corners. Cut a lath into the same lengths as those of the frame and glue the lath flat side down to the top edges of the base upon which to rest the "keys." Cover the top of the laths with felt by gluing it on.

To make the "keys," cut eight strips of wood into graduated lengths. The dimensions will vary depending upon the kind of wood and the pitch. A good workable size, however, is $7/8$ inch wide x $1/4$ inch thick, and about 8 inches long for middle C. The octave above middle C will be about $4\frac{1}{2}$ inches. Cut the lengths somewhat longer than you expect to use. Then adjust the length by tuning the key with a pitch pipe or piano. To determine the

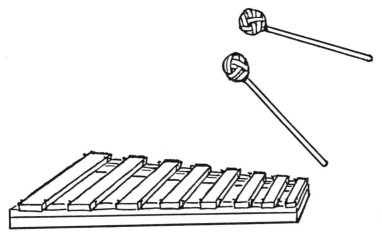

tone, hold the key loosely between your thumb and forefinger and strike it with a hammer. (The hammer is described below.) Cut down the key to the right length with a coping saw, then file to exact size and sandpaper smooth. Do this with all eight keys. Fasten each key in place with 4 small-headed nails as in the picture. Allow space for a little play by not driving the nails in all the way.

To make the hammers used for tuning and playing the marimba, select two sticks about 10 inches in length. Wind one end of each stick with cloth cut into strips until it is about the size of a golf ball. Sew the strips of cloth in place as you wind.

If you wish to make an instrument with a greater range, make a larger base and add more keys of graduated lengths.

MASKS FOR FANCIFUL CHARACTERS

Many characters in plays for children call for fanciful costumes. Characters, such as animals, brownies, gnomes, can be suggested or enhanced with masks. Among the simplest masks are those made with brown paper bags or flour sacking. Select a bag to fit down over the head of the actor. Mark the position for eyes, nose,

and mouth with chalk. Take the bag off to cut the openings. Put it on again and crumple the end in around the wearer's neck to mark the chin line. Remove and decorate the face, using calcimine paint or crayon pencil. Yarn or crepe paper cut into strips makes excellent hair and whiskers. To make ears tie the corners of the bag. Tie a string around the neck to hold the mask in place as in the illustration at the right.

MATCHSTICK PROJECTS

Here is a use for burned kitchen matches. They may be used for social studies projects. Matchsticks, for example, make excellent fences for miniature pioneer and present-day communities. They also make good miniature snow fences which are set up along the windward side of highways and railroad tracks to serve as a barrier for drifting snows. Matches may be used as logs in building tiny log cabins and stockades.

To make a fence, fasten the matchsticks together at regular intervals with thread. Use two rows of thread, one near the top and one near the bottom to hold the sticks in place. Tie the thread to the sticks as you proceed.

MATS FOR HOT DISHES

A mat for use under a hot dish or hot pot of tea may be made from heavy cardboard, cork, or rubber. Cut the material into a square, rectangle, oval, or any shape desired. Embellish the mat with squash seeds, pumpkin seeds, or corn kernels. To color the seeds, dip them in calcimine or tempera paint. When they are dry, glue the seeds to the mat.

Appropriate mats also may be made for various holidays. A shamrock-shaped mat may be made for St. Patrick's Day, a heart for St. Valentine's Day, a turkey gobbler for Thanksgiving, a poinsettia for Christmas.

MAY BASKETS

A pretty May Day custom is the hanging of baskets on the doorknobs of unsuspecting friends. Small baskets are filled with flowers gathered in the woods or in your yard.

PAPER DOILY BASKET

An exquisite May basket may be made from a round paper doily about 8 inches in diameter. Take hold of one edge of the doily and fold over to a point on the opposite edge. *Do not crease the fold.* Tie the two edges together with narrow, crinkled paper ribbon. Tie in a bow and allow for ends about 12 inches long, and also for a loop for hanging the basket. Curl the ends after the bow is tied by drawing the ends of the ribbon between  your thumb and one blade of your scissors. The paper ribbon and doily may be purchased at variety and general stores. A doily

6 or 7 inches square is equally suitable. Take hold of a corner and fold over to the one diagonally opposite and tie them together with ribbon. Then proceed as with the round doily.

Stick half a dozen flowers that happen to be in season into the open ends of the basket. Select small flowers, such as violets, pansies, sweet peas, flowering shrubs, or any of the wild flowers. Pick flowers ahead of time and put them in water for several hours or overnight to keep them fresh longer. If you wish to add a May Day greeting make a small card from a scrap of light-colored construction paper, and pink the edges with pinking scissors. This type of basket can be duplicated quickly, and you can hang one on the door of every friend before he is aware that it is May Day.

PAPER LACE DOILY

A lacy basket for May flowers may be made from lightweight construction paper. Select a pastel color and cut a 5-inch square as in *A*. Take hold of corner 1 and put it on 2, folding on the dotted line. This makes the figure in *B*.

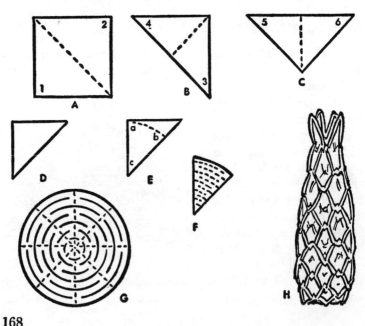

Fold again from 3 to 4 to get the figure in *C*.

Fold once more from 5 to 6 and you have the figure in *D*.

Figures *D* and *E* are the same. In figure *E*, dot an arc *ab* so that *ac* is the same length as *bc*. Cut on the dotted line *ab*.

Make dotted lines as in *F* and perforate the lines at short intervals. Unfold the paper and you have a circular lace doily as in *G*. Gather four outer strips into handles. Drop a marble or a rubber eraser into the doily, and watch the doily lengthen into a long lacy basket as in *H*. Fill the basket with flowers that are in season and hang on a friend's doorknob.

SERPENTINE MAY BASKET

An attractive May basket may be made with crepe paper streamers. Use two colors—white and light green—and wind into a flat coil about 6 inches in diameter. Begin in the center by winding with two streamers at the same time. Overlap them and paste together lightly as you proceed.

When it is about the desired size, shape the flat coil into a round basket. The shaping can be done easily by grasping the circle with both hands and putting your thumbs in the center. Make a handle by using a streamer of each color. Fold the streamers lengthwise for thickness and paste the ends to the basket. Make a bow from narrow strips of crepe paper and tie to the handle of the basket. If it is necessary to hold it in shape, shellac the basket on both sides. This adds a finishing touch.

A MINIATURE HARP

If you are a collector of pocket-size musical instruments, you will want to add a harp to your collection. Select a clean, dry wishbone and about half a dozen thin rubber bands depending upon the size of the wishbone. Stretch the rubber bands across the wishbone and the harp is ready.

Another harp may be made from a small forked branch of a bush. String the harp with green thread or twine depending upon the size of branch.

A MINIATURE SOLAR SYSTEM

In studying the solar system, it is helpful if boys and girls can visualize the relative sizes of the sun and its family of planets. Represent the nine planets—Mercury, Venus, Earth, Mars, Jupiter, Saturn, Uranus, Neptune, Pluto—in their relative sizes. Make them from modeling clay. Begin with the largest and smallest, Jupiter and Mercury. If you make the diameter of Jupiter 4 inches, the diameter of Mercury will be 1/29 as large, about the size of a BB shot. Cut cardboard circles to represent the diam-

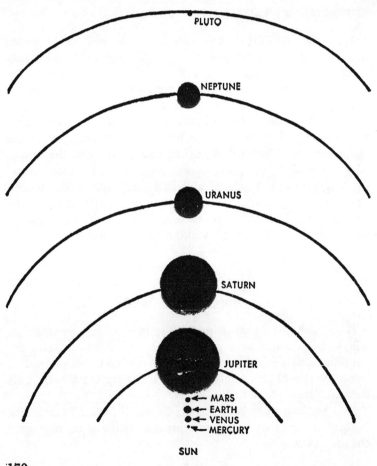

eters of the planets, and use the circles as patterns or, guides. Model a clay ball 4 inches in diameter to represent Jupiter. Then make a hole through which to thread a wire for suspending the ball. Work a metal darning needle or similar instrument, through the center of the ball before the clay sets too much. Pull out the needle and thread a wire through. Hold a nail in a horizontal position and fasten one end of the wire to the middle of the nail. Pull on the other end of the wire so that the nail is pressed into the clay. Cover the nail and close the hole by pressing the clay. Label Jupiter by lettering on adhesive tape and sticking it on.

Follow the same procedure for modeling the other planets. Pierce the smaller planets with a needle and stout thread. Tie a knot in the thread to keep it from slipping through. Close the hole by pressing the clay. Label the smaller planets by cutting a triangular pennant from paper. Use the thread at the top of the ball as a staff by sewing through the wide end of the pennant.

THE SUN

The sun is so large that it is difficult to make a ball large enough to represent it. The diameter of the sun is ten times larger than that of Jupiter, and therefore 40 inches according to our scale. Let's represent Jupiter with a circle and imagine that it is a ball.

From yellow cardboard cut a circle 40 inches in diameter. You may need to use 2 pieces of cardboard and to splice them by overlapping and pasting. Reinforce the circle with two flat, 40-inch sticks. Two yardsticks will do, even though they are not quite long enough. Lay one across the other at right angles in the middle and paste to the cardboard. The color, however, is optional. White cardboard will do equally well.

To suspend the circle punch 4 small holes in button fashion in the center of the cardboard. Thread 2 stout strings or wires through and back to form a loop. Tie the ends in a knot, and fasten a longer string to the loop. Suspend the sun and its planets from the ceiling so that they clear the heads of the people in the room. Hang the sun in the center and the planets in the order of their orbits. Do not attempt to show the relative distances between the sun and planets.

MINIATURE STORY STAGES

Miniature reconstructions of scenes from stories are excellent devises for stimulating children to read. A series of stages and sets placed about the schoolroom afford intriguing glimpses into favorite books with the hope of encouraging reading.

Wooden and cardboard boxes make ideal stages for miniature scenes. A boy or girl who has enjoyed reading *Hansel and Gretel,* for instance, may enjoy building a forest scene. Paint the interior of the box to represent sky, clouds, and mountains. Use papier-mâché for the ground covering, and steel wool dipped in tempera paint for trees and underbrush.

Hansel and Gretel may be fashioned from pipe cleaners and dressed in crepe paper or yarn. To portray the children scattering bread crumbs to the birds in the forest, model the birds from clay and add touches of color with paint. Use real bread crumbs.

The elaborateness of the scenes will depend upon the grade level of the group. The stage sets may be prepared by the group working in committees or smaller groups. A group project of this type provides an opportunity for a report to the class.

MISS MOUSE AND MR. MOLE

A GAME FOR THE PRIMARY GRADES

This is one of the many varieties of Blindman's Buff. The children form a circle and choose a girl to be Miss Mouse and a boy for Mr. Mole. Both go to the center of the circle. Mr. Mole is blindfolded and tries to catch Miss Mouse. He calls, "Miss Mouse, Miss Mouse, where are you?"

"I'm right here, Mr. Mole," replies Miss Mouse.

When he finally catches her, both choose replacements for themselves. For variety's sake, Miss Mouse may choose someone to be Mr. Mole, and Mr. Mole chooses the next Miss Mouse. The mole, however, always chases the mouse.

This game may also be played by blindfolding both Miss Mouse and Mr. Mole.

MOLDING VASES FROM PHONOGRAPH RECORDS

Have you ever fashioned a vase or low flower bowl from an old phonograph record? Begin by heating the record in boiling water until it is pliable. Test the record frequently by raising the edges with a fork or pliers. When it is soft, remove the record from the water and then remove the labels. Wear fabric gloves to protect your hands.

Select a mold for a bowl ahead of time. Look for a broad tin can, such as a small Crisco can. Place the can upside down on several thicknesses of newspapers. While the record is still very hot and pliable, mold it quickly over the can. Flute the edges carefully, working as rapidly as possible before the record begins to harden. If you need to soften it again, reheat the record in boiling water, and then remold quickly.

After the bowl has hardened, cover the hole in the bottom of the record with adhesive tape on the outside. Fill the hole from the inside with hot sealing wax. Lacquer the bowl if you wish to give it a glossy finish.

MORACAS

RHYTHM INSTRUMENTS

A popular Latin American percussion instrument is a pair of moracas. Moracas are used to accentuate rhythm, and may be made with pop bottle caps, a stick, and a nail. Remove the cork from six bottle caps. Nail three of the caps loosely to the end of a handle made from a stick as in the picture. Make a pair of moracas and shake them to accentuate rhythm.

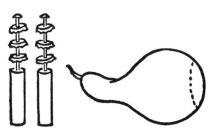

Small gourds also make excellent moracas. Select a pair with natural handles. Be sure that the gourds are dry. Cut the gourds

173

open crosswise toward the bottom, and scrape out the seeds and pith. Put in some coarse gravel or tiny pebbles. Glue the two sections together and shellac. Use them as described.

A MOSAIC IN CORK

An attractive mosaic can be made by inlaying a picture with small pieces of colored cork. Sketch a large picture on a sheet of colored construction paper. Select a piece of sheet cork somewhat larger than the sketch. Decide on two or three colors for your picture, and cut a piece of cork for each color. With calcimine or tempera paint, color each piece a separate color. Now cut the cork into small pieces. Arrange and paste the small pieces of variously colored cork on the sketch to create a mosaic, such as an autumn scene, a balloon vendor, an organ grinder, a Christmas tree, a baby elephant, a boy or girl on skis.

MOVING PICTURES

In this project boys and girls prepare a stage for moving pictures and then draw pictures to fit the stage.

THE STAGE

Select an orange or apple crate, or a packing box for a stage. Study the illustration carefully for the next steps. Make two rollers, one for each side of the stage, on which to wind the pictures. Make the rollers from an old broomstick, or from a similar stick or rod. Cut two lengths as long as the stage is high and allow for an additional inch at the bottom and 4 inches at the top for a handle.

Drill four holes in the box slightly larger than the diameter of the rollers to allow for play. Drill the holes 3 inches from the front and side edges. Drive a nail horizontally through each roller near the end at the bottom. Let both ends of the nail stick out to keep the roller from slipping out at the bottom. Put the rollers in place from the ceiling of the stage; that is, from the inside of the box, by pushing up through the holes at the top. Let the bottom end of the rollers drop into position.

To make a handle for turning the rollers, drill a hole through each roller about 1 inch from the top. Drill it large enough for a sucker stick or large nail. Remove the rollers from the box to facilitate drilling. Then put them back in place and put the sucker sticks or nails through the holes for handles. Use adhesive tape for fastening the sticks or nails in place. Also paste tape over the pointed ends as a safety measure.

THE PICTURES

This part of the project requires careful planning. Make the "screen" of wrapping or butcher paper, and draw pictures on the screen. The width of the screen should be slightly less than the inside height of the stage. Then accommodate the size and shape of the picture to that of the paper "screen." Allow a margin around the pictures. Draw a sequence of pictures either on a long strip of paper or on shorter strips. If you use short strips, more boys and girls can work on the project at the same time.

Many subjects lend themselves to the "movies," such as a safari in Africa, a day at the county fair, the gold rush to California in 1849, or a sequence of scenes from one's favorite story. The pictures may be drawn in pencil and colored with crayons or tempera paints. Titles or short descriptions may be written to accompany the pictures or given orally as a commentary.

If the pictures are drawn on short strips, paste them together in sequence. Then fasten the end of the strip to the roller on the right side with Scotch tape, glue, or with staples. Wind the picture strip backwards on the roller. Unroll enough strip to fasten the front end to the roller at the left. The movie gets under way by turning the left-hand roller.

The curtain is optional and may be added for effect. Make it from cheesecloth, an old bedsheet, or from crepe paper. For a simplified version, the stage may also be omitted. The broomstick rollers may be operated without the stage box.

MUSICAL GLASSES

A set of tumblers or glass bowls can be tuned to a musical scale by filling the glasses with graduated amounts of water. Test the note that each glass produces on a piano or with a pitch pipe. Label the glasses with the letter designating the notes of the octave. If you prefer, write the notes instead of the letter.

To make a hammer for striking the glasses, wind strips of cloth around the end of a small stick and sew to keep the knob in place. Simple tunes may be played on the glasses.

MUSICAL LOTTO

A GAME FOR THE UPPER GRADES

Like the game of lotto, musical lotto is also played with cards. The cards, however, bear an assortment of notes, signs or symbols used in music. These notes and signs are known collectively as "notation."

This game calls for advance preparation before the game can be played the first time. Ask as many boys and girls to help as you can use conveniently. For each player prepare five blank cardboard markers ½-inch square. Make as many musical lotto cards as there are players. Also prepare a list for the teacher or caller.

To make the cards, tear a sheet of writing paper in half and rule off fifteen ½-inch squares in three rows as in the picture. Write in the sharps, flats, clef, half notes, whole notes, rests, time, and key signatures. Be sure to arrange these symbols and notes in a different order on every card.

Begin play by distributing a card and set of markers to each player. The teacher calls a symbol or note aloud, and each player covers the identical symbol with a marker. The game is won by the first player to cover five squares in a row. He raises his hand and calls, "Lotto."

NAME BINGO

A GAME FOR THE INTERMEDIATE GRADES

Name Bingo is excellent for learning to spell the names of one's classmates. It is a good game for the first weeks of school.

Each player prepares his own bingo card. On a piece of paper he rules off five 1-inch squares across and four 1-inch squares down, making a total of 20 squares. He writes the name of a classmate in each square. It is well to have a list of the names on the blackboard to enable the players to get the correct spelling. If there are fewer than twenty in the room, add enough names to make twenty. If there are more, omit the easiest names such as Mary, John. Make it a point, however, to retain all names pronounced alike but spelled differently as John, Jon or Edith, Edythe, the various spellings for Jean, Kathryn, or whatever names may come up in the classroom.

Each player makes a set of five markers somewhat smaller than 1-inch square. Make them from construction paper or lightweight cardboard.

Then write each name on a separate slip of paper. There must be at least twenty slips and there may be as many as thirty or forty. Put the slips in a hat and mix them thoroughly. Then the teacher or leader draws a name and calls it aloud. Each player covers the corresponding name on his card, or skips the name if it is not on his card. The first player to cover five in a row wins. He raises his hand and calls, "Bingo!"

NAME PIN

FOR THE INTERMEDIATE GRADES

To make a pin bearing your name, you will need a package of dry alphabet macaroni, a small piece of balsam or other soft wood, and a safety pin. Select the letters that you need for your name. Color them with calcimine or tempera paint and allow them to dry thoroughly.

To cut the wood into desirable dimensions, lay out the letters of the name as you want them to appear on the pin. Then cut the wood accordingly, allowing for a margin of about ¼ inch around the name. Carve a narrow groove or slot in the back side of the pin to accommodate the back of a safety pin. Varnish the wood block and allow to dry for twenty-four hours.

Glue the letters of the name on the pin. Take pains to space the letters so that the name is easy to read. Straight-sided letters like *I* and *L* should be placed farther apart than rounded letters like *O* and *G*. The space between letters should be judged with the eye rather than measured with a ruler.

Glue the safety pin in place for a fastener. Then shellac both sides of the pin including the letters. When it is dry, the pin is ready to wear.

NAPKIN RINGS

Napkin rings may be made from a variety of materials and articles. A few suggestions are given below.

RINGS MADE FROM LINOLEUM

With a sharp knife or tinner's shears cut a strip of linoleum 1¼ inches wide and 4 to 4¼ inches long depending upon the size of the napkin generally used. Line the strip with pastel chintz or glazed pastel shelf paper by pasting it to the wrong side of the linoleum. This will be the inside of the napkin ring. If the linoleum is a plain color on the outside, select a small all-over pattern in chintz for the lining. To make the ring, splice the ends of the linoleum strip with Scotch tape. Then shellac the ring to make a smooth finish.

If you are making a set of napkin rings for a family, try to vary the color of the linings or of the linoleum so that the rings can be identified easily.

RINGS MADE FROM BABY FOOD CANS

Remove both ends of a baby food can, and you have a ring about the right width. Smooth off and polish the rough edges. Write or letter the name or initials of the prospective owner with fingernail polish or sealing wax. Then apply a coat of lacquer.

RINGS MADE FROM PASTEBOARD ROLL

Slice a paper towel roll into sections 1¼ inches wide for a set of napkin rings. Cover the ring with small-figured wallpaper. This is an excellent use for small scraps.

RINGS MADE FROM MODELING CLAY

You can model a set of napkin rings easily with clay. Paint the rings in pastel colors. If you wish to add a personal touch, decorate the ring by writing or lettering the name or initials of the owners. Apply a coat of shellac as a finish.

A NATURE CALENDAR

Boys and girls often enjoy working on a calendar project. In addition to showing the days, weeks, and months embellish the calendar with pictures of seasonal occurrences. If it is too time consuming to make a calendar for every month, make one for each season of the school year. Choose a month that most nearly typifies the season in your region.

Make the calendar on a large sheet of wrapping paper 5 feet (60 inches) square. Allow for a 2-inch margin on the right and left sides of the sheet, and divide the remaining 56 inches into seven 8-inch squares, one for each day of the week. Since there will be only five squares up and down instead of seven as across, allow for larger margins at the top and bottom of the sheet.

To allow as much space as possible for illustration, write the numbers for the days of the month rather small, possibly 1-inch figures. Place them in the upper left-hand corner of the 8-inch squares. Suggestions for illustrating seasonal occurrences are given below and on the following page:

FALL

children going to school
fall foliage
falling leaves
bonfires
seeds flying in the air
nuts falling from trees
pumpkins
field mice
cocoons
harvest moon
corn in crib
squirrel storing acorns
turkey gobblers

apples
clusters of grapes
migrations of birds including
    wild ducks and geese
fall flowers and berries
    wild sunflower
    asters
    goldenrod
    cardinal flower
    jack-in-the-pulpit
    common barberry
    Oregon hollygrape
    bittersweet

WINTER

thermometer showing 20°
snowflakes
popcorn

snow falling
sleds
squirrel asleep in hole

180

cranberries
ice skates
long shadows
frost on windows
bare trees
evergreens
snowdrifts

cocoons
frozen pond
animals with long hair
snow man
children playing inside
icicles
house flowers

SPRING

green grass
pussy willows
robins
frogs
spring showers
dandelions
farmers plowing
farmers planting
boys playing marbles
children rollerskating
eating breakfast by
  daylight
bird nests
moth leaving cocoon

blossom-laden fruit trees
baby birds
baby animals
  opossum
  lamb
  pigs
  colt
wild flowers
  crocus
  violet
  jack-in-the-pulpit
  May apple
  Dutchman's-breeches
boys flying kites

NATURE RIDDLES

Riddles are fun, and nature offers a wealth of subject matter. Encourage boys and girls to make up rhymes containing riddles. When a class gets into the swing of making up riddles, there is no end to this type of activity. The rhyme about the pussy willow is an example.

> My fur is as soft as a kitten
> And could be the color of your mitten
> I'm the earliest thing
> That awakens in the spring
> What am I?

NEIGHBORHOOD MAPS

FOR THE PRIMARY GRADES

One of the best introductions to the study of maps on the primary level is for children to map their own neighborhood. This may be done by making a replica of a neighborhood in the sandbox. Children work as a group on a project of this type.

Decide on the boundaries of the area that are to be mapped. If you live in a city, it may be well to limit the area to a city block, perhaps to the block in which the school is located. Chart items, such as streets, alleys, stores, libraries, churches, and houses. If you decide to locate the larger buildings only, it may be more practical to include several city blocks.

If you live in a rural community, decide on a convenient area and limit your boundaries accordingly. Chart hills, valleys, streams, highways, farm sites, fields, pasture areas, wood plots.

Should the children like to show population on their sandbox map, they may fashion people from clothespins or mold them from clay. In a rural area, in addition to showing population, children may want to show sheep, cattle, and pigs in the pastures.

NEWSPAPER DOLLS

To make a doll from newspapers, wad or crush sheets of newspaper. Shape the wadded paper into a body, head, arms, and legs. Cover these with smooth sheets of newspaper or tissue paper.

To indicate the joints, tie the neck, waist, elbows, wrists, knees, and ankles with string. Paint in the features with calcimine paints. Instead of painting the features, you may wish to cut out the eyes, nose, and mouth from colored paper and paste them on. For hair glue on yarn, ravelled rope, or string. These string materials lend themselves well to braiding. Dress the doll in crepe paper, chintz, or calico. If the doll's dress calls for buttons, cut them from cardboard. Color the buttons with crayon and sew them on. You may make boy and girl dolls or perhaps an entire family.

NEWSPAPER SEATWORK

FOR THE ELEMENTARY GRADES

For a bit of variety in English or reading classes, the teacher may pass out newspapers for seatwork. There are a number of activities that children may undertake. They, for example, may list words that they have had in spelling. They may underline names of persons, places, or things (nouns), or action and doing words (verbs). They may find synonyms for words that the teacher lists on the board or words that rhyme. They may want to list unfamiliar words to be looked up in the dictionary.

Other possibilities will suggest themselves to the teacher.

NEW YORK

A CHANTING AND RUNNING GAME FOR THE PRIMARY GRADES

This game is a simple form of charades which may be played indoors or outdoors. The players choose sides. The sides are called Team 1 and Team 2. Each team has a goal, or home base.

Team 1 secretly decides upon an episode to pantomime, or act out, such as hanging the washing on the line, carrying on a telephone conversation, dialing on the radio or television set, driving a car, watching a motion picture.

Then Team 1 approaches Team 2 chanting and running.

"Here we come."

"Where from?" questions Team 2.

"New York," replies No. 1.

"What's your trade?" asks Team 2.

"Lemonade," says Team 1.

"Show us some if you're not afraid," challenges Team 2.

Team 1 pantomimes the action which it has decided upon and Team 2 tries to guess what it is. When Team 2 guesses correctly, Team 1 runs for home base. The members of Team 2 try to tag as many players as they can. Tagged players must join the other side. The play now reverts to the other side.

NUMBER AIDS

FOR THE PRIMARY GRADES

To enable children on the primary level to understand number concepts more easily, arrange to have concrete objects on hand. Objects that the children can collect easily and keep in a box in their desks are acorns, pebbles, sucker sticks, toothpicks, used kitchen matches with the burned ends cut off.

When difficulty in addition or subtraction arises, the pupil can "call" upon the acorns and pebbles to help him out.

NUMBER RECOGNITION DRILL

FOR THE PRIMARY GRADES

Distribute a set of flash cards to the class, each bearing a number from 1 to 100. Begin counting aloud slowly. The children bring up their cards as the numbers are called. If someone fails, repeat the number only once. Those who still hold cards at the end come to the front of the room and state the number before and after their own. Pupils usually have one or two cards left.

NUT CUPS

Attractive nut cups may be made from cotton cloth. If you are making them for a party for St. Valentine's or St. Patrick's Day use red or green cloth.

To make a cup, cut a circle 5 to 8 inches in diameter depending upon the size of the cup that you desire. Starch the cloth very stiff. Select a fruit juice glass or a tumbler with a small base. Set the glass in the center of the circle. Draw up the edges of the cloth to fit the glass. Hold the cloth in place around the glass with a rubber band or string. Allow the cloth to dry. Then remove it and finish the edge with pinking shears. The cup is ready for use.

OLD-FASHIONED SUGAR COOKIES

Elementary school children sometimes enjoy baking cookies. They enjoy having cookies as a special treat, or as a treat for their mothers and other special guests.

Following a recipe gives children experience in purposeful reading. It gives them experience in measuring ingredients and helps them to visualize measurements, such as a cupful, teaspoonful, tablespoonful, and fractions thereof.

RECIPE

½ cup of butter or margarine	2 cups flour
1 cup sugar	3 teaspoons baking powder
2 eggs	¼ teaspoon salt
3 tablespoons milk	½ teaspoon grated nutmeg

Cream the butter and add the sugar gradually. Beat the eggs well. Add the baking powder and nutmeg by sifting it in the flour. Mix by stirring and combine with eggs and milk. Place a small amount of dough on a well-floured board. Pat and roll the dough to ⅛-inch thickness. Cut with a cooky cutter and place in a buttered baking tin. Bake in a moderate oven of 325° F.

This recipe make about thirty cookies.

OLD MOTHER WITCH

AN OUTDOOR GAME FOR THE PRIMARY GRADES

To prepare for the fascinating game of Old Mother Witch, trace the outline of a lake on the playground. Draw the shoreline with deep indentations, such as capes, harbors, inlets. Use a stick for tracing on a dirt playground and chalk on a hard-surfaced playground. Lay the chalk sidewise to draw a heavy line. Since it will be used for "swimming," adapt the size of the lake to the number of swimmers. A lake 20 feet across will accommodate ten to fifteen swimmers.

One of the players volunteers to be the Old Witch. All the other children are swimmers. They "swim" in a stooped running position and paddle with their hands and arms. The players try to tantalize the Old Witch by swimming quite near the shoreline, but they *must avoid* being caught by her. Meanwhile the Old Witch is furiously practicing her black magic on the banks of the lake. Her magic is to catch swimmers. By darting in and out on the indentations, the witch usually can panic a swimmer into getting caught.

As they are caught, the swimmers come ashore. The last swimmer to be caught becomes the next Old Witch.

ORIGINAL LEGENDS

From time immemorial children have enjoyed hearing legends and tales, such as how the rabbit lost his long tail, how fire came upon the earth; how Paul Bunyan's footsteps filled with water to form the Great Lakes, why the robin's breast is red.

Encourage children to use their vivid imaginations to compose original legends. Their legends, for example, may explain some of the local surroundings, such as a flat-topped mountain or mesa, or a picturesque wild flower. Children, for example, may tell in legend about the habits of a gopher, a grasshopper, or a bird. They may explain why the days are long in summer and what makes the hailstones.

To help create a background and to stimulate children's imaginations to make up their own stories, read aloud to them legends and tales of our own country and of peoples from other lands. Below is a list of books that may be of help to the teacher from which to select stories for reading aloud.

CHASE, RICHARD (Editor). *Jack Tales.* Boston: Houghton, Mifflin Co.

HOGNER, DOROTHY. *Navajo Winter Nights.* New York: Thomas Nelson & Sons, 1935.

McCORMICK, D. J. *Tall Timber Tales.* Caldwell, Idaho: Caxton Printers, 1939.

MALCOLMSON, ANNE. *Yankee Doodle's Cousins.* Boston: Houghton, Mifflin & Co., 1941.

SCOTT, FRANCES MARY (Editor). *Legends of the United Nations.* New York: McGraw-Hill Book Co., Inc., 1943.

AN OUTDOOR LESSON IN ART

FOR THE ELEMENTARY GRADES

Every neighborhood whether it be rural or urban offers interesting subjects for an art lesson. Plan an excursion with the class to a nearby neighborhood or community. If the surroundings are suitable for sketching on the spot, have the class take their drawing materials with them. If they are not, help the boys and girls to train their memories so that when they return to class they can recapture the essential elements of the scene.

COLOR, LIGHT, AND SHADOWS

Point out such values as color, light, and shadows. Call the attention of the class, for example, to the soft, misty blues and purples in the shadows of the distant hills and mountains, the filagree pattern formed by the sun shining through leaves, the shafts of light streaming down as the sun emerges from storm clouds, the sparkle of sunshine on water, the ripples on a pond, the morning dew on grass, the delicate sculptured effect of snowdrifts, the mellow reds and mauves in old brick, the changes in light that afternoon shadows have wrought on a scene visited earlier in the day. Call attention to the color of the sky, explaining the difference in the color at various seasons of the year.

PERSPECTIVE

An outdoor lesson is also the ideal time for teaching boys and girls to draw objects in perspective. Ask them to draw the horizon line first, the line across the picture where the sky and earth seem to meet. Point out, for example, that the horizon is always far in the distance, that any object on the horizon looks no larger than a tiny spot, and that the same object close at hand looks large.

A railroad track is an excellent object for studying perspective (page 188). Notice that the railroad track becomes narrower with distance until the two rails meet on the horizon. Notice that the trees, telegraph poles, and buildings along the track look smaller and smaller the closer they are to the horizon.

187

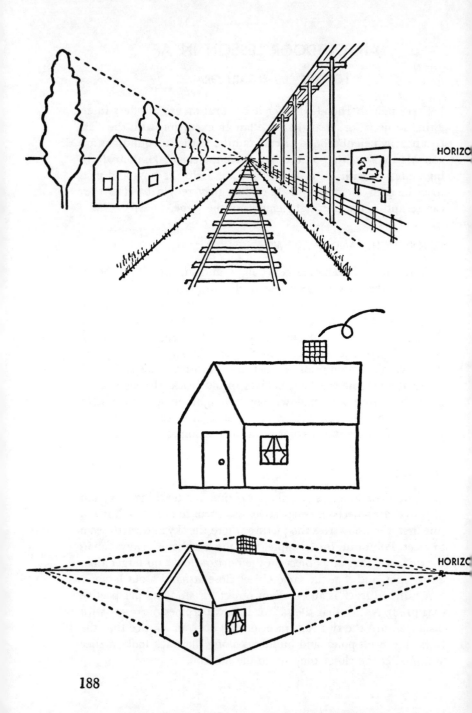

HORIZON

HORIZON

Let us take another example. In the picture of the middle house on the opposite page perspective has been disregarded, but the lower house has been drawn in perspective. Look at one of the corners only. It is just a perpendicular line. Now place two dots, on the horizon at opposite sides in the picture. Call the dots vanishing points. All the horizontal lines of the house converge at one of the two points as in the illustration. Draw the front part of the roof and slant the ridge in the direction of the vanishing point. Even the doors, windows, and chimney slant toward the vanishing point.

To be exact in drawing the roof lines, one could project a third vanishing point high above the house, but for all practical purposes teach boys and girls to slant both roof lines parallel to one another.

PADDED CLOTHES HANGER

FOR A GIFT

Clothes hangers may be attractive as well as useful. Both wooden and metal hangers lend themselves to decoration. Form a base by padding the hanger with cotton batting and fasten it in place by winding with strips torn from old cloth. Tack the strips securely with needle and thread. Cover the hanger by winding ribbon around the padding and the hook, too. Sew the ribbon in place as you wind. Then tie a ribbon bow around the base.

Winding the hanger with crepe paper instead of ribbon is equally attractive. Paste the edges of the paper as you wind.

PAINTING ON COLORED PAPER

When boys and girls tire of painting on white paper or of working with it on handicraft projects, it is time to switch to colored paper. They enjoy experimenting with color, and with guidance they soon develop a color sense of their own.

Color is one of the deepest influences in creating feelings and moods. Red, for example, is an exciting color. It is generally used for danger signals. Yellow gives a feeling of warmth, a feeling of the tropics. Blue is a cool, calm color. It suggests snow scenes. It is a good color to use in a room during the summertime. Green suggests growth, freshness, and spring. Brown is soft and rich.

"PAINTING" WHEN BLINDFOLDED

AN INDOOR GAME

This is a good game for a rainy recess. All the players except one are "painters." They go to the blackboard where they are blindfolded. Inexpensive blindfolds may be made by folding butcher paper into bands and fastening the blindfold with paper clips.

A leader is appointed to direct the "blind" in their painting activities. He may direct them to draw an elephant and say, "Draw the elephant's eye. Draw the other eye. Now his tail. His left hind foot." The leader continues giving directions. When the final touches have been added, the artists sign their names.

The players remove the blindfolds, take their seats, and take a look at their efforts. Everyone has a good laugh since most of the pictures resemble nothing at all, much less an elephant.

"PAINTING PORTRAITS" WHEN BLINDFOLDED

This game may be used as an additional assignment to supplement the "art work" in the previous game. The "artists" need not wear a blindfold in this game. The leader instructs the players to hold 8½ x 11-inch sheets of white paper against their faces. He gives instructions by saying, "Draw the outline of your face. Your right eyebrow. Now your chin. Your left ear." The leader continues in this manner until all the features have been drawn. Then the portraits are displayed on the blackboard.

PAINTING WITH SPONGES

FOR THE PRIMARY GRADES

Painting on the blackboard with wet sponges is fun for the small fry. Large circular up and down motions help to develop rhythm and co-ordination.

After experimenting on the blackboard, children are ready to transfer the sponge technique to paper. Instead of water, they use calcimine or poster paints and a small sponge. Make provision for protecting children's clothing. Dad's old shirt worn backwards serves as an excellent protector. Use newspapers on desks.

PANTOMIME RHYMING

A GAME

Divide the players into two teams. Team 1 leaves the room while Team 2 chooses a word that has rhyming possibilities, such as the word "hill." When Team 1 returns, Team 2 starts off with a clue word that rhymes with hill, such as mill, bill, pill, rill. Then Team 1 pantomimes every word its players can recall that rhymes with "mill." When they finally get to "hill," Team 2 has a turn at leaving the room, and the procedure is repeated.

PAPER-BAG CAPS, CROWNS, AND HATS

FOR THE PRIMARY GRADES

At times children enjoy "just wearing" caps, hats, and even royal crowns as they go about their business in school. They imagine themselves as soldiers or kings, or they may want to be "just a bunny." They also may wear the "hats" to represent a character in a play, in a story, or in a lesson. Paper bags lend themselves readily to making headgear of this type.

191

SOLDIER'S CAP

Boys are fascinated by the caps and hats worn by postmen, policemen, firemen, and soldiers. A soldier's cap is easy to make.

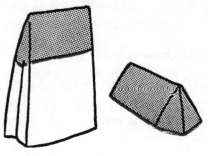

Select a clean, brown paper grocery bag, size 10 or 12. The size is printed at the top. Size 10 makes a 21¼-inch headband and size 12 a 22¾-inch band. Flatten the bag by folding the bottom into its unopened size. Draw the corners on each side together. Staple the corners and the bottom fold. Cut the bag off 4 inches from the bottom and the cap is ready for an eager wearer.

KING'S CROWN

To make a crown, worn by kings as a symbol of authority and distinction, cut a band 4 inches wide. Make the triangular points of the crown 1 inch high and 1½ inches wide at the base. Draw the side lines of the point and cut out. The crown is ready.

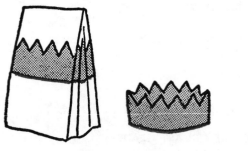

KING'S CROWN   BUNNY HAT

BUNNY HAT

If you need to represent a rabbit as a character in a play or lesson, or if someone just wants to be a bunny, a rabbit ears' hat suggests the character to children. Flatten and staple a bag as

192

you did in making the soldier's cap. Turn the bag bottom side up. To make an ear, start at the corner and cut toward the center 5 or 6 inches as in the illustration. Cut through both thicknesses of paper. Make the other ear in the same way. Allow a strip about 4 inches wide for the headband. Cut off the rest of the bag.

PAPER COSTUME DOLLS

Girls' love for paper dolls can be put to advantage as they progress through the primary and elementary grades. During the early school years children may want to reproduce the characters that they learn to know in their reading. Later they learn about people as a unit of society, about the family and group living.

These projects in the social studies may be enhanced by the portrayal of people in their geographical, historical, and present-

BACK   FRONT

day setting. Dolls of the flat cutout variety lend themselves to this type of project. Stiff cardboard or tagboard is excellent for cutouts. Six to ten inches are good, workable heights. Encourage the children to design their own dolls.

PAPER LANTERNS

Children enjoy carrying lanterns around much in the same way as a girl enjoys carrying a handbag. Then, too, lanterns are attractive when hung from a string or thin wire strung across a corner of the classroom. Tiny lanterns also make attractive Christmas tree ornaments.

To make a tall lantern, fold a piece of colored paper 7 x 8 inches lengthwise. Cut slits as indicated in the picture. To guide

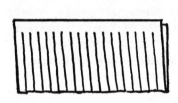 

the children in cutting even slits, encourage them to measure and draw lines ½ inch apart. Unfold the paper, shape it into a cylinder widthwise, and paste the ends of the paper together. Squash down the top of the lantern to form the rounded bulge in the middle. Make a suitable paper handle and paste it on.

Vary the size of the lanterns by changing the dimensions. Keep in mind that the width of the rectangle determines the height of the lantern.

PAPER WEIGHTS

FOR GIFTS

Small, squat glass jars, such as commercial houses use for putting up gift jellies and marmalades, make useful paper weights. Small attractively shaped bottles may be added to the list, too. Fill the jar or bottle with sand from your favorite beach. Plaster of Paris is another excellent filler. For color add calcimine or tempera paints to the plaster mixture. Fill the container with the mixture and allow to dry. If you are using a low jar, decorate the cover with the picture of a small flower cut from a magazine or old seed catalogue. Shellac and allow to dry.

If the jar is deep enough and the neck of the bottle wide enough, you may use marbles for a filler.

PAPIER-MÂCHÉ

Papier-mâché is a French word meaning "chewed paper" or "pulped paper." It is a strong substance made from paper pulp and paste or glue. It is used in making pails, boxes, tubs, trays, vases, relief maps, and for sandbox projects.

To make papier-mâché, soak old newspapers in water in a tub or in any large container. Reduce the paper to pulp by tearing it into bits and by stirring the mixture with a stick or wooden spoon. Make a heavy, thick paste with flour, water, and a small quantity of salt. Mix the paste with paper pulp. Stir until the papier-mâché begins to feel pliable like modeling clay. It is now ready for use. There will be some shrinkage, however, as the papier-mâché dries.

If you desire color, paint the papier-mâché with calcimine or poster paint. Be sure, however, that the papier-mâché is thoroughly dry before you apply paint.

PASTE FOR FINGER PAINTING

Finger painting is a form of painting so popular with children in which paste is applied directly to paper with the fingertips. To make the paste, boil household starch until it is the thickness of pea soup. Mix calcimine or other dry paint with warm water and add to the boiled starch.

The paste is used as paint, and one cup of paint for every two painters is a generous amount. A glossy paper works best. Apply the paint fairly thick in large sweeping motions.

PATCHWORK QUILT

Begin early in the semester to build up a collection of patches for a quilt. Encourage children to collect scraps of clean, pressed cloth. Scraps of material left over from sewing are very suitable. Make the quilt either of cotton or wool patches. Do not mix the two. Piece the patches together to form a cover for a quilt. Sew the various colors and shapes to a foundation. An old blanket, for instance, serves as an excellent foundation.

Plan to make a child's size blanket. It can be finished in a comparatively short time, and children will not loose interest in the project. Add the quilt to a box that is being prepared for the needy at home or abroad. (See page 216.)

PEANUT FIGURES

DAPPER DAN

Here's a way to have fun with peanuts. You can eat the nuts and have fun with the shells, too. Peanuts are quite versatile and may be used for almost any type of figure, tall or squat.

Select a large well-shaped peanut for Dapper Dan. With a small, sharp knife, cut the peanut lengthwise into unequal halves. Use the larger half for the front of the figurine. Cut and remove the shell in one piece so that you can put it back again.

Draw the features and spectacles with India ink. Use a gumdrop for the crown of the hat and construction paper for the brim. Cut the brim slightly oval based on a circle about the size of a fifty-cent piece. Cut the opening for the head to fit the peanut. Then fashion the crown. Use a strand of yarn or a narrow paper strip for a headband.

Make the arms with a wire hairpin. Spread the pin and poke the forks through the shell from the inside. Bend to form the elbows, wrists, and hands. Complete the hands with gum. Make the cane from pipe cleaner. With a sharp-pointed tool or large needle make two holes in the end of the shell and run a pipe cleaner through to form the legs. Bend slightly to indicate the knees. Fashion the feet with chewing gum. The gum will enable Dan "to stand on his own." Paste the two halves of the peanut together, and Dapper Dan is ready to step out!

HOUSEFLY

Select a medium-sized peanut. With a small sharp knife open the shell lengthwise and remove the nut. Use the shell for the body of the fly. Make three pairs of legs with short fine wire hairpins. Poke the hairpins through the shell from the inside and bend to form the 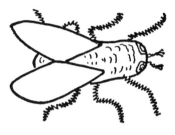 legs. With a needle draw two short ends of black thread through to form the antennae. Fray the ends. Draw the eyes with India ink. Paste the shell together. Cut the wings from white paper.

A PEEKABOO BIRDHOUSE

Build a small birdhouse out of a chalk box. Remove one end of the chalk box. Use tacks to nail the end to the bottom of the box so that a small board extends out to form a "porch." Cut a round opening in the other end of the box for an entrance. Place the house on a window sill outside the schoolroom so that the open end is against the windowpane. Anchor the house with adhesive tape. From dark colored, heavy paper cut a piece large enough to cover the open end of the birdhouse. Cut a peephole, and make a paper flap to cover the peephole, fastening it with a roundhead (brass paper fastener).

If birds build their nest inside and if the children are quiet, they will have a bird's-eye view of the proceedings. To attract birds, sprinkle corn or bread crumbs near the birdhouse.

A PEEP SHOW

An excellent peep show may be made with a shoe box. Cut rectangular or square openings in the sides of the box for windows and another opening in the cover for a skylight. Then cut a peephole in one end of the box.

To help dramatize a social studies unit or to portray characters and scenes from books, encourage boys and girls to draw scenery and people. The peeper, for example, may look in upon Pinocchio inside the whale's stomach, Ali Baba in the cave of the Forty Thieves, or perhaps a Mexican fiesta. Mount the pictures on cardboard. Make bases or back supports to hold the pictures upright. To add to the effect, arrange the pictures in tiers in the shoe box. A series of these peep shows may add great interest to a library corner.

PEN AND PENCIL HOLDER

To make an inexpensive pen and pencil holder, cut corrugated paper into a strip about 2 inches high and 2 feet long. Roll it with the corrugated surface on the inside. Then tie a ribbon around the roll to hold it together. It is now ready to have pens and pencils stuck into it.

PERSONAL STATIONERY

Children take pride in decorating their own stationery. Embellishment may take the form of a hand-painted initial or of an original design. Small floral pictures cut from magazines pasted neatly in place with rubber cement add variety to note paper or cards.

Children also enjoy decorating stationery for particular seasons and holidays. Designs made into seals representing a sprig of holly, a poinsettia, a Santa Claus head, a heart for Valentine Day, a shamrock for St. Patrick's Day, an Easter bunny, an

American flag for Independence Day, or a turkey gobbler for Thanksgiving lend an air of festivity.

Draw or paint the design on lightweight construction paper. Then cut out the design and paste it on the stationery. In case of a heart or shamrock, cut out a small heart from red construction paper or a shamrock from green paper. Paste on the stationery with rubber cement to insure a smoother finished product.

PHONOGRAPH RECORD ALBUM

FOR THE UPPER GRADES

Use strong paper, such as butcher paper, to make the pockets for the pages of a phonograph record album. Measure, draw, and cut a rectangle that is slightly wider than the diameter of a phonograph record and that is a little longer than twice the diameter of the record. Allow a $\frac{1}{2}$-inch margin on all four sides. Fold the paper so that the fold is at the bottom of the record pocket as the illustration at the left.

Follow the picture and cut out a circle so that the name of the record can be seen. Cut out a semicircular piece at the top to facilitate handling the record. Reinforce the right edge with tape on both sides. Make as many pockets as you think are practical. From three to six records is the average for one album.

Use heavy cardboard for the cover of the album. Make the top, bottom, and right edges of the cover $\frac{1}{4}$ inch wider than the pages of the album. Crease a fold on the front cover 1 inch from the left side and reinforce the folded part with tape. Punch holes through the left edge of the record pages and through both covers. Bind the album by lacing with shoestrings or strong cord. Letter the title PHONOGRAPH RECORDS on the cover.

PHONOGRAPH RECORD RACK

To make a rack for phonograph records like the one in *D*, select a sturdy cardboard carton that is 24 inches long, 18 inches wide and 18 inches thick. Cut off the two ends as indicated by the dotted lines in *A*. Now cut along the dotted line as in *B*. Bend the box into a triangular shape as in *C*. Overlap the two sides to form the base. Fasten the overlaps together with brass paper fasteners (roundheads) or by sewing them together with string. With a sharp knife, cut slots to hold the records as in *D*. Cut the slots about 2 inches apart.

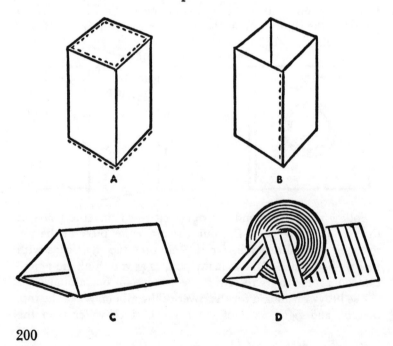

A

B

C

D

PICTURE FRAMES

A picture frame may be made from cardboard. Select a heavy piece and cut it to fit the picture that you wish to frame. The frame may be covered with wallpaper, cotton print, or chintz. Choose a small allover design in these materials. A ruffle may be made for around the edge of the frame. A mosaic effect, for instance, may be achieved with pumpkin seeds. Dip the seeds in calcimine or tempera paint of different colors, and arrange the seeds closely together on the frame to give the effect of a mosaic. Glue them in place.

Use papier-mâché if you wish to work out a raised design. Cellophane may be used instead of glass to protect the pictures.

PICTURES IN COPPER

FOR THE UPPER GRADES

To make a picture on copper sheeting you need these materials:

A sheet of 36-gauge copper obtainable at a store carrying art supplies. ("Gauge" refers to the thickness of the copper.)

A small amount of plaster of Paris to fill indentations

Small brass-plated nails called "escutcheon" pins and generally used for upholstering furniture

A small bag of liver of sulphur (potassium sulphide)

1 box of steel wool

Thin wood for the back of the picture

Tools: a nut-pick, screw driver, orange stick. A putty knife may come in handy.

Work out a picture on paper that you wish to put on copper; such as a lily, an iris, a daffodil, a tulip; tropical fish; vases; a Spanish dancer; a sailboat.

Then cut a copper sheet somewhat larger than the picture. Make a line drawing (a drawing without shadings) of the picture on tracing paper. Trace the drawing on the copper sheet with a lead pencil. *Do not use carbon paper.* Remove the tracing paper and sharpen the outline on the copper with a copper working tool.

Place the copper sheet upside down on a pile of soft newspapers. With the flat end of a tool, press the design down so that the right side of the copper shows an embossed effect. Be careful not to press the tool through the copper. Lay the copper sheet right side up and go over the outline of the design again. Fill in some of the outline with stippling, which is to engrave with dots.

Remove the fingerprints from the copper with steel wool. Dissolve the liver of sulphur in water and apply the solution to the copper to preserve the copper tone and to darken the picture. Dip in clear water to remove any excess solution. Dry the copper and polish again with steel wool. Pour plaster of Paris into the indentations on the back side of the copper sheet to strengthen the picture. Prepare a back and frame for the picture from thin wood. Cut the board enough larger than the copper to allow for a suitable margin or frame. Fasten the copper to the frame with brass-plated nails (escutcheon pins). Lacquer the copper.

PICTURE SPELLING

FOR THE PRIMARY GRADES

Pictures of objects suggested by the class and drawn spontaneously by the teacher on the blackboard is an entertaining visual aid in learning the sounds of letters. If the drill, for example, is on the sound of the letter "b," children may suggest words such as ball, bat, balloon, basket, box, bear, bell.

PIGGY BANK

To make a piggy bank you will need a small tin can and some modeling clay. Cut a slot large enough in the side of the can to take coins. Use the can for the body of the pig and cover it with a thin layer of clay. Keep the coin slot at the top of the pig's back. Mold the head, feet, and tail. When the clay is dry, paint the pig any color that you like and tie a ribbon around its neck.

PIÑATA

A LATIN-AMERICAN CHRISTMAS CUSTOM

Children in countries south of the United States border—in Mexico, Honduras, Central America—look forward to the breaking of the piñata at Christmas time. The piñata is an earthenware jug filled with sweetmeats and small gifts. It is elaborately decorated to resemble a rooster, peacock, or some other large bird, and hung from a tree. The children gather near the tree and take turns at trying to break the piñata. As his turn comes up, the child is blindfolded and given a stout stick. He is given only one turn at striking the piñata. When someone succeeds in breaking it, the piñata crashes to the ground with its load of goodies and all the children share in it.

This interesting custom has been adapted to fit in with the holiday season festivities carried on in our classrooms. Instead of using an earthenware container, however, use a strong paper bag, such as a shopping bag. Fill the bag with nuts, candy, and inexpensive games and trinkets. Wrap the candy.

Plan, for example, to make the piñata in the form of a rooster. Crumple newspapers, fashion and pad out the body with the papers. Then stitch the padding to the bag near the top. Make the rooster large enough so that you can conceal the width of the bag behind the bird. The length of the bag can be hidden behind crepe paper streamers. Make the feathers by cutting crepe paper into strips 1½ inches wide. Make a fringe 1 inch wide by snipping the edge of the strips. Then paste the strips to the newspaper padding fringe side up. Begin pasting at the bottom of the rooster and work up strip by strip. The fringe will tend to hang downward, giving a soft feathery effect. Cut the feathers for the wing and tail from colored construction paper, and paste and stitch into place. Frill a piece of crepe paper and make the comb and wattle, and fold construction paper for the beak. For an eye cut a small circle from black paper and a larger one from white paper. Paste the black circle on the white one. Make another eye and paste in place. Then paste crepe paper streamers to conceal the bottom of the bag as in the illustration.

Tie a long string to the piñata (to the handles of the shopping bag) and suspend it from a hook in the ceiling. Use a string that is long enough so that the piñata can be pulled up and down with one end of the string.

When the time for breaking of the piñata is at hand, the boys and girls gather about and take turns at trying to break the piñata by hitting it with a stick. As his turn comes up, the player is blindfolded and given a stick. By pulling the string, the teacher moves the swaying piñata up and down. The other players stand well away from the danger zone until someone succeeds in breaking the piñata. Then the load crashes down, and everyone scrambles for a share.

PIN CUSHIONS

Here are two types of pin cushions that are easy to make at school: (1) the yucca plant cushion, and (2) conventional types.

YUCCA PLANT CUSHION

People living in the Southwest use the dry stalks of the yucca plant for handicraft pursuits. Be sure, however, not to cut the yucca during its period of growth because it is protected by law while it is in bloom. But there is no objection to gathering the stalks after they are dry.

The yucca has beautiful natural markings and a pithy center, hence it is ideal for a pin cushion. Cut off a slice of the stalk the thickness desired for the cushion. Paint it and it is ready.

CONVENTIONAL TYPES OF CUSHIONS

Select a low jar, such as a cold cream jar. Squat medicine bottles are excellent, too. Clean the jar or bottle and fill it with sawdust, cotton batting, or wool. If you use cotton batting or wool, stuff it in firmly. Choose a scrap of felt, velvet, or heavy satin. Put it over the jar and tie a string around it. Make a skirt from small-figured chintz. Finish the top of the skirt with an attractive binding.

The dressed-up jar also makes an excellent seat for a doll house. Stick in three or four pins to form the back of the seat. (For doll house furniture, see page 92.)

PINE CONE CHRISTMAS TREES

FOR THE PRIMARY AND ELEMENTARY GRADES

If you live in a region where pine cones are plentiful, encourage children to collect them for Christmas trees. They may be used in their natural state or they may be painted green with calcimine paint. Select a large cone, stand it firmly on its base, and trim it with gilded or silvered acorns, eucalyptus burrs, or berries. Press them in place between the spiny scales.

Large and small trees may be grouped to make an attractive set or "forest." The pine cone trees are a holiday decoration that can be made easily by primary grade children.

PIN-POINT PICTURES

Lacy greeting cards and invitations may be made by pricking out designs with coarse sewing needles or hat pins. Designs and pictures may be pricked out on any kind of paper that has some body and a fairly smooth surface, such as typewriter or construction paper.

Pictures cut from magazines make excellent patterns. Choose a picture that is fairly simple in composition. Ask the children to cover the tops of their desks with protective materials, such as newspapers or linoleum mats. Place the picture and paper together on the desk protector. Put the picture on top and prick through both papers at the same time. Do the outline of the picture first. Closely spaced pinpricks make for a lacier effect than widely spaced pinpricks.

Printed and handwritten initials and monograms may be reproduced attractively with pinpricking.

PINWHEEL

To make a pinwheel that will whirl, cut out a 6-inch square from colored paper and draw two diagonal lines from corner to corner. Three-fourths of an inch from the center, put a small mark on each line as in the picture at the left. Start from a corner

and cut toward the center until you reach the mark. Do this with the other three corners, too. Take hold of one of the corners and curve it toward the center, and then pull the other three. Stick a pin through the four corners and through the center of the paper. Then push the pin into a stick about 12 inches long.

Whisk the pinwheel through the air or blow into it.

PIPE RACK

A GIFT FOR DAD

Select a sturdy cardboard box about 8 inches long, 5 inches wide, and 5 inches deep. Choose a box with a flap cover. Study the picture carefully. Cut off the cover lengthwise along a line ¾ inch from the hinge. Fasten the ¾-inch strip securely at the corners with Scotch tape. This is the front of the pipe rack. Cut off the top of the rack except for a strip 2 inches wide. Cut three or four U-shaped notches to hold the pipe stems in place. 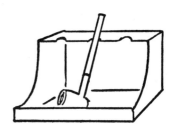 Cut off an arc on each end as in the illustration above. Paint the pipe rack and then shellac for a smooth finish.

THE PIPES OF PAN

Pan, the merry Greek god of flocks, pastures, forests, and wild life, is credited with the invention of pipes. According to legend Pan made the pipes, a primitive wind instrument, from a reed. Attended by nymphs, Pan wandered through the mountainous regions of ancient Greece, playing his pipes.

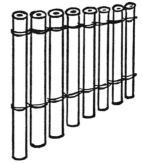

You, too, can make pipes from cane stalks, such as sugar cane or sweet sorghum (sorgo). The latter is common in many regions of the United States. Cut the stalks into graduated lengths as in the illustration. Cut the stalk near a joint so that one end is blocked off, or plug it with wax or chewing gum. Place the pipes side by side with the open ends at the top. Tie the pipes together with raffia and the instrument is ready. Blow across the tops of the holes as you would on the mouth of a bottle.

PLACE MATS

FOR GIFTS AND FOR USE IN SCHOOL

Place mats for the dining table are an important accessory in present-day living. They may be made from a variety of materials and everyone has a few favorites. However, a number of suggestions for materials and how to make mats are given here. Place mats vary in size, but a good size for children is 10 x 14 inches and for adults 12 x 18 inches. Make as many as you need for a set.

CARDBOARD MATS

Cut a mat from a cardboard carton. Select a heavy cardboard or a carton made from corrugated paper. If the cardboard has printing on it, cover the mat with wrapping paper. If it does not, use the cardboard as it is, and decorate it with pictures cut from magazines, decals, or cutouts from colored paper. Instead of decorating the cardboard, you may cover it with small-figured wallpaper, chintz or calico. For a finish, shellac the mat or cover it with cellophane. Wax paper makes a good finish. Press it on the mat with a warm iron. Border the edges with wide adhesive tape, or punch a border of small holes and blanket stitch with yarn.

CORNHUSK MATS

If you live in an area where corn is plentiful and where cornhusks are easily obtained, you have an inexpensive substitute for raffia. Select cornhusks at harvest time when they are dry and store them until needed. Then soak them in water until soft and wrap in a Turkish towel to take up the excess moisture. Cut or tear the husks into narrow strips and braid while still pliant. To make an oval mat, start at the center by arranging the braid into an oval coil. Sew the edges of the braid together.

LINOLEUM MATS

Mats made from odds and ends of linoleum are handsome and practical for use in the classroom or school cafeteria. Linoleum

208

needs no additional decoration. Stores dealing in linoleum sometimes give a limited number of scraps to children for school use.

INNER TUBING MATS

Mats made from an old inner tube are practical for use in the
classroom or school cafeteria. Cut small-sized mats from the tubing and then wash thoroughly. Decorate with a border of brightly
colored drops of sealing wax.

OILCLOTH MATS

Select an allover pattern in oilcloth. Cut out the mats and
ornament the edge by cutting with pinking shears. Make the mats
either rectangular or oval. Oval-shaped mats are attractive.

PLANTS FOR SALE!

To grow plants for a sale, encourage boys and girls to bring
seeds, bulbs, and slips of plants to school early in the school year.
They plant the seeds and bulbs and start the slips in water for
transplanting. They nurture the young seedlings and shoots until
they have grown into strong plants.

Then the class advertises a plant sale, inviting parents, neigh-
bors, and friends. The money obtained from the sale may be used
for a party, a charitable cause, an expedition, or for some useful
bit of equipment for the classroom.

PLANTS FOR THE SCHOOLROOM

Many of us have discovered that a carrot or a sweet potato
makes an inexpensive and decorative plant for the schoolroom.
Almost any root vegetable, such as a beet or radish, may be used
with equal success. Select a vase or bottle with a narrow neck,
a neck with a diameter less than the length of a toothpick. Stick

two toothpicks through the vegetable so that the ends stick out. Place the vegetable in the vase or bottle in a way so that the ends of the toothpick rest on the neck and the root end of the vegetable is submerged in water.

Acorns will sprout in a bowl of water. Later they may be transplanted out of doors. The seeds of oranges, lemons, grapefruit, and tomatoes make beautiful plants when started in a soil box. Growing peanuts is another interesting project. Peanuts require a sandy soil. Be sure to plant the unroasted ones.

A PLAQUE OF A HAND

FOR A GIFT

To make a plaque of a hand, prepare a layer of modeling clay or plaster of Paris about ½-inch thick. The boy or girl who wishes to make a plaque presses his hand into the pliable mixture evenly and holds it there for about a minute. Write the name and date below with a pointed tool or pencil. Work two small holes through at the top about three inches apart for hanging the plaque. Let the clay or plaster of Paris dry thoroughly and paint the plaque any color you like. Hang the plaque by putting a fine wire or cord through the holes.

A POEM BOX

FOR THE INTERMEDIATE AND UPPER GRADES

Boys and girls are often shy and reluctant about handing in original poems. This feeling may be overcome by setting aside a special drawer or box in which poems may be placed inconspicuously. As the poems are shared in class and as the children become more accustomed to this procedure, the more confident members of the class will begin to establish their authorship. The others will soon follow suit.

210

A POEM FOR THE DAYS OF THE WEEK

FOR THE PRIMARY GRADES

An easy way to learn the days of the week is to repeat "Solomon Grundy," an Old Mother Goose rhyme. Better still and more fun, too, is to compose one of your own.

> Wash clothes on Monday,
> Iron on Tuesday,
> Sew on Wednesday,
> Play on Thursday,
> Shop on Friday,
> Clean house on Saturday,
> Go to church on Sunday,
> What's your fun day?

POETRY FIELD TRIP

FOR THE INTERMEDIATE AND UPPER GRADES

When inspiration for creating poems is at a low ebb, the time has come to take the class on a field trip. A short excursion around the neighborhood will usually suffice. Encourage boys and girls to take pencils and notebooks to jot down ideas and suggestions for poems.

Either on the trip or after they return to the classroom, only a few of the children will pay attention to rhyme and meter and produce a verse, such as the following:

> There goes a butterfly
> Stopping to smell a rose;
> It may be on its way to see
> A butterfly friend it knows.

The majority, however, will not come up with verse. Encourage them to formulate descriptive words and phrases and to express their observations. Examples follow on the next page.

a narrow vacant lot
a noisy, boisterous crowd of boys and girls
Suddenly a cloud appeared.

Waiting on the frozen doorstep, the cold
milk bottle was stretching its neck to peek
through the keyhole into the warm kitchen.

POSTCARD AND LETTER CLUB

FOR THE INTERMEDIATE AND UPPER GRADES

Boys and girls usually are eager to correspond with those in other parts of the United States or in foreign countries. Magazines and newspapers, such as *Junior Scholastic, The Instructor,* and Sunday school papers, frequently carry names and addresses of boys and girls in foreign countries who wish to correspond with those of their own age. Lasting friendships are sometimes formed through correspondence of this kind.

Encourage the class to form a club in which the members share the letters which they receive. An interesting scrapbook may be made of letters, pictures, and postcards.

POTATO-BLOCK PRINTING

An effective block print may be made from a raw potato. To print a design with a potato, cut away the parts of the surface that you do not want to print. Select a long, medium-sized potato, and slice off a piece from the thick end. This cut end will form the surface from which you print. The rest of the potato is the block or base.

Work out a design on paper, cut it out, and press it on the sliced surface. The cutout serves as a guide to the carver. With a penknife cut away the unnecessary parts of the design in the potato to a depth of about one-sixteenth of an inch. Use a stamp pad for inking. The pads come in various colors. Press the design end of the potato gently on the pad and then on the article to be printed.

Simple allover designs, such as you may use in a border or to decorate gift wrapping paper, lend themselves best to printing with a potato. Plan to do the printing within a day or two after you make the block print because the potato will shrink and will need to be discarded in favor of a new one.

POT HOLDERS

FOR GIFTS

Pot holders make useful gifts. They may be made from cloth, felt, inner tubing, oilcloth, raffia, or any other suitable material that your ingenuity may devise.

CLOTH POT HOLDER

Cut two 6- or 6½-inch squares from cloth. Use one square for the front and the other for the back. Pad the holder with cotton batting or with several layers of outing flannel. Bind the edges with yarn, using a blanket stitch, or with a narrow strip of material cut on the bias, or with bias tape which may be purchased at a notions counter. Quilt the holder to keep the padding in place. Sew a small ring on one corner for a hanger.

BRAIDED CLOTH HOLDER

A good use for cotton rags is to tear the cloth into strips for braiding. You will need perhaps three strips 10 feet long to make a braid. Braid and make a 6-inch square by arranging the braids across and back as in the picture of the raffia holder on page 215. If you wish, arrange the braids into a coil instead. Start at the center and sew the edges of the braids together firmly as you proceed. Fashion a loop and sew it in place for a hanger.

FELT TEAPOT-SHAPED HOLDER

The felt from old hats may be put to good use for making pot holders. Draw an outline of a teapot large enough for a holder.

Make it 8 inches from the tip of the spout to the end of the handle and about 6 inches from the top to the base. Work out a pattern for the teapot on paper, cut it out and place it on two thicknesses of felt, one for the front and one for the back. Cut out and put cotton batting between the felt for insulation. Whip the two pieces of felt together with a blanket stitch. Use yarn of a contrasting color. Outline the bottom of the lid with yarn, using a running stitch. Sew a small ring to the top of the holder for a hanger.

FELT BUTTERFLY HOLDER

Work out on paper a butterfly large enough for a pot holder. Make it 6 inches from wing to wing. Place the pattern on two

layers of felt and cut it out. Make the body of the butterfly from brown or black felt. Make it 2½ inches long and ½-inch wide, and place it in position on the larger piece of felt and sew it on. Embroider the rest of the contours and decorations with yarn or heavy embroidery thread.

After you have finished the details, place cotton batting between the two pieces of felt for insulation, and whip the seams together with a blanket stitch. Sew on a small ring for the butterfly's head. The ring will also serve as a hanger for the pot holder.

214

INNER TUBING HOLDER

Cut a paper pattern of a star that measures about 6½ inches across from point to point. Place the pattern on inner tubing and cut two stars, one for the front and one for the back. You need not pad holders made from rubber tubing. Sew the edges together with yarn, using a blanket stitch. Sew on a small ring.

OILCLOTH HOLDER

Oilcloth is a coarse fabric that has been waterproofed with heavy paint. It is usually used for table, wall, and shelf covering.
Attractive pot holders may be made from small-figured oilcloth. Cut two 6½-inch squares from oilcloth, one for the front and the other for the back. Pad the holder with cotton batting or with several layers of outing flannel. Place the squares and padding in position and hold in place with paper clips. Bind the edges with yarn. Remove the clips, and quilt the holder enough so that
the padding will stay in place. Sew on a small ring for a hanger.

RAFFIA HOLDER

Raffia fiber makes rather unique holders. Braid about 10 feet of raffia. Put several fibers in each strip as one fiber to a strip is not enough. Make a 6-inch square by arranging the braid across and back as in the picture. Lace or sew the edges of the braids together firmly with a strand of raffia. You will need a special needle, a stout needle with a very large eye. It may be purchased at a fancy goods counter. Fashion a loop from raffia for a hanger.

Raffia is a strong fiber obtained from the leafstalks of the raffia palm, which grows abundantly in Madagascar. The natives of Madagascar use raffia for making clothing. It is also exported for use in weaving baskets.

215

PREPARING BOXES FOR THE NEEDY

FOR THE INTERMEDIATE GRADES

The preparation of boxes for the needy, whether for those at home or abroad, involves a variety of skills and experiences. It involves making lists, trips to the grocery store, a knowledge of food values, and a consideration of prices.

If the box is for shipment to a foreign country, problems in packing are involved, skill in estimating weights and measurements, and a trip to the post office for mailing. Before plans for sending a box abroad are too far advanced, it is wise to check with the post office about the size and weight of parcels and other packing and shipping instructions. Food, of course, should be sent separately, and care should be taken to avoid glass containers. If toys, clothing, and household items are sent, they should be assembled and prepared well in advance.

PRESSED FLOWERS

FOR THE INTERMEDIATE AND UPPER GRADES

A plant study may culminate in a classroom display of pressed flowers. Encourage the children to gather the flowers and to identify them with the help of flower books from the school or public library.

To press the flowers and to keep them from staining the pages of the book, place each flower between two sheets of tissue paper and place between the pages of a book. Do not place the tissue paper and flowers near the binding of the book, because it will weaken the binding. Then weight the book down with something heavy like a larger book. Let the flowers remain in the "press" for several days.

When they are thoroughly dry, mount the flowers on white tagboard. Label each specimen clearly with its name, and cover it with cellophane. A border of colored tape adds to the effectiveness of the decoration.

PRINCE OF PARIS

AN INDOOR GAME

The Prince of Paris is an old favorite. It is a hilarious game and one that demands constant attention and quick thinking on the part of the players.

The players number off quickly by beginning with one and continuing until everyone has a number. Number 1 is the leader, and he starts play by saying, "The Prince of Paris has lost his hat and I say Number 9 has it. Number 9 go to the head of the class."

However, before the leader has time to add, "Number 9 go to the end of the line," Number 9 retorts, "Who sir? I, sir?"

If he is too slow, Number 9 must go to the end of the line, and everyone below him moves up one number.

"Yes, sir, you sir!" answers Number 1, if he is first.

"Oh, no, sir, not I, sir!"

"Who then, sir?" questions Number 1.

"Number 5," replies Number 9 naming someone else.

Before Number 1 can beat him to it, Number 5 must say, "Who, sir; I, sir?"

"Number 5, go to the end of the line," commands Number 1.

So the game continues. The object is to unseat Number 1, the leader, by calling upon him frequently.

THE PROFESSORS' CLUB

Membership in the classroom Professors' Club requires that the members read two books a month. To make the club tick, prepare a wall chart of a picture of a round table. Also prepare a cutout of a professor for each member. Someone who is apt at drawing will enjoy making a cutout. Make as many duplicates as there are members. Ask each member to write or letter his name on his cutout. Arrange the professors to "sit" around the table. Do this by tacking the cutouts to the wall chart.

As long as he continues to read two books a month, a member's professor stays at the table.

PROMOTING INTEREST IN HYGIENE AND HEALTH

Interest in personal hygiene and in the health of the school and community may be stimulated by allotting bulletin board space to these subjects. The children may clip articles and bring them to school. Have them write the name of the periodical and the date on which it appeared on the clipping.

Newspapers are the readiest source for up-to-date information. In fact, in addition to articles reporting new discoveries in medicine, the metropolitan dailies have established columns on health. The articles often give advice about personal hygiene, how to avoid communicable diseases, and how to maintain the health of the individual and community.

PUPPETS

The art of puppetry is one of the most fascinating of dramatic presentations. It requires considerable skill to manipulate the puppets artistically and entertainingly. Puppets are figures used to imitate live characters and their actions. There are different kinds, such as the finger puppet, the hand puppet, the paper-sack puppet, and the marionette, which is worked with strings.

FINGER PUPPETS

This kind of puppet is easy to make. It needs only a head fastened to the puppeteer's forefinger to make it work. The finger

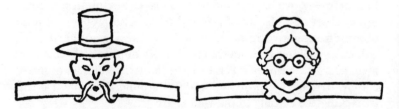

puppets illustrated are drawn either on white or colored paper. Draw the head of any character that you wish to portray. Cut

out the puppet including the band and paste the band around the forefinger of the puppeteer. One end of a peanut shell makes an interesting puppet, too. Draw the features with India ink.

HAND PUPPETS

The hand puppet is also easy to make but somewhat more difficult to work than the finger puppet. It requires a head, arms and hands, and a narrow costume that fits over the hand of the puppeteer like a loose glove. The puppeteer works the head with his forefinger and the arms with his thumb and third finger. Mold the head and hands with modeling clay or with papier-mâché. Leave room in the head for the puppeteer's forefinger. After the puppet is dry, draw the hair and features.

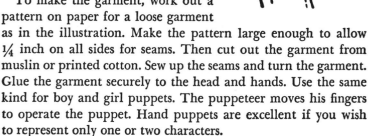

To make the garment, work out a pattern on paper for a loose garment as in the illustration. Make the pattern large enough to allow ¼ inch on all sides for seams. Then cut out the garment from muslin or printed cotton. Sew up the seams and turn the garment. Glue the garment securely to the head and hands. Use the same kind for boy and girl puppets. The puppeteer moves his fingers to operate the puppet. Hand puppets are excellent if you wish to represent only one or two characters.

MARIONETTES

Marionettes are puppets worked with strings. To make the head, select a sock and stuff the toe with a burned-out light bulb or with a rubber ball. Stuff the rest of the sock with crumpled newspaper or cotton batting. Avoid stuffing the joints, but tie them with string so that they are flexible.

Turn the sock upside down. To make the arms, start below the waistline and cut a strip upward on each side and pull back. Do not cut the strips off at the shoulder. Stitch up a seam for

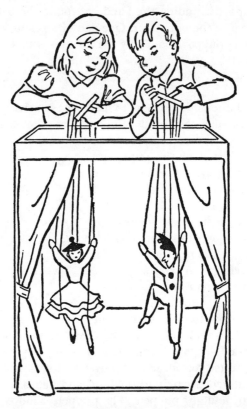

each arm. Stuff the arms and tie at the elbows. Stitch the sides of the body together to hold in the stuffing. Make the legs by slitting up the sock in the middle and stitching the seams. Weight the feet with pebbles or marbles so that the puppet will stay down. Stuff the legs. Use buttons for the eyes and yarn for the hair. Paint the features and make clothes from crepe paper.

The puppet is ready to be strung. Make the strings about 3 feet long and attach the strings to the head, waist, hands, and knees.

The fewer joints that you string, the easier will be the manipulation of the marionette. The number of strings will depend upon what you expect the marionette to do. To keep the strings from getting tangled make a "control" to which to fasten the strings. Make the control of wood in the shape of a cross. Make the longer piece about 8 inches and the shorter piece about 6 inches.

PAPER-SACK MARIONETTE

Select a small paper sack, size 6 or 8. The size is printed at the top of the bag. Stuff the bottom of the bag with crumpled newspaper to make the head and tie a string tightly around the neck. Turn the bag upside down and cut a strip wide enough on each side for arms. Stuff the arms with crumpled paper and fasten the stuffing to the strip by winding with string. Slit up the bottom of the bag to form the legs. Stuff the bag with crumpled paper to form the body. Pad the joints lightly or not at all to keep them flexible. Tie a string around the waist, knees, and elbows to form the joints. Paint or draw the features. Dress the marionette in crepe paper. Fit the garment loose enough so that it will not interfere with the motion. Attach strings to arms, head, and waist and the marionette is ready for the stage!

PUPPET STAGES

To give boys and girls an opportunity to try their skill at manipulating marionettes, make a stage from a cardboard packing box. The height of the stage needs to be greater than the width. Select a box that is from 18 to 24 inches deep, depending upon the size of the puppets. Use the top opening of the box for the top of the stage, and cut away most of one side for the front of the stage. Allow a 2-inch strip to remain across the top for the proscenium.

A simple stage may be made with a card table. Open the table, and place it on its side with the legs extended toward the audience. For background scenery drape the table and legs with two small tablecloths. Place the stage on a bench or on two chairs.

Another simple stage may be made with an armchair. Place the chair so that the back is away from the audience. Use the seat for the stage. Drape the back and arms for background scenery. The manipulator stands behind the back of the chair to work the marionettes. A chair makes a good stage for finger and hand puppets, too. Turn the chairs so that the back will be toward the audience. Kneel on the seat and work over the back of the chair.

PURITAN COSTUMES

Costumes for Puritans may be based on basic clothes and given the Puritan "touch" by adding accessories. Children may dress at home for the day. This eliminates the bothersome detail of changing into costumes at school except for adding accessories.

PURITAN GIRL

Choose a dress with a simple bodice, long sleeves, and a long skirt gathered at the waist. Select a plain dark color, such as black, dark blue, or brown. A small-size adult dress sometimes fits girls well enough to serve the purpose. The Puritan collar may be a three-cornered fichu, or it may be made like the pattern on this page or the one on the Puritan doll on the next page. The

cuffs may be plain bands or turned back. Make the collar and cuffs of thin white cotton or crepe paper. Whether you use cloth or paper, make the collar and cuffs double to give them body. Make an apron like the one on the Puritan doll. Aprons usually were not worn outdoors; however, they add to the effect.

PURITAN BOY

If he has a dark suit with knickers, a boy can be a Puritan by adding some accessories. Make band cuffs and a wide, round collar that opens in front. Use a man's wide-brimmed felt hat and make a tall crown 6 or 8 inches high to fit over the regular one. Make a cylinder from black cardboard and draw it in a bit at the top. Tack it in place with needle and thread. Trim the hat with a wide band and buckle. Cover the buckle with silver paper, and make similar buckles for the shoes.

A PURITAN DOLL

To make a Puritan doll you will need an onion about the size of a golf ball, 1 or 2 cornhusks, black and white crepe paper, and a large nail. Use the onion for the head of the doll. Push the nail into the top of the onion. Invert the onion so that the nail is at the bottom. Use a blade or two of the husk to cover the onion. Paste down smoothly with glue and cellophane tape. Arrange cornhusks around the nail to form a long, full dress. If the husks from one ear of corn make a skimpy dress, use two. With scissors cut the husks to form the arms. Cut up on each side of the dress and pull the cut section away. Do not cut the husk at the top of the arm. Tie string around the neck, waist, and wrists to complete the dress. Make the hair from black crepe paper cut into strips. Make the bonnet, collar, and apron from white crepe paper. Draw the eyes, nose, and mouth with India ink.

QUIETING A CLASSROOM

FOR THE PRIMARY AND INTERMEDIATE GRADES

When she steps into a noisy classroom, a teacher may restore order by asking the children to close their eyes and to listen for a pin to drop. Children raise their hands as soon as they hear the pin. Sometimes the teacher may need to drop it several times.

Another technique is giving instructions in a whisper. The teacher may say, "Betty, please go to the blackboard and draw a flower. Dick, balance an eraser on your head and walk around the table. Sue, hold up as many fingers as there are days in the week." Soon the children begin to listen for their names.

A RACK FOR POT HOLDERS

FOR A GIFT

A good rack for pot holders may be made with a wooden coat hanger. Remove the metal hook from the hanger. Cut oilcloth

 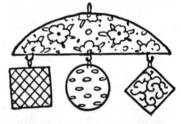

in the shape of the hanger. Allow for an overlap all the way around. Place the oilcloth over the hanger, and tack or glue the overlap to the back. Put a row of three hooks across the bottom on which to hang the holders. If you are using screw hooks, screw them in place. If you are using S-shaped hooks, drill three small holes in the bottom bar large enough to accommodate the hooks. S-shaped hooks may be purchased at a hardware store or they may be made from wire. Put the hooks in place and the rack is ready to be hung in a convenient spot.

RADIO BROADCASTS

Assimilated radio broadcasts provide excellent learning experiences for boys and girls. Children, for example, may plan a quiz program in the social studies, a spelldown, or vocal and instrumental music. An original play or poem may be given on the "broadcast." Current events may be presented in the form of newscasts. Announcements and advertising "blurbs" for such occasions as Book Week, PTA programs, school plays, and programs for other special occasions may be given publicity on the classroom radio. Good usage in English should not be overlooked on any of the programs and announcements.

To make the broadcasts more realistic, boys and girls may make a microphone. Select a 1-gallon paint can and fill it about ¾ full with sand or plaster of Paris. Sink a discarded broomstick or a 4½-foot pipe length into the sand or plaster of Paris. For a mouthpiece use a shower spray or a perforated tin can lid or a cardboard circle. Fasten the mouthpiece to the standard with wire or string. Name the broadcasting station and paint its letters on the microphone.

RAG DOLLS

FOR THE PRIMARY GRADES

Children always enjoy having "just one more doll," and the most popular of dolls is apt to be a rag doll that a child has made himself. Boys especially like rag boy dolls, such as the gingerbread man, a fireman, or a policeman.

Work out a pattern on paper and then cut out the doll from cloth. Flour or sugar sacks make excellent materials. Sew up the sides. Allow about ¼ inch for seams and an opening large enough to put the stuffing through. Turn the doll inside out and stuff with sawdust, rags, or shredded newspaper. Make the hair from yarn and the eyes with buttons. The mouth and nose may be painted or stitched with colored thread or yarn. Dress the doll to suit your fancy.

225

RAINBOW PICTURES

Work out a pattern of a butterfly on paper. Then cut three identical butterflies from construction paper. Choose a different color for each butterfly. Paste the three together so that a narrow margin of each color shows. The result is a pleasing sense of color.

Another object that lends itself to this type of picture is a rainbow. Cut three or more identical rainbows from construction paper, selecting a different color for each one. Paste them together in a manner so that a bit of each color shows.

Fasten a string to the rainbow picture and hang it from a globe or window fastener. It also makes a beautiful Christmas tree ornament; or, it may be mounted on construction paper to make a plaque.

RAMONA STRINGS

For years Indian and Mexican homes in the Southwest were brightened by strings of gay peppers and gourds hung in the corner to dry. In time the custom spread to other parts of the country, and the purpose of the strings changed from the utilitarian to the ornamental. In addition to being called Ramona strings, the strings also are known as patio strings, fiesta chains, or gourd strings.

To make a string, select gourds, pods, peppers, cones, burrs, berries, or other ornamental plants that grow in your region. Shellac or lacquer to heighten and to preserve the colors. Arrange and tie with a strong cord. Ramona strings vary in length from 1 to 4 feet.

READING DISTANCES ON A MAP

METHOD NO. 1

The project on page 114, "Figuring Distances on a Map," makes us realize the problem that confronts mapmakers. Distances are greatly reduced or squeezed down to get them on a map. The method by which they are proportionately squeezed down is called "scale" or a "scale of miles."

In this project let us try to read a map; that is, to determine how far it is from one place to another. Use a wall map or a large road map of your state. Look at the scale of miles at the bottom of the map or in one of the lower corners. It may read, "1 inch = 3 miles," which means that the distance had to be reduced 190,080 times.

With a ruler measure the distance on the wall map between two towns or cities. Choose two places that you know about and between which you probably have ridden in an automobile. Now use the scale of miles given on the map and change the measurement on the ruler into miles.

This way of showing scale is called the "inch-to-the-mile" method. Another method of determining distance on a map is explained in the next project.

READING DISTANCES ON A MAP

METHOD NO. 2

We learned in the preceding project how to read distances on a map according to the "inch-to-the-mile scale." We also learned that scale shows how much the distance on the earth's surface has been reduced in order to represent it on the map. The reduction of distance varies from map to map and therefore it is always important to consult the key at the bottom or in one of the corners of the map.

Another way of showing scale, and one that is in common use, is with a line or bar. The line is marked off into parts. Each part represents a certain number of miles on the earth's surface. This also is a scale of miles.

Again use the wall map of your state. Study the key to see if the line or bar scale is used. If you do not find it on the wall map, look for a map in an atlas or encyclopedia that does show this kind of scale. Take a piece of paper and place the edge of the paper on the line of the scale and mark the scale on the paper. Now place the paper between two towns or cities. From your scale and data in the key, figure how many miles apart the towns or cities are.

If you wish to learn more about reading distances on a map and about the methods that mapmakers use in showing the scale of miles, look in an encyclopedia under the subject of "Maps."

A READING TREE

A "reading tree" is a device for encouraging boys and girls to read. After reading a book and making a satisfactory report, a reader has the privilege of hanging his name on the tree.

Work out a pattern for a tree on brown construction paper. Make the tree about two feet high. Cut out the tree, mount it on butcher paper, and hang it on the wall. Draw and cut out a supply of leaves. Make them of red, green, and yellow paper. Then as soon as a reader qualifies, give him a leaf. He prints the title of the book, the author's name, and his own name on the tree. Paste the leaf on a branch of the tree.

REBUS WRITING

Rebus writing is a form of picture writing that is very old. It is a source of fun and fascination. In a way it is a form of riddle, since words are expressed by pictures of objects that resemble those words or letters. The pictures often are made somewhat obscure to add to the riddle element. At the top of the next page is an example of a message in rebus writing.

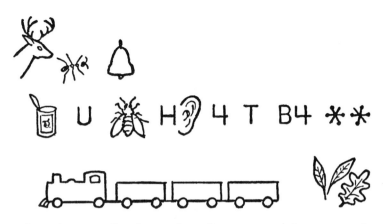

As a timesaver for the teacher, the answer to the message in rebus writing is given at the bottom of page 230.

A RECIPE BOOK

A notebook with cardboard covers and bound so that it will lie open easily makes a handy recipe book. A blank book of this type can usually be purchased in a store that sells school supplies.

The appearance and usefulness of the book may be enhanced by giving it a pretty cover and by providing alphabet index tabs for quick reference. Choose an attractive chintz, cotton print, or oilcloth. Cut the print the size of the book and glue it to the covers. Make index tabs from the gummed paper. Stiffen the centers with cardboard. Print the letters of the alphabet on the tabs and put them in place in the book.

A RELAY RACE

A SPELLING GAME

Here is a way to have fun and an incentive for learning to spell correctly at the same time. Appoint a leader for each row in the classroom. Each leader pronounces words to be spelled by

229

his row or team. The spellers on each team, beginning with the first one in the row, hurry to the blackboard to write the words as fast as they can. If a word is misspelled, the next speller corrects it. If he, too, misses it, then it is up to the next speller to uphold the honor of the team.

To eliminate the chance of copying, each leader should have a different list of words. The team that finishes its list first correctly wins the relay. The word lists may be exchanged and play resumed.

A RELIEF MAP

A relief map shows the land formations, such as hills, valleys, mountains, streams, lakes. To build up a relief map, use heavy cardboard or tagboard. Draw the outline of the area to be mapped. Coat the area to be worked with glue. To build up the elevations and to make the depressions, apply modeling clay, papier-mâché, or a salt and flour mixture. Continue to spread additional areas with glue and molding material.

When it is dry, spread the surface of the map lightly with glue. Color by sprinkling with colored sawdust. To color sawdust, mix it in a jar with dry calcimine paint. To make the flour and salt mixture, use these proportions:

$\frac{1}{2}$ cup salt
1 cup flour
Add enough water to make a paste

Answer to the message in rebus writing at the top of page 229.

Dear Aunt Bell,

Can you be here for tea before Jack's train leaves?

REMOVING COLOR

In preparing costumes and stage settings, it is sometimes necessary to remove color from a fabric. To remove color, wash the cloth with soap and water, and then boil it in soda water. If this does not remove all the color, bleach the cloth in a solution of chloride of lime. Make a solution by adding one tablespoon of chloride of lime to one-half gallon of water. Immerse the fabric in the solution for about fifteen minutes. Then boil the fabric in soda water again. If the fabric will not stand this drastic treatment, use hydrosulphite of soda. Make a solution by adding one tablespoon of hydrosulphite of soda to one-half gallon of warm water. Stir until well mixed.

There are several excellent commercial dye removers on the market. These usually can be secured at drug, variety, or department stores. Select one to suit your purpose and follow directions.

When using a color remover or a bleaching solution, wear rubber gloves to protect your hands. Be careful not to let the solution come in contact with your eyes, skin, or clothing.

See also "Dyeing," page 98.

A RETURNING BOOMERANG

To make this fascinating toy, select a can with a removable top so that you can restore the top after the contents have been emptied. With a hammer and nail drive two holes an inch apart through the top of the can and two through the bottom. Cut a heavy rubber band apart so that it is in one piece. Thread it through the holes to form an 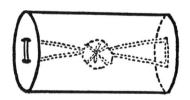 "X" as in the picture. Then tie the ends of the band together. With a string, tie a stone or a piece of metal to the rubber band at the place where it crosses on the inside of the can. Roll the can away from you; and, as if by magic, it will roll back to the starting point.

RHYMING

Children in the primary grades enjoy supplying the rhyming word in a couplet. Make up the couplet and leave a blank for the rhyming word. For example, compose couplets like these:

1. "It's eight o'clock," Dick's mother said
   "It's time you children were in _____."
2. On moccasined feet the red men come
   To dance to the beating of the big war _____.
3. With a putt-putt clearing of its throat,
   Across the lake came the motor _____.
4. It's spring! The circus has come to town
   Lion, tiger, and funny-faced _____.
5. The sky is black, the thunder roars,
   The wind bangs windows and rattles _____.

Answers:
   1. bed   2. drum   3. boat   4. clown   5. doors

RHYTHM GAME

The teacher claps out the rhythm of a well-known song. The children listen carefully to identify the song. As soon as someone succeeds, everyone joins in singing. Children then take turns in clapping out familiar rhythms.

RHYTHM STICKS

FOR THE PRIMARY GRADES

If you have a rhythm band, you will need several pairs of rhythm sticks. The sticks may be made from sparerib bones. Select two rib bones. Clean and dry the bones. Then lacquer them. To use the rhythm sticks, hold one with the left hand. Place one end of the stick on the thumb and hold it with the forefinger. Tap the stick with the one held loosely in the right hand.

ROLLING PEBBLES

A GAME FOR THE INTERMEDIATE GRADES

Divide the class into small groups of about six to ten. Each group plays by itself. Have a bucketful of pebbles on hand and have someone distribute an equal number to each player.

To play the game, the players in each group form a circle and seat themselves on the ground. With a stick or chalk the player draws a line between any two pebbles. He selects one of the two pebbles as a shooter with which he shoots the other pebble. If he is successful in hitting the pebble, the player picks up both pebbles and has another turn. If he misses, the next player picks up all the pebbles on the ground and continues to play in the same way. The player who has the most pebbles after everyone has taken his turn is the winner.

SAFETY *DO'S* AND *DON'TS*

From time to time it is well to point out the great loss of lives caused by accidents. About 100,000 people lose their lives by accidents each year in the United States and many more are injured and permanently handicapped. Many of these accidents can be prevented by getting rid of the causes and by observing a few *do's* and *don'ts*.

Encourage boys and girls to formulate their own *do's* and *don'ts* for preventing accidents and to keep them in the form of a check sheet. Keep the list short so that the pupils will not feel overwhelmed by the list. Call attention to it from time to time and add an item as the need arises.

DO'S AND DON'TS FOR SCHOOL

1. Do walk up and down stairs one step at a time.
2. Do keep your feet under the desk so that you will not trip anyone.
3. Do use a handkerchief when sneezing or coughing.

4. Do keep the scissors in a safe place.
5. Do report broken chains on playground swings and rings.
6. Don't run in the school building.
7. Don't walk with a pencil in your mouth.
8. Don't block doorways.

DO'S AND DON'TS FOR PEDESTRIANS

1. Do cross the street at corners where you can be seen.
2. Do look to the left and right before crossing a street.
3. Do face traffic on country roads. Do step off the roadway when cars come at high speed.
4. Do judge traffic by speed and not by distance alone.
5. Do be cautious.
6. Don't run or step out from behind a parked car.
7. Don't run after a ball in the street.
8. Don't loiter or play in the street.
9. Don't concentrate on one object when crossing a street.
10. Don't take a chance when crossing a street.

DO'S AND DON'TS FOR BICYCLISTS

Bicyclists need to exercise special care in guarding against accidents. Many bicycle clubs have adopted rules for safe driving formulated by the Cycle Trades of America. The *do's* and *don'ts* which follow are based on those rules.

1. Do obey all traffic regulations, such as red and green lights, one-way streets, stop signs, and hand signals.
2. Do ride in a straight line.
3. Do have a white light on the front of the bicycle, and a danger signal on the rear for night riding.
4. Do have a signaling device to warn of your approach.
5. Do give pedestrians the right of way.
6. Do look out for cars at crossings and when you pull out of a parking place.
7. Do keep your bicycle in good condition.
8. Don't carry another person on your bicycle.
9. Don't weave in and out of traffic.
10. Don't hitch on vehicles.

234

SALT AND PEPPER SHAKERS

FOR A GIFT

Small tin cans and glass jars make excellent salt and pepper shakers. Paprika cans, spice cans, small olive oil and shampoo bottles work well, too. With a hammer and small nail or tack perforate the tops of the shakers. Try to make small perforations for the pepper by using only the end of the tack. Make larger perforations for the salt.

Decorate the shakers with any design that you like. This may be done with lacquer, enamel, or nail polish. Twisted or braided raffia glued on coil by coil is also an effective decoration. Label the shakers *S* and *P*.

A SAVINGS BANK

FOR THE PRIMARY GRADES

A glass jar makes an excellent savings bank. A child can watch his pennies and nickels accumulate. Select a jar that is suitable in size and shape and one with a tin lid. Cut a slot large enough in the lid to take a coin. Decorate the glass bank with lacquer, nail polish, or sealing wax.

SAVING SCRATCH PAPER

Thrift and neatness may be encouraged in the classroom by providing a box for scratch paper. Ask boys and girls to deposit partly used sheets of paper in the box at the end of a study period. The paper may be used for work that does not require a full-size sheet, such as arithmetic and spelling drills. This activity helps children to clear their desks of paper clutter and encourages them to save partially used sheets of tablet paper.

SAWDUST ANIMAL SILHOUETTES

Attractive animal silhouettes may be made with cardboard and colored sawdust. The sawdust gives an interesting texture. Fill several quart jars about two thirds full with sawdust. Use a different jar for each color that you plan to use. Mix calcimine or tempera paint with water to a thin consistency. Pour the paint over the sawdust and stir well. Then spread the colored sawdust on newspapers to dry.

Work out a pattern of the animals on paper. Make them large or small depending upon how you want to use them. Six inches high is a good height for an elephant if you want to use it for the classroom zoo, or if you want to let it parade in a border. If you prefer, however, to gather a group of animals into a loose-leaf scrapbook, make them smaller. Cut out the pattern and transfer it to cardboard. Then cut out the animal, spread glue on the surface, and sprinkle with dry, colored sawdust. Allow the glue to dry and the animal is ready.

You probably will want to include a bear, a panda, an elephant, a giraffe, and your favorite dog and cat in your collection. If you run out of varieties, you may vary the poses and positions of the animals. A gallon of sawdust will sprinkle about 20 areas 8 x 4 inches or 35 to 40 areas 4 x 2 inches. Sawdust for handicraft projects can usually be obtained at lumberyards.

SAWDUST PICTURES

Attractive pictures may be made by sprinkling a drawing with colored sawdust. Work out a picture in pencil in which there is an opportunity to blend one color into another, such as a sunrise or sunset scene.

To color the sawdust fill several small glass jars, such as peanut-butter jars or old glass tumblers, nearly full with sawdust. Use a different jar for each color that you plan to use. Mix calcimine or tempera paint with water to a thin consistency. Pour the paint over the sawdust and stir well. Then spread the colored sawdust on newspapers to dry.

Spread with glue all areas of the picture that should have the same color. Sprinkle with sawdust and allow to dry thoroughly. Shake off the excess sawdust, and coat with glue the areas for the next color. Again allow to dry, and again shake off the excess sawdust. Repeat the process for every color that you use. The hills may take shades of green and black or blue and purple.

A SCISSORS BOX

A box for scissors is a convenience as well as a safety device. Select a cardboard tube that is somewhat larger in diameter than the width of the scissors. You may find a tube that is just the right length. If you do not, cut a tube from a longer one. Close one end with a disc cut from heavy cardboard and fasten it in place with adhesive tape. Make a cover for the other end by cutting another disc and fastening it to the tube with a hinge made from adhesive tape. Make a tab or pull from a scrap of cotton tape or ribbon about an inch long. Glue one end to the under edge of the cover opposite the hinge. Then pull up on the other end. Decorate the tube with small-figured wallpaper or chintz or in any way that you wish.

If you prefer a scissors case that does not roll, use a flat box large enough to accommodate the scissors. Children keep the scissors boxes in their desks.

SCRAMBLED PUZZLES

A GAME FOR THE ELEMENTARY GRADES

Divide the class into three or four teams. Give each team pieces from a different jigsaw puzzle. However, give each player only one piece. Throw the remaining pieces of all the puzzles in a pile on a table. Mix them thoroughly. The trick is for the members of each team to sort out and put together the pieces for their puzzle. The team that puts its puzzle together first wins.

SCRAMBLED STORIES

Children enjoy piecing together stories that have been scrambled. Type a number of fairy tales with which the children are familiar. Make enough carbon copies so that each child can work on a separate story. Some of the children, of course, will be working on duplicate stories. Cut the stories into 1-line strips. Mix the strips in a box and put them in a pile on a table.

To unscramble a story, assign one to each pupil. Ask the children to gather around the table. Each one sorts out his story and arranges it in order on art paper.

A contest may be made of this activity by dividing the pupils into teams. Divide them into several teams if you prefer to have them work in small groups. Put each team to work at a separate table and give each the same story to unscramble. The first team to finish wins.

If you wish to use this activity as seatwork, put the strips for one story in an envelope, and give it to the child to unscramble and to piece together.

SEALING WAX PICTURES

Applying sealing wax to paper or tin is an enjoyable art experience. Select a paper plate or a pie tin, and let it serve as a

foundation for a wall plaque. Work out a drawing on paper, and then transfer it lightly in pencil. If you are working on tin, use chalk.

Heat one end of a stick of sealing wax over a low flame. Heat one color at a time and dribble the wax on the areas that should have the same color. Let the wax dry, and repeat the process for every color that you use.

Let the rim of the plate form the frame and paint it a solid color with calcimine paint. To hang the plaque, fasten a string across the back with adhesive tape.

SECRET TAG

AN OUTDOOR GAME FOR ANY NUMBER OF PLAYERS

Secret Tag is a delightful game because of the element of mystery and suspense that prevails. The teacher, or leader, secretly chooses someone to be "it." She circulates among the players, pretending to give them a small article, such as an eraser, a piece of chalk, a marble, or a button. The player into whose hands the article is actually slipped becomes "it." But in order not to reveal his identity, "it" maintains a poker face until the leader has completed his rounds.

On a signal from the teacher, the players disperse. "It" tries to tag someone secretly and to slip the article into his hand. Once he is tagged, the new "it" accepts the article as secretly as possible and the old "it" soon retires from the game and watches from the sidelines. The player who stays in longest wins.

SEED CHARTS

To make a seed chart, encourage the children to collect seeds and to mount them on a large cardboard for display purposes. Put the tiny seeds in small cellophane bags or envelopes. Glue the bag or envelope to the chart. Group under headings, such as:

Seeds We Eat (corn, peas, beans, peanuts, poppy seeds)
Vegetable Seeds (onions, carrots, radishes, lettuce, tomatoes)
Flower Seeds (sweet pea, petunia, pansy, four-o'clocks)
Seeds for Squirrels (nuts, acorns)
Seeds for Birds (flowers, grains, such as wheat, rye, oats)
Seeds That Give Us Clothing (cotton, flax)

A SEWING KIT

A handy little sewing kit may be made from a small round box, such as an ice-cream carton. To make the pockets for the inside of the kit, cut a strip of cloth to fit the box. Allow enough material at the bottom to turn in the raw edge and enough at the

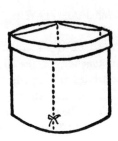 

top for a hem. Hem the top and put the material in place. Make about three pockets by stitching the cloth vertically to the box as in the illustration.

Cover the outside of the box with a decorative paper, such as a small-figured wallpaper. Apply a coat of shellac. A pin cushion may be added to the top by padding the cover with cotton and covering it with cloth.

SHADOW ACTING

Shadow acting is a drama activity that lends encouragement to the diffident and retiring. It is the same as pantomime except that the performance is given behind a curtain. The curtain must be sheer enough so that the audience can see the shadows of the actors performing on the other side of the curtain.

The stage area behind the curtain should be well lighted while the audience room is darkened. If the performance is in the daytime, use a curtain made from a transparent material, such as cheesecloth. If it is in the evening, a bed sheet may be used if a more transparent curtain is not available.

A SHAMROCK LAPEL PIN

FOR ST. PATRICK'S DAY

To make a lapel pin shaped like a shamrock, you will need a foot of wire the thickness of a fine hairpin, several feet of finer wire, a needle and green silk thread, and a snitch of green crepe paper. Bend the thick wire into the shape of a shamrock and allow for a stem. Wind the perimeter closely with the fine wire. With the needle and green silk thread, fill in the leaves as in the illustration. Fasten the thread to the edge and take it across. Take the second thread across at right angles to the first one. Then weave the other threads through the center as you take them across. Cut a bit of green crepe paper into a narrow strip and wind the stem. The shamrock lapel pin is ready to wear.

SHUFFLEBOARD

AN ARITHMETIC GAME FOR THE INTERMEDIATE GRADES

Use a large calendar for a shuffleboard. Choose any calendar month, tear off the sheet, mount it on cardboard, and place it on the floor for a shuffleboard. One board accommodates from two to five players. The object of the game is to toss beans on squares that have high numbers, and the first player to score 100 wins.

The players take turns at the shuffleboard. A turn consists of throwing two beans one at a time on the board. The sum of the two numbers on which the beans fall is the players score for his turn. Each player keeps his own score on paper and picks up his beans after each turn. Play may continue for several turns until someone wins. The score made at each turn, of course, is added to that made in the previous turn.

It is desirable to prepare several shuffleboards to accommodate the class. The game may be played quietly in the rear of the room by those who finish their seatwork early. It is also an excellent game for a rainy recess. Shuffleboards provide an excellent use for the large old calendars that you have been saving.

SILENT BRASS BAND

AN INDOOR GAME

In Silent Brass Band, the instruments—trumpets, trombones, flutes, clarinets, piccolos, drums, cymbals—are imaginary. The game is a great deal of fun and "acquaints" boys and girls with band instruments and the way in which they are played. Each player chooses an "instrument." The trombone is reserved for the teacher, or for a leader who is wide awake and a good showman. As the band is about to begin to "play," the leader looks to see that everyone is holding his "instrument" in position.

With a gesture, the leader signals "Begin." He looks around to see that everyone is "playing" his instrument properly. Suddenly he trades his "trombone" for the "instrument" of one of the players. The player must take up the trombone or pay a forfeit. The forfeit may be an item, such as a marble, ring, pencil, watch, eraser. If the player accepts the trombone promptly, the leader continues to lead the band, resuming his trombone playing and trading it unexpectedly for other instruments to catch players unaware.

At the end of the game, the owners may redeem their forfeits by reciting a poem, singing a song, carrying on an imaginary telephone conversation, or anything that the teacher prescribes.

SILENT BUTLER

A silent butler is a handy device to have around the house, and one that boys and girls enjoy making for a gift. A silent butler is convenient for emptying ash trays, papers from candy boxes and other small waste materials. Use a cigar box and make a handle from a piece of light-weight wood about 27 inches long and 1 inch wide. Nail it to the cover as in the picture. Do not nail the cover down. Then gild or shellac.

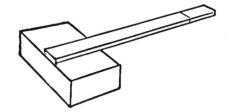

SILHOUETTE PORTRAITS

FOR THE PRIMARY AND INTERMEDIATE GRADES

Making silhouette portraits—especially of one's classmates—is a project that boys and girls thoroughly enjoy and one that is easy to do. A silhouette is an outline of a person's head in profile. Pose the boy or girl between a sunny window and a smooth wall or between a lighted candle and wall. Hang a light colored paper on the wall. Focus the model's shadow on the paper. Experiment until the silhouette is the desired size by moving the model closer or farther away from the wall. Then draw the outline of the silhouette directly on the paper on which the shadow is cast and cut out carefully.

To be effective, mount the cutout on dark paper. Should you prefer a dark cutout, transfer the silhouette from light to dark paper by putting the two together. Pin or clip them together to keep them from slipping. Cut out the two at the same time by following the outline on the light paper.

Instead of drawing the outline of the shadow directly on the paper on which it is cast, the class may copy the silhouette at their desks. This type of art activity is a fascinating experience and one of which children seldom tire.

To delight the class, arrange the silhouettes into a border. Allow about 4 inches between each one. Then on some special occasion, such as Parents' Day, parents, aunts, uncles, and friends will enjoy identifying the portraits.

A SIPHON

AN EXPERIMENT THAT DEMONSTRATES AIR PRESSURE

A siphon is a bent tube with unequal arms through which a liquid can be drawn up over the edge of a container into another at a lower level. It is useful for drawing water from a container that cannot be overturned.

Fill a bowl with water and put it on a table or chair. Place a bucket on the floor, and fill a rubber tube that is about 18 inches long with water. Put one end of the tube under a faucet and hold the tube in a U shape. Pinch the ends shut by holding them tightly. Then put one end into the bowl and let the other hang into the bucket. Water will start to flow from the bowl up over the edge and down into the bucket.

It is air pressure that makes the siphon work. The water in the long arm of the tube weighs more than the water in the short arm. The air presses down on the surface of the water in the bowl. The pressure is strong enough to push water up into the short arm and over the bend into the long arm where the water falls into the bucket.

SKETCHING TO ENLIVEN STORIES

FOR A TEACHER WHO LIKES TO SKETCH

In addition to enlivening subject matter as described on page 246, the teacher may wish to use freehand drawings as a relaxing game. She may do the sketching on a large easel or on the blackboard with colored chalk, crayons, or calcimine paint. Pupils are fascinated and delighted with this type of entertainment. It works especially well with an original story, as in the one that follows.

"Boys and girls," begins the teacher, "I know of two little children who came to school this afternoon across a big vacant lot. The grass was very tall, and as they walked through it, Betty said to Peter, 'Peter, do you see the tall grass moving?'

"The children stopped and listened a moment, and Peter said, 'Yes, Betty, I do.'

" 'Oh, Peter,' said Betty, 'Do you suppose there's a big animal hiding in the grass?'

"Just then they both saw one long ear sticking up, and then another ear.

"Peter said to Betty, 'I bet it's a rabbit,' and then a rabbit did appear!

" 'A cottontail!' they cried. 'Look at his cute little white tail.'

"Just then, the school bell rang. And as the children started to run, the rabbit saw them and hippety-hopped away.

"All that afternoon Peter and Betty couldn't wait for school to be over so that they could go back to the vacant lot to see if the rabbit was still there."

SKETCHING TO ENLIVEN SUBJECT MATTER

Freehand sketches drawn on the blackboard as the lesson progresses may make subject matter more meaningful and enjoyable. In studying a lesson in science, the class, for example, may come upon the words "lever" and "fulcrum." Pupils may not realize that they have any practical knowledge of these words.

Draw a large rock that is being pried loose with a pole, with the pole resting on a smaller stone. Lead the pupils into recognizing the pole as the lever and the smaller stone as the fulcrum.

Another illustration of the lever and fulcrum with which the children are familiar is the teeter-totter.

Keep the sketches simple and to the point. Sketching is a great aid in sustaining interest.

A SKI POLE

The young skier, using barrel stave skis described in the next project, will need a pole to help him keep his balance. Cut a broomstick into a 3-foot length, depending upon the height of the skier. In the center of a tin coffee-can cover, punch a hole large enough through which to force the broomstick. Anchor the can lid about 3 inches from the bottom of the pole by driving a nail through the broom above the lid and another below the lid.

SKIS

A pair of skis for a small boy or girl can be made by cutting a wooden barrel stave into two pieces, one for each runner or ski. To make straps for slipping the feet through, cut a strip from inner tubing about 2 to 3 inches wide. Cut the strip long enough to make a circle. Tack the strap securely about 6 inches from the end of the runner. If the tacks stick through the runner, bend the points by pounding them with the hammer. Tack a strap to the second runner in the same manner.

If they curl too much, flatten the barrel staves by weighting them down for twenty-four hours or so before using them. Do not straighten the front ends, as these need to turn up slightly. Wax the bottom of the runners so that they will glide smoothly over the snow. Older boys often enjoy making skis or a snow scooter (page 249) for younger brothers and sisters.

A SLED

For a hand sled you will need a pair of runners made from barrel staves; a 2 x 4-inch board 16 inches long; a box for the sled. An apple box is about right. Cut the 2 x 4 into four 4-inch lengths for legs to support the sled. Nail one to each corner of the box. Drive the nails through from the inside of the box.

For runners select two wooden barrel staves that are about 9 inches longer than the box. Wax the bottom of the runners so that they will slide smoothly through the snow. To fasten the runners to the box, turn the box upside down. Place the runners so that the box will ride toward the back of the staves; that is, allow about 6 inches of the runner sticking out in front. Nail the runners in place and then drill two holes through the front for tying the tow rope.

A SNAKE TRICK

FOR APRIL FOOLS' DAY

Fooling your friends with a make-believe snake is a harmless April Fools' Day trick. To make the snake, have the children bring discarded stockings to school. Fill them loosely with grass, shredded newspapers, or crumpled tissue paper. Fasten a long string to the snake and it is ready.

The trick is to hide behind a clump of bushes and slyly pull the snake across the path of an unsuspecting friend, parent, or uncle. Children think this is great fun.

SNAPPY ARTISTS

A FREEHAND ART CONTEST

For a "Snappy Artists" contest divide the class into teams composed of about five members. Appoint a leader for each team. Someone from each team goes to the blackboard to draw an object or animal, such as a cat, rabbit, clock, drum, bird, teacup, fork, flower, tree, star. The leaders whisper the assignments to the players as they leave their desks.

Each team tries to identify the object its player is drawing. As soon as a player has an idea about the identity of the object, he raises his hand, and the first one to come up with the right answer wins a point for his team. The game continues until each player has had a turn at the blackboard.

If you have a large class and if you have a lot of blackboard space, several teams may be put in play at the same time.

SNIFFING FLOWERS AND AROMATIC PLANTS

AN INDOOR SEAT GAME

This game gives boys and girls experience in distinguishing flowers and plants through the sense of smell. Divide the class into two groups, or let the class choose sides. The players remain in their seats and are blindfolded. Inexpensive blindfolds may be made on a wholesale scale from butcher paper folded into bands and fastened with paper clips.

Give each player a flower or a cutting from an aromatic plant, such as pine, eucalyptus, sage, dill, pepper tree, onion, geranium leaf, rose, violet, or any plant and flower that is at hand. A player scores a point for his team for each correct answer. The team with the higher score wins.

The game should not be concluded until everyone has had several turns at sniffing. To insure a fresh start after each turn, shift the cuttings up or back or across the aisle several seats instead of one and begin the game again.

SNOW SCOOTER

To make a child's snow scooter, you need a wooden barrel stave about 3 feet long and 3 pieces of softwood for the steering pole, handle, and brace. Make the steering pole 2 feet long, 2 to 2½ inches wide, and 2 inches thick; the brace about 1 foot long; the handle bar 10 inches long and a convenient thickness and width. Ten inches of an old broomstick makes a good handle.

Wax the bottom of the runner so that it will glide smoothly. Nail the handle to the steering pole; or, if you use the broomstick, screw it to the pole. Nail the steering pole to the runner about 1 foot from the front end. Place the brace against the steering pole and runner, mark the angles, and saw to make the brace fit. Nail the brace in place and the scooter is ready.

SOAP CARVING

Partly used bars of soap and small scraps may be used for this project. Work out a pattern on paper of an object, such as a cowboy hat, a maple leaf, an elephant, a sailboat. Transfer the design to the soap on carbon paper. Then, with a penknife or small paring knife, carve the figure. Cut away the parts that you do not need for the decorative form. Smooth off the rough edges with a damp cloth. If you need to add finishing touches in color, use a mixture of sealing wax and denatured alcohol.

249

SOAP FOR CLASSROOM USE

"Soap scraps" is one of the items on the list of materials, page 307, that the boys and girls have been saving for "just the right project." So for this project and the preceding one get out the scraps. Put them into a large-sized cold cream or glass jar with a metal top. Perforate the top to make a shaker. Add enough wate to soften the soap. Keep it on hand to use as extra soap.

SOIL STUDY

FOR THE ELEMENTARY GRADES

For a study of soils, have the class collect specimens of loam, gravel, sand, clay, and humus. The class will discover that soils are usually a mixture of two or more kinds of soil. For a soil to be considered sandy, clay, or any other kind, it should be more than half sand, more than half clay, etc. Loam is a mixture of soils. If it contains humus, loam is considered an excellent soil.

Test the soils for their ability to absorb and to retain moisture. Put each specimen into a separate container, such as a flower pot or tin can. Make sure that the containers are the same size and that the same amount of soil is put into each. Add water to the soils to determine their absorption qualities. Be sure to add the same amount to each. The class will notice immediately that in the coarser soils—gravel and sand—the water disappears quickly and that very little moisture clings to either. The finer soils— clay, humus, and loam—may even present a flooded appearance.

Set the soils in a sunshiny spot and do not add any more moisture. At the end of a week examine the soils to see what has happened. The class will discover that the water in the bottom of the gravel can may have disappeared completely. The sandy soil may be dry; the clay may be caked and hard; and the loam may still be moist.

If the class is interested in carrying the study further, plant seeds in each kind of soil. Add the same amount of moisture to each and at identical times. Watch to see what happens.

A SPANISH SHAWL

FOR SCHOOL DRAMATICS

A striking Spanish shawl may be made from cheesecloth and trimmed with a flower design and wide fringe. Cut and sew together strips of cheesecloth to make a 36-inch square. Dye the material black or a brilliant red. White also is a favorite. Plan to use a stylized flower since it is easy to make. Use red or rose on a black or white shawl. A brilliant orange is also good on black. Use black flowers on a red shawl.

Make the flowers from crepe paper. Cut 6 circles 2 inches in diameter for the center. Put the flower together by overlapping the circles as in the picture and tack the circles in place with a dab of paste here and there. Make as many flowers as you like. Group them in twos and threes and sew the flowers on securely enough so that the edges will not curl up.

For the fringe, select crepe paper that is the same color as the shawl. Make a 6-inch fringe by folding a 12-inch strip of paper double. A fringe of two thicknesses will give body to the shawl. You will need at least 4 yards of fringe, and be sure to allow for the corners. Fringe by cutting to a depth of 5 inches. This allows for a 1-inch band for sewing the fringe to the shawl. The shawl is ready and awaits the call of a señorita.

SPATTER PRINTS

Greeting cards, classroom projects, and articles described in this book may be decorated with spatter painting. Spatter painting is a way of producing a design by laying it on paper or cloth and spattering the exposed parts or perforations with paint. To do this you will need to cut a stencil of the design. Make one on paper or cardboard that has a glossy finish. Work out the design on paper and transfer it to the cardboard by tracing on carbon paper. Then cut away the cardboard within the design and leave only the outline, and the stencil is ready. If you do not wish to work out an original one, select and cut out a design from an old magazine or greeting card. Discard the cutout portion as this forms the perforation of the stencil.

Place the stencil on the paper that you wish to decorate. Then prepare a screen for spatter painting. Make a wooden frame (a discarded picture frame will do) about 1 foot square and tack window screening to the frame. It will resemble a sieve. Place the screen over the stencil and hold or prop it about 3/4 inch above the surface. Use a stiff brush, as a toothbrush, for example, and paint across the screen, brushing the paint through. The spattering of the paint through the perforations of the stencil and on the paper underneath forms the picture.

SPECTACLE CASE

A convenient case for glasses may be made from the felt in an old hat. Cut the felt according to the dimensions given in the

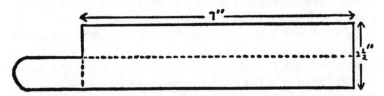

pattern. Fold the felt lengthwise and whip the edges together with yarn, using a blanket stitch. Sew on a snap to fasten the flap.

SPELLING CHARADES

Spelling Charades is a guessing game in which a verb is acted out. From a recent spelling lesson choose a doing verb, such as hit, bat, rub, wash, walk, halt, prance, cry, scratch, knock. Whisper the word to one of the players and he acts it out for the class while the players try to identify it. The first one to come up with the answer, raises his hand, goes to the board, and writes the word. If he spells it correctly, he becomes the next actor. If he misses it, the player looses his turn at acting and calls upon another to become the next actor.

A SPELLING GAME

FOR THE PRIMARY GRADES

Here is a game in which children bounce a rubber ball and learn to spell at the same time. In spelling out a word, a player bounces the ball once for each letter. If he spells the word correctly, the player tosses the ball to the next player, and pronounces a word for him "to spell and bounce." If he misspells the word, the player is given two additional chances. The game continues until every player has had a turn.

If it is large, divide the class into several groups and have a "spell and bounce" game going in each group.

SPIDER AND THE FLIES

A GAME FOR ANY NUMBER OF PLAYERS

This is a game in which one player, the "spider" tries to catch one of the "flies" as they run around in the spider's web. The game requires a large play area, such as an outdoor playground or a gymnasium. Trace a large spider's web with a stick or chalk. Make the web 25 to 30 feet across.

The player chosen "spider" goes to the center of the web. The flies take their positions on the goals throughout the web. Each intersection is a goal. The flies race from goal to goal along the threads or runways while the spider leaps from his den in an attempt to catch a fly. A fly is safe as long as she stays on a goal. As soon as he catches a fly, the spider takes her to the center where she is held prisoner. The play continues until everyone is caught. The last fly to be captured becomes the next spider.

A variation of this game is Fox and Geese, which is usually played in snow. Draw or tramp out in the snow, a large wheel 25 to 30 feet in diameter with spokes, rim, and hub. The hub is the fox's den and the goals are at the intersections of the spokes and rim. The fox corresponds to the spider, and the geese to the flies. The game is played the same as Spider and the Flies.

SPINNING YARNS

FOR THE PRIMARY GRADES

This activity affords variety for the story hour. Have on hand a ball of yarn, or string, wound with pieces of varying lengths. Vary the lengths from 10 to 20 feet. The storytellers sit in a circle. Someone picks up the ball, begins to unwind the yarn, and to tell an original tale, which may be something like this:

Frankie Mouse jumped into his little red wagon and started up the mountain. Since he knew he would be gone all day, Frankie packed a lunch of cheese and crackers. But long before noon he was so hungry that he pulled up under a big pine tree and unpacked his lunch.

Just as he was about to take his first bite, Frankie heard a faint tapping behind him. He looked around and discovered that the tapping seemed to come from a big hole in the tree. He looked into the hole and down, down, down. There he saw a little light gleaming in the dark——

When he comes to the end of his piece of yarn, the storyteller passes the ball to his neighbor at the right.

The new spinner of tales continues to unwind yarn and to add to the story, making it up as he goes along. Continue until everyone has had a turn. Keep the length of yarn and the story short.

SPOOL RACKS

A clay model of a head and a replica of a steering wheel for a ship can be made into handy racks for holding spools of thread.

CLAY MODEL

Draw a head on paper to serve as a guide in molding. Try to give it a comic touch. With modeling clay, mold a head the size of a large grapefruit. Then model the ears. Flatten the bottom of the ball to give the head a base so that it will not roll. While the clay is still pliable, press in the ends of 8 or 10 sucker sticks to serve as spindles. Allow the clay to dry thoroughly. Paint in the features with calcimine paint and then shellac the head to give a glossy finish. The model is ready for spools.

If, however, you have a kiln and you wish to "fire" the clay, allow the unpainted clay head to dry for about a week. Remove the sucker sticks while the clay is still damp. Heat the kiln for at least three hours at a temperature of 1350 to 1500° centigrade. Place the clay in the kiln and bake it for about six hours. Then remove and allow the clay to cool. Now paint the head with glaze, a glossy substance used in coating pottery. Fire again in the kiln. Remove and allow to cool. Put the sucker sticks back in place and the spool holder is finished.

Local potteries usually will give helpful information and will help you to obtain "cones," which you may place in the kiln to help time the firing. When it becomes hot enough, the cone falls over indicating that the clay is ready to be removed.

A clever spool rack may be made in the shape of a half steering wheel of a ship. Use the cover or bottom of a cigar box. Paint the

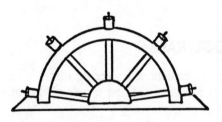

cigar box board and let dry. Work out the design of the wheel on paper. The width or base of the wheel is the diameter of the circle and the height the radius. Then transfer the pattern to both sides of the board.

Then paint in the hub, spokes, and rim. On the rim drive in large pins or small finishing nails (nails without heads) to hold the spools of thread.

Make a base 2 inches wide and somewhat longer than the length of the rack. Nail the base to the wheel by driving in the nails from the bottom of the base.

STAGE FOOTGEAR

Many a footgear problem may be solved by painting the shoes right on the actors' feet. It not only eliminates the problem of making footgear but it enables actors to tread silently, which usually is an important factor even for a classroom play. Sandals especially are easy to simulate. Use calcimine or tempera paint, which washes off easily.

Shoes with pointed toes for medieval warriors and for peasants of many periods may be made from old stockings. Cotton or wool stockings or a mixture of cotton and wool are most suitable. Select a stocking that is long in the foot. If the toe needs stiffening, cut a sole with pointed toe from cardboard. Use the actor's foot as a guide for drawing the outline of the sole. Insert the stiffening in the stocking. Curve the cardboard upward if the pointed toe needs to be accentuated. If it does not, merely pulling the toe of a stocking that is too long will suffice. Roll the tops of the stockings to the ankles.

256

STAGE PROPERTIES

Stage properties for school plays are usually difficult to come by because of their occasional use and expense. So it is often up to the class to improvise furniture, dishes, silverware, and the other adjuncts that are needed for a play. Costumes, however, are not considered "property" and may be made the responsibility of the actors.

Apple boxes, orange and lemon crates, and cardboard cartons may be readily assembled into realistic furniture. Later they can be dismantled and put to other uses.

FIREPLACE

Many a dramatization is centered around a fireplace, and a fireplace is usually hard to come by in the schoolroom. A convincing one, however, may be made by arranging and stacking 6 orange crates as in the picture. The effect of brick may be achieved by drawing a brick pattern on butcher paper. Paint or color the brick red and the mortar either white or black. 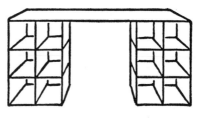 Use calcimine paint or crayons. Tack the brickwork around three sides of the fireplace with thumbtacks. Supply a mantelpiece in keeping with the setting of the play.

DAVENPORT

Place 4 orange crates as in the illustration on the next page. Place the two lower crates with open tops to the back and the upper crates with open tops to the front. Take the two upper crates down; remove the sides marked *A* and *B*; the two ends *C*; and the partitions *D* and *E*. Nail the boards *A* and *B*, to the back of the davenport for added support. Put the top crates back in position and nail to the lower two. Be sure to nail the ends down, too. Make colorful pads from cloth and stuff with crumpled newspapers. Add pillows if they are needed for effect.

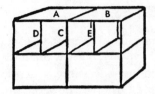 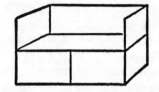

While davenports made from orange crates give the desired effect, they are not intended for seating or lounging purposes.

CHAIR

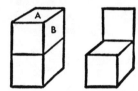

Stand an orange crate on end with the top of the crate facing front. With a hammer, knock off the end *A*. Then saw off *B* and the section opposite *B*. Make a colorful pad for the chair.

CUPBOARDS AND BOOK CASES

Set together 4 orange crates for a cupboard. If you need to go higher, tack the crates together to keep them from toppling over. Add a curtain if you need that kind of cupboard.

Orange crates are extremely adaptable for high or low book cases and library shelving. The possibilities for arrangements are numerous.

BROOM AND LANTERN

You will need a broomstick, or a bamboo pole, and a bundle of hazel brush or willow switches. Arrange the bundle so that it gives the effect of a broom. Stick a broom handle into the center and tie with string or fasten with wire. This type of broom was

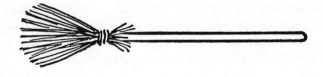

used by the American pioneers and the early European peasants. It is also suitable for a witch's broom.

A lantern may be made from a shoe box or oatmeal carton. Cut a design in the side and cover the openings with colored cellophane. Place an electric light in the lantern. You will need a long cord to permit freedom of movement.

TABLEWARE

Paper plates may be decorated or banded with color to serve as china for most situations in school dramatizations. For banquets of bygone days, paper plates, cups, forks, and spoons may be gilded or silvered with paint. The paper "ware" may be obtained at variety, drug, and grocery stores, and the gold and silver at paint stores and counters. To work out the tableware project, select children who have a knack for this sort of thing. Forks and knives came into use in Italy during the 1500's.

STAINED GLASS WINDOWS

The effect of stained glass windows may be achieved with a mixture of Bon Ami, alabastine, and dry paint and by applying the mixture directly to the window.

Work out a design on paper. Plan the colors carefully. Then mix equal parts of Bon Ami, alabastine and dry tempera paint. (Alabastine is another name for glass paint or whiting. It comes in powder form and is obtainable at hardware or paint stores.) Add enough water to make a creamy paste. The paint, of course, supplies the color. Experiment until you get the exact color that you want and then mix small batches for each color that you plan to use. Follow the sketch that you have worked out and apply the paste to the window with a small brush or clean rag in a freehand manner.

Although any subject may be used, this style of painting lends itself especially well to Thanksgiving, Christmas, and Easter themes. Later, the art work may be wiped off easily with a damp cloth without marring the window in any way.

STALKING THE BEAR

AN INDOOR GAME OF BLINDMAN'S BUFF

Two players are blindfolded. One is the bear and the other the hunter. They play a lively game of catch and tag around the table with the hunter doing the stalking. Select a table large enough, or make a barrier of teacher's desk and several chairs placed beside it, so that neither player can easily touch the other by reaching across. When the bear is caught, both players choose replacements from the group. This is a good game for a rainy recess.

STAMPED DESIGNS

Designs for gift wrapping paper, art folders, booklet covers, personal stationery, greeting cards, and other gift items may be stamped with ink. Small allover patterns lend themselves especially well to this technique.

Use a stamp pad for inking. The pads come in several colors. To transfer the ink and to create variations in design, use objects, such as the eraser end of a pencil, a wooden button, a potato-block print (pages 212–13), a rubber washer, a cork, a thimble, a eucalyptus burr, or the end of your finger. A piece of rough burlap makes an interesting variation in a pattern, too.

A STAMP MAP

To make a stamp map, you will need a world map, several yards of yarn of various colors, and stamps from as many countries as the class can collect. World maps may be purchased at most bookstores. Airline and steamship companies sometimes will supply a map to school children. A class, however, should be considerate in its request and should not ask for more than one. World maps also may be salvaged from discarded atlases and geography books. Mount the map on heavy cardboard. Cut the cardboard large enough to allow for a border around the map that will accommodate the largest stamp. Paste the stamps in the border and use yarn to connect the stamps with the countries of their origins.

It is more fun, if children acquire their foreign stamps on letters that they receive from pen pals in other countries.

STARCH

Making starch is one of several projects in this book to acquaint boys and girls with processes that they otherwise may take for granted. A good starch can be made from a sweet potato. Select a large one; peel and grate it. Wrap the gratings in cheesecloth and dip into a bowl of cold water, squeezing the starch, a milky-looking substance, into the water. Allow the starch to settle in the bowl for several hours. Then pour off the clear water, and wash the starch with fresh water. Allow the starch to settle again. Pour off the clear water a second time, and allow the starch to dry. This may take several hours.

Other projects of this type are casein glue, pages 37–38; cottage cheese, pages 70–71; making butter, pages 163–64.

STEALING ROSES

A GAME FOR ANY NUMBER OF PLAYERS

Divide the class into two teams. Each team chooses either a red rose or a white one as an emblem. Encourage the class to prepare paper roses well in advance.

Every player wears two roses, one on his chest and one on his back. Fasten them lightly with gummed paper in a manner so that the clothing will not get torn during the heat of the game. The point is for one team to steal as many roses as possible from the other without losing its own flowers. Limit the playing time to 5 minutes or less. The team with the larger number of roses wins. Count the team's own roses and those that it acquired.

STEALING THE DOG'S BONE

AN INDOOR GAME FOR THE PRIMARY GRADES

Someone is chosen to be the dog. He hides a bone under a chair in the corner of the room. Use an eraser for the bone. The dog sits in the chair with his back to the class, trying to protect his bone from being stolen.

The teacher signals to a player to begin. The player sneaks up stealthily behind the dog. If he hears the thief coming, the dog barks "Bowwow!" and the player returns to his seat empty handed. If the thief succeeds in stealing the bone, the dog tries to guess who the thief is. He has three guesses. If he fails in three turns, the dog becomes a player and the thief becomes the next dog. This game is also suitable for a rainy recess.

STENCILING LETTERS AND NUMBERS

Make a stencil from cardboard that has a glossy finish. Work out letters and numbers on paper and transfer them to the cardboard on carbon paper. Cut away the cardboard and you have the perforations of the letters and numbers. Lay the stencil on the paper that you wish to letter. Use a sponge, or brush, and stroke across the stencil with paint that is fairly thick.

Stencils are excellent for lettering scrapbooks, notebooks, headlines for bulletin boards, and large packages for mailing.

STENCIL WORK AND STIPPLING

Plan to make the stencil from cardboard that has a glossy finish. Work out the design on paper and transfer it to the cardboard by tracing it on carbon paper. Cut away the cardboard and you have the perforations that will carry the design. Mix the paint to the consistency of molasses. Use oil paint, lacquer, or showcard colors. Much of the success in stencil work depends upon the thick consistency of the paint and upon daubing the paint on instead of brushing it on.

Lay the stencil on the surface of the material that is to take the design. Then apply the paint to the perforations by stippling. To stipple is to paint or daub in separate touches. Use a small paint brush or tie a wad of cloth to a stick and use it for applying paint. Another way of stippling is to use an ink pad instead of paint. Transfer the ink with the eraser end of a pencil, or with a cork. Use this method if you want bold dots.

Artistic results also can be achieved by placing the stencil on drawing paper and applying glue. Then remove the stencil, sprinkle the glue areas with sawdust, and allow to dry.

Stencil designs are effective for making border designs for scrapbooks and for decorating paper, cloth, and furniture.

STORYLAND MAP

To learn the geographical settings of stories that children come across in their reading in and out of school, encourage them to work out a storyland map. You will need a world map, which may be purchased at most bookstores, or which may be drawn on butcher paper. To aid in drawing the outline, fasten the butcher paper on the wall and project the map on paper with an opaque projector. Use a small map in the projector, project the map the size you want, and then trace the outline on paper. If a projector is not available and if you have no suitable map on hand, try to draw one freehand.

Allow space for a border of squares around the outside of the map for illustrations. Encourage the children to select characters and places to illustrate. Use colored yarn, string, or ribbon to connect the illustration with the country in which the story is laid. Thumbtacks with colored heads may be used to tack the ends of the yarn or ribbon in place both on the map and on the border. A scene from *Hans Brinker, or the Silver Skates,* for example, would be connected with Holland, *Young Fu of the Upper Yangtze* with China, and *Alice's Adventures in Wonderland* with England, the birthplace of the author.

SUMMING UP THE DAY'S WORK

When boys and girls come home from school, parents often ask, "What did you learn today?" Teachers can prepare children for the question by asking the question of children at the end of the day and by helping them to recall and to evaluate their work. This procedure gives the child a sense of accomplishment. It also is good public relations between the school and home.

SUNDIAL

FOR THE ELEMENTARY GRADES

To make a sundial you will need a smooth board about 8 inches long and a long nail. The board will serve as the dial face and the nail as the indicator or gnomon. Drive in the nail vertically in the center of the board. Fasten the board outside the window on the south side of the room or school building. Or place the board in an open area away from the building.

Have the class note the position of the shadow cast by the indicator at nine o'clock in the forenoon. Mark the position on the dial face with a pencil. Do the same at 12 M (noon) and again at three o'clock. Then mark the six o'clock position opposite the noon position. The dial is now divided into quarters. On the next sunny day mark the hours.

THE SUN'S EFFECT ON PLANT GROWTH

FOR THE PRIMARY GRADES

In separate flower pots, plant identical seeds of radishes or lettuce. Set one pot where it receives the maximum amount of sunlight. Set the other in a dark corner, closet, or cupboard. Give each the same amount of moisture. Compare the growth and development of the young plants from time to time.

SURPRISE BOX

Keep a large decorated box on hand in the classroom. Call it the Surprise Box, and let it serve as a clearinghouse for short stories clipped from children's magazines, materials mounted on cardboard, activities for seatwork, picture puzzles, flashcards, and cutouts of all sorts. Keep the materials lively and entertaining and children will enjoy using them during their spare time. Arrange to have children take turns as custodian, whose duty it is to keep the box in order.

A "SWIMMING" MAGNET

The strength of a magnet may be shown in an entertaining way. Melt a cake of wax and soak a piece of rope in the wax. Wrap some iron around one end of the rope. Then float a rope in a dish of water. Hold a magnet close to the rope. The rope will wriggle toward the magnet like a snake.

TABLEAU

Scenes from fairy tales, stories, historical events, and episodes from the lives of people lend themselves to effective representation in tableau. In tableau the actors take the position, or a characteristic pose, of the people they represent and remain motionless and silent.

Boys and girls, for example, may enjoy representing the disenchantment of the Princess by the young Prince in a scene from the charming fairy tale *The Sleeping Beauty*. The Princess, shut up by enchantment in a castle, sleeps a hundred years. A great thick forest grows up around the castle. Finally, the young Prince penetrates the wood, disenchants, and awakens the Princess.

Another favorite tableau scene is the return of ragged, tottering Rip Van Winkle to his native village after a twenty-year sleep in the Catskill Mountains.

Famous paintings make excellent tableaux in which persons take the same positions as those portrayed in the paintings. Sir Joshua Reynolds' "The Age of Innocence" lends itself well to tableau. Another is Whistler's "At the Piano" which shows the painter's sister in a black dress seated at the piano and her small daughter Annie in a white dress standing at the piano.

An impressive tableau scene for the closing of an Armistice Day program is the raising of the American flag on Mount Suribachi, Iwo Jima.

To present a tableau of somewhat more pretentious proportions, a Lincoln's Birthday program may feature a series of scenes on the life of Lincoln. Encourage boys and girls to collect information about Lincoln and to plan scenes, such as Lincoln's boyhood in the log cabin, Lincoln splitting rails, and his political career with perhaps a Lincoln-Douglas debate.

Similar tableau scenes may be planned from the lives of Robert E. Lee, for example. Child actors, football, basketball, and baseball heroes also are interesting subjects.

To end a tableau effectively, the actors hold their positions for a moment. The curtain is lowered or drawn and the actors come to life in response to a curtain call.

A TAMBOURINE

To make a tambourine, you will need 6 or 8 tops from pop bottles, a pie tin, and as many nails as you have bottle tops. Remove the cork centers from the tops, and nail the tops loosely to the pie tin by bending the ends of the nails. Brass paper fasteners, often known as roundheads, may be used in the place of nails. Another way of fastening the tops is with wire. With hammer and nail, punch a hole through the top and a corresponding one through the pie tin. Then draw a wire through the holes and twist the ends of the wire together. Be sure to allow for slack so that the tops rattle.

The tambourine may be decorated gaily with ribbon and bows. Fasten the ribbon to the pie tin with cellophane tape, or with rubber cement.

TELEGRAM PUZZLES

FOR THE UPPER ELEMENTARY GRADES

Boys and girls never tire of deciphering the mysteries involved in secret writing and code puzzles. Here are two telegrams in a form of code.

1. Bruises hurt. Erased afford. Analysis hurt, too. Infectious dead.
2. Jackal becoming hereafter the truculent. Canoe locket forum afterwards?

Code puzzles offer a challenge to students who finish their work ahead of the others and who are always ready for more work. Encourage them to make up puzzles for others to solve. It is an excellent activity for someone who likes mysteries.

For the answer to the telegram puzzles above, see page 268.

A TELEPHONE DIRECTORY

FOR A GIFT

A booklet containing the names and telephone numbers of the people and business concerns that you call frequently is a time-saver. Plan a booklet 3¾ inches wide x 5½ inches long, consisting of 8 leaves or 16 pages. Use typewriter paper or odds and ends of paper. Several shades of colored paper used in the same booklet are interesting. Cut 4 strips 3¾ inches wide x 11 inches long. Put the strips together and fold across the middle to make a page 3¾ x 5½ inches. Plan to bind the booklet at the top. This type of booklet is convenient to use.

Make a cover from cardboard, construction paper, or small-figured wallpaper. Cut the paper for the cover 4 inches wide and 11¼ inches long to allow for an overlap at the edges. Fold the cover in the middle. To bind the booklet, punch two holes 2 inches apart at the top. Thread yarn, colored string, or ribbon through the holes and tie in a bow.

TELLING TIME AROUND THE WORLD

Cardboard clocks with movable hands are an aid in learning about the differences in time Encourage everyone to make his own clock. Cut a cardboard circle at least 6 inches in diameter. Write the numerals of the clock in black crayon. Cut the hour and minute hands from cardboard and color them black. Fasten the hands in place in the center of the clock with brass paper fasteners (roundheads).

After a study of how standard time is determined around the world, the class will learn, for instance, when it is 12 noon in London, it is 7:00 A.M. in New York, 6:00 A.M. in Chicago, 4:00 A.M. in Portland, Oregon, and 9:00 P.M. in Tokyo. Appoint people to represent these cities. Ask the "cities" to form into a circle and to space themselves roughly according to the distance between the cities which they represent. Then each "city" sets his clock according to the time given above.

For additional drill, appoint pupils to represent each of the 24 hours of the day. Each "hour" sets his clock. Then the "hours," carrying their clocks, form into a circle. Assign "12 noon" to London, and let the other "hours" determine where they should be. Eleven A.M., 10:00 A.M., 9:00 A.M., and 8:00 A.M. will be in the Atlantic Ocean; 7:00 A.M. in New York; 6:00 A.M. in Illinois; 5:00 A.M. in Utah; 4:00 A.M. in Oregon; 3:00 A.M., 2:00 A.M., and 1:00 A.M. in the Pacific Ocean; 12 midnight at the International Date Line in the Pacific where it is today and tomorrow; 11:00 P.M., 10:00 P.M. in the Pacific; 9:00 P.M., in Japan; 8:00 P.M. in Peiping; 7:00 P.M. in Mongolia; 6:00 P.M. in Lhasa, Tibet; 5:00 P.M. in Bombay, India; 4:00 P.M. in the Ural Mountains; 3:00 P.M. in the Caspian Sea; 2:00 P.M. in Istanbul; and 1:00 P.M. in Stockholm.

Answers to "Telegram Puzzles" on page 267.

1. Bruce is hurt. He raced a Ford. And Alice is hurt, too. In fact, she is dead.

2. Jack will be coming here after the truck you lent. Can you lock it for him afterwards?

A TEMPERATURE GRAPH

FOR THE INTERMEDIATE AND UPPER GRADES

This activity provides experience in reading the thermometer and in plotting the readings on a graph. Appoint someone to read the thermometer several times daily. Read it at 9:00 A.M.,

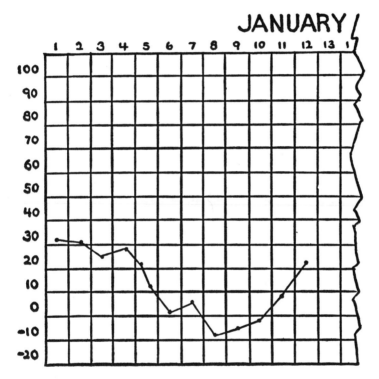

12:00 noon, and 3:00 P.M. Average the three readings to get the mean temperature reading between the hours of 9:00 A.M. and 3:00 P.M. Plot the daily mean on a graph. Have someone do this for a stated period of time, as for a week or for a month, and then pass the assignment on to another. Determine at the outset whether or not to include Saturdays and Sundays in the readings. Try to read the same thermometer every time and keep it in the same location out of doors.

To prepare the graph paper, use a sheet of unruled paper 8½ x 11 inches, which is the size of typewriter paper. Put the paper on the desk with the broadside towards you. With your ruler and pencil draw ¼-inch squares. You will need 15 squares up and down and as many across as there are days in the month.

Try to place your graph so that the left- and right-hand margins are about equal. Write the scale of the thermometer on the left side as on the graph on page 269. Write the figures for the days of the month across the top. On the previous page a partly finished graph is given to get you started. Complete the graph for the month by extending it on the right and writing in the figures for the remainder of the month.

Now you are ready to plot the graph. If the mean temperature reading between 9:00 A.M. and 3:00 P.M. is 30° on a certain day, put a dot on the line marked 30° on the date that the temperature occurred. If the mean temperature reading is 25° put the dot in the middle halfway between 20° and 30°. If the reading is 32°, put the dot a bit above the line labeled 30°, etc.

At the end of the month, connect the dots with a line. This will show the temperature readings at a glance.

TIGER

A GAME FOR THE PRIMARY AND INTERMEDIATE GRADES

This is a run-and-catch game in which someone is chosen to be the "tiger." The game begins with the tiger crouching in his lair, which is an imaginary one off to one side or in a corner behind a chair or two. The other players hover around the tiger, inviting him to come out.

"Tiger, come out and play," they beg.

"I'm still in bed," replies Mr. Tiger.

The players dance away but soon return.

"Tiger, when are you coming out?"

"I'm dressing," replies the tiger.

The players call again. This time the tiger is washing his face or perhaps combing his hair.

After a number of excuses the tiger suddenly dashes out to catch someone. The player who is caught becomes the next tiger.

A TIN CAN TELEPHONE

A toy telephone may be made from two tin cans. Remove the tops of the cans in a way so that there are no rough edges. With hammer and nail punch a hole through the bottom of each can. Wax a string about 30 feet long or whatever distance you want to telephone. Thread the ends through the holes in the can. Make a "knot" by tying each end to a match, toothpick, or nail.

The telephone is ready for use. Two boys, for instance, can have fun telephoning from one room to another or from the house to the garage. Each takes his telephone far enough away so that the string is taut. The boy holding the first "telephone" talks into the can in a low, natural voice. If he holds his "telephone" to his ear, the second boy will be able to hear. He may send a message back by speaking into his "telephone."

TIPCAT

AN OUTDOOR GAME

For tipcat you will need two sticks, a very small one called the "cat" and a longer one to be used as a bat. Someone is chosen to be the batter. He tosses the "cat" into the air, hitting it with his bat and driving it as far as possible. The players chase the "cat" and the one catching it throws it at the batter, hoping to hit him below the waist. If he is successful, the player becomes the next batter. If he is not, the batter has another chance.

A slightly different way of playing Tipcat is to make the "cat" of a small piece of wood pointed at both ends. Instead of throwing it into the air, the batter tips or strikes the "cat" lightly to make it fly high enough into the air so that he can bat it and drive it as far as possible.

TIT-TAT FIVE IN A ROW

Tit-Tat Five in a Row is very similar to tit-tat-toe (tit-tat-to). As in the illustration, draw 7 squares across and 7 squares up and

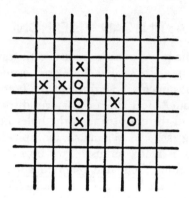

down, making a total of 49 squares. The game is played like tit-tat-toe. But to win you must succeed in getting five *x*'s or five *0*'s in a row before your opponent does.

TONGUE TWISTERS

Tongue Twisters afford excellent drill in enunciation and pronunciation. Read them slowly and articulate clearly.

No. 1

Betty borrowed Benny's broken bicycle
But Benny's brother Bobby had borrowed it before.
Benny blamed Betty; Betty blamed brother Bobby
But Benny bade Betty to borrow it no more.

No. 2

"Tweet, twit, titter," twittered the throaty tomtit
As he teetered on the thistly twig so long.
He tweeted and tittered and teetered and twittered
To the twisty tune of the tomtit song.

"Cluck, cluck," cackled the crotchety hen,
"Cockle crow's caught the croup."
"Cheep, cheep," chirped the chattering, scattering chicks,
"If he kicks the corn bucket, who'll rule the coop?"

TOOTHPICK STAR

An interesting little star trick may be done with toothpicks. Bend 5 toothpicks in the middle as in the illustration at the left.

Be careful not to break any of them. Arrange them in a circle with the bent parts in the center. Place a drop of water in the center, and watch the toothpicks straighten out to form a star.

A TOP

To make a toy top, draw a circle on cardboard 3 inches in diameter. Cut out the circle carefully and stick a pencil about 3 inches long through the center. Cut a notch in the pencil above the cardboard. Tie a knot in one end of a string. Place the knot in the notch, and wind the string tightly around the pencil.

273

TOSSING THE RING

Tossing the Ring is a game in which the players develop skill in hitting the mark. It is played by tossing rubber rings from a foul line onto hooks on a wallboard. Make a rectangular wallboard 3 x 1½ feet. Use thin board, such as plywood. Paint or varnish the board to give it a finish.

Screw clothes hooks, the size used in closets, into the board. Arrange the hooks in two rows with 5 in a row. Allow about 6 inches between the hooks and 10 to 12 inches between the rows. Nails may be used instead of hooks. Number the board from 0 to 9 by painting the numbers above the hooks. Hang the board at eye level for the group using it.

Should the members of the group become interested in determining their exact eye level, encourage them to measure the distance between their eyes and floor. Add the figures and divide by the number of players to get the average for the group and hang the board accordingly. Screw in two screw eyes to hang the board.

You will need 10 rings. Use fruit jar rings or cut rings from inner tubing. Establish a foul line across which players may not step while tossing a ring. Have the foul line 6 feet from the board for third graders and 8 feet for fourth or fifth graders. However, vary it as you see fit. Draw the line with chalk. Players take turns at tossing the ring. A turn may consist of ten tosses. A player scores each time that he "rings" a hook. Each player keeps his own score. Set the game at 25 or 50 depending upon the number of tosses a player is allowed at each turn.

To vary the game, encourage the group to choose sides. Alternate the turns at play between the two teams. The first team to score 100 points wins. This is an excellent indoor game.

A TOY DRIVE

Boys and girls often enjoy carrying on a drive for abandoned and broken toys for the purpose of giving them to an orphanage or to a children's ward in a hospital. They enjoy repairing and renovating the toys or engaging the help of parents, who are usually eager to help.

A good time to open a toy drive is about November 1. Encourage the class to organize the campaign and to carry it on throughout the school. The drive may well continue beyond the holiday season into January.

A TREASURE HUNT

Boys and girls love treasure hunts perhaps because of the mystery that surrounds the solution of the clues. The hunts are usually carried on in the fall, especially around Halloween time.

Prepare for a classroom treasure hunt at a time when the children are not in the room. Hide the treasure, which may be a bag of jelly beans or some other special treat. On separate slips of paper, prepare five or six clues guiding the hunters to the treasure. Write the clues on white paper with invisible ink. Use lemon juice for ink and a clean, steel pen point. When the paper is pressed with a warm iron or held over a hot radiator, the ink turns brown. An example of a set of clues is given below.

1. At the bottom of the world
2. Under the briny deep
3. In a small forest
4. In a spot of no worth
5. Behind a small grinder
6. Hiding like one of the Forty Thieves

Either before or after the children return to the classroom, write a clue on the blackboard guiding them to the first paper clue. And the treasure hunt is on! The boys and girls try to fathom the clue, and soon hands are waving. The teacher calls upon volunteers to take turns in searching for the first hidden clue.

The clues should lead the hunters to look in these places:

1. under the globe	4. in the wastebasket
2. under the aquarium	5. behind the pencil sharpener
3. in a potted plant	6. in a bowl or jug

The finder has the privilege of handling the clue and exposing the invisible writing by holding the paper over a hot radiator or by pressing with a *warm* iron. The ink turns brown, seemingly as if by magic! The treasure hunters try to solve the clue and then take turns again in searching and solving the next one. The hunt for the clues continues until the treasure is found.

A TREE MAP

FOR THE PRIMARY GRADES

A good introduction to the study of trees is to make a map of the school grounds and to chart the trees on the map. Make the trees from modeling clay or papier-mâché. Use burned kitchen matches or sucker sticks as a base for trees, and mold around the sticks. After the clay is dry, glue the tree to the map. If you prefer to make them flat, instead of upright, cut the trees from inner tubing or cork. Paint them in their natural colors with calcimine paint and paste them on the map. Whichever way you make them, try to identify the trees with labels.

TRICKS WITH VINEGAR

Interesting tricks may be performed with vinegar. Egg shells, for example, may be softened by putting them in vinegar. The acetic acid in vinegar reacts on eggs and makes them pliable.

PUTTING AN EGG INTO A BOTTLE

To do this trick soak a hard-boiled egg in vinegar for several days. Do not remove the shell. Select a bottle with a neck smaller than the egg. A milk bottle will serve the purpose. When the shell has softened, squeeze the egg through the bottle. The egg will reharden and return to its normal size so that it will be impossible to remove the egg without breaking it.

TYING SPARERIBS INTO KNOTS

Rib bones left from a meal may be used for this trick. Clean and dry several bones, and place them in vinegar for a week. Do not use a metal container, since the vinegar may "eat" holes in the metal. It may also form a poison. Use a glass or a pottery container. At the end of a week the bones will be soft enough so that you can tie them into a knot.

HORSEHAIR SNAKES

Place a horsehair in some vinegar. The hair will wriggle like a snake almost immediately and continue for about a minute.

A TRIP AROUND THE SCHOOLROOM

A GAME FOR ANY NUMBER OF PLAYERS

This game is a good exercise in memory training. Someone is chosen to begin the game. He walks to the front of the schoolroom and touches an object so that everyone can see. He may touch perhaps a desk, the wastebasket, a book, a plant, a map case, a doorknob. The player chooses someone to replace him. The second player touches the same object and an additional one.

The second player names a third player. The third player touches both objects in the right sequence and adds another of his own. This continues until the sequence becomes so long that someone gets mixed up and makes a mistake.

TRUTHFUL COMPLIMENTS

A CLASSROOM GAME

Truthful compliments is a game which encourages sincerity and generosity. One of the players is elected to leave the room.

The players in the room volunteer two or three compliments. Someone writes them on the blackboard. The player returns and tries to guess who complimented him. If he identifies any of the complimenters, the player wins. Win or lose, another player is chosen to leave the room.

This game is excellent as a fill-in just before recess or at the close of the day. Children enjoy the spontaneity of the game.

TRYOUTS FOR CLASSROOM DRAMATICS

The teacher announces that she is a talent scout looking for actors and actresses to participate in class dramatics and that she will give everyone a chance to try out for a part. She has on hand a boxful of assignments, which she has prepared or which were prepared with the help of the class. The assignments may consist of incidents like these:

1. You come home one evening to find that you have locked yourself out. What steps do you take to arouse the family?
2. You find a lost child crying in a store. Comfort and entertain the child until its mother arrives.
3. You are a barker at a circus trying to sell tickets for a lion tamer's act.
4. You are a barker at a newspaper stand. The latest edition has just arrived. Bark your wares!

The incidents are written on slips of paper, and pupils draw them from a box. Give the members of the class time enough to organize their interpretations. Then close the preparation period and ask for a volunteer to give his performance.

TURKEYS

Turkeys for favors or schoolroom decorations can be made with apples, toothpicks, cornhusks or construction paper, and gumdrops. Using the illustration on page 279 as a guide, draw a pattern of the turkey's head and tail feathers and then cut them out from cornhusks or construction paper. With a knife make slits in the apple and insert the head and tail. Stick two toothpicks into the apple for legs and use a large gumdrop for a pedestal. Or combine several smaller ones by shaping them into a pedestal large enough to support the turkey.

TURKEY TALES

Using the illustration as a guide, work out a paper pattern of a turkey without a tail. Make the body 2 inches across and cut out from cardboard or construction paper. Then draw and cut out 8 tail feathers. Choose paper about the weight of typewriter paper, a paper stiff enough to stand out but not too heavy for pasting to the cardboard turkey.

Encourage everyone to think of reasons for being thankful. Everyone writes his reasons on the tail feathers and adds them to the turkey.

USING THE TELEPHONE

Boys and girls should learn to use the telephone efficiently and courteously and to say words clearly. Talk over the following questions in class and decide how you would answer them.

1. Do you have a telephone in your home? If you have, what is your number?
2. Do you ever call your friends? How often? Should you ever call at mealtime or late at night? Why should your telephone conversation usually be short?

3. Do you have a telephone at your school? When might it be all right for pupils to use the school telephone?

Do you answer the telephone at home? Perhaps you do if you are given permission. The following conversation may take place:

Bob (answering the telephone): This is Lake 6349, Bob Hall speaking.

Mr. Smith: This is Mr. Smith, Bob. May I speak to your father please?

Bob: Yes, Mr. Smith. I'll call him. He will be here in a minute.

1. Notice that Bob gave his number and name instead of saying "hello" when he answered.
2. What could Bob have said if his father had not been at home when Mr. Smith called?
3. If Mr. Smith left his message with you, what would you do? Would you make a note about it?
   When your father comes in, please ask him to call me at Main 3852. Thank you."

Whenever you take a message over the telephone be sure to check yourself on these points:

1. Find out who is calling.
2. Get the exact message.
3. Make a note about the message so that you will not forget it. Tell who called.
4. Be sure the message is received by the person who was called.

If you wish practice in using the telephone, someone probably has a toy telephone at home that he will be glad to bring to school. If none is available, pretend that you have a telephone. Choose partners and dramatize one of the conversations below.

1. Billy Grant's number is 274. Call him and ask him to go to a movie with you on Saturday.
2. Call Alice Woods at Walnut 6459 and thank her for bringing a book to your house.
3. Bob Smith has been sick. Call B3402 and ask his mother how he is.[1]

[1] Harry A. Greene, Maude McBroom, Ruth Moscrip, and Norma Gillett. *Building Better English*, Grade IV, pp. 84–85 (adapted somewhat). Evanston, Illinois: Row, Peterson and Company, 1947.

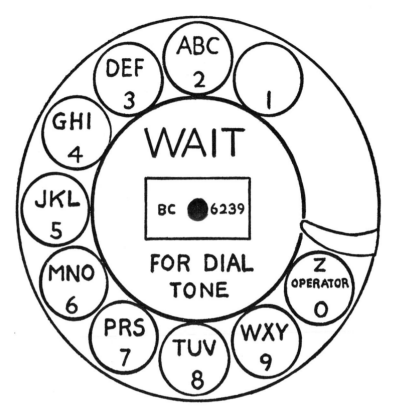

You will want to practice making a call on a dial telephone, too. The teacher will make a cardboard telephone dial by cutting two cardboard circles, 4 inches in diameter. On one of the cardboards she will draw ten circles, each ¾ inch in diameter. She will letter the letters and numbers as in the illustration. In the other card she will cut holes ¾ inch in diameter to correspond with the circles on the first card. She will place the two cards together, putting the one with the holes on top. She will fasten the cards together in the center with a brass paper fastener (roundhead). The dial is ready and your teacher will give practice in its use until everyone is proficient.

You will not need a telephone operator in using a dial telephone. Make sure to call the correct number. If you have made a mistake, say, "I am sorry, I have the wrong number."

A VALENTINE DOLL

This valentine doll can be made easily by following the illustration. Cut a large heart from red paper for the body. If you feel

that you need a pattern, make one from paper. Fold the paper and cut out one half of the heart. Then unfold and the two sides of the heart will be the same shape and size.

Cut a small heart for the head and two smaller ones for the legs. From white paper cut two hearts somewhat smaller than the leg hearts to serve as a decoration for the body. Draw features with white or black ink. Paste the head, legs, and decorations in position.

A VALENTINE LAPEL PIN

A heart-shaped valentine lapel pin may be made from a scrap of linoleum. Pull off the burlap backing on the linoleum. If some of the burlap still sticks, sandpaper it smooth.

Draw a heart pattern about 1½ inches wide on paper. Tack the pattern to the linoleum with dabs of paste and cut out with a coping saw or sharp, pointed knife. Cut a groove in the back to accommodate the back of a safety pin. Glue the pin in place for a fastener. Paint the heart red with tempera paint and shellac.

A VALENTINE MESSAGE IN A NUTSHELL

A nutshell can be made into an ingenious carrier for a valentine message. Crack an English walnut carefully in half and remove the meat. Use the shells in their natural form; or gild, silver, paint, or varnish them.

Compose a valentine message on tissue paper. Fold it, put it into the shell, and glue the two halves of the shell together. Decorate the nutshell by tying a ribbon around it. Allow a long end for fastening a name card. Cut a small triangular (pennant shaped) name card from red paper. Pink the edges with pinking shears, and thread the end of the ribbon through a small hole punched in the card. Tie a knot and a small, perky bow.

VALENTINES

There is no end to the making of valentines, and everyone has a few favorite ideas of his own. However, here is one "to hang up" and one "to weave." Both kinds are fun to make.

A VALENTINE TO HANG UP

From red construction paper, cut four hearts in graduated sizes. Cut slits and string the hearts with red ribbon as in the illustration at the left. Additional decoration is an individual matter. If you wish, add a valentine greeting. Use a white crayon.

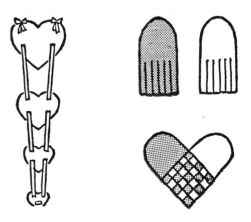

WEAVING A HEART

From construction paper cut two pieces in the shape shown at the right. Cut one of red paper and the other of white. Cut slits along the dark lines about half way up. Weave the strips together to form a heart. Paste down the ends of the strips neatly.

A VALENTINE PUZZLE

Encourage the children to prepare a valentine puzzle. Cut out a red paper heart any size you wish, large or small. Then write a valentine greeting or message, and sign your name if you wish. Cut the heart into jigsaw puzzle pieces, and put the puzzle into an envelope. Decorate the envelope with tiny hearts and drop into a box set up for this purpose.

Then on St. Valentine's Day everyone receives an envelope containing a puzzle. He pieces his puzzle together and pastes it on paper to form a valentine. He, of course, will discover the message and perhaps the name of the sender.

A VANISHING TIGER

To make the tiger vanish, you need to make one side of a cage. Cut out a rectangle 7½ x 5 inches from lightweight cardboard. Draw 7 bars on the side of the cage ½-inch wide and ½-inch apart. Cut a slit at each end along the dotted lines. Prepare a

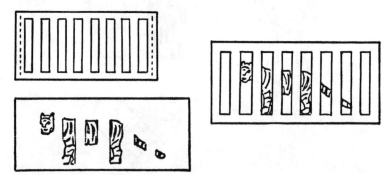

piece of paper 9 x 4 inches and draw it through the slits so that the bars of the cage are in front. Mark the position of the bars with pencil dots. Remove the slip and draw those parts of the tiger which are visible between the bars. Put the paper back in place with the tiger in his cage. Pull the paper to one side and watch Mr. Tiger vanish.

VEGETABLE PARADE

FOR THE PRIMARY AND LOWER ELEMENTARY GRADES

There are times when vegetables and fruits dress up and go on parade. Here are Potato Pete, Lemon Pig, Celery Spook, and Miss Ear of Corn. These interesting figurines are fun to make.

POTATO PETE

To dress Potato Pete, you will need a potato, a flat round cooky, a marshmallow, 2 black-eyed peas or navy beans, 2 lima beans, a radish, several toothpicks, and a scrap of cornhusk or crepe paper for hair. Use the potato for the head. Make a wide slit in the potato for the mouth and two smaller ones for the ears. Press a lima bean in each ear to complete it. Spear a radish with a toothpick and stick the other end of the toothpick into the potato for a nose. Cut slits for the eyes and put in a pea or bean in each slit to complete the eyes.

Use the cooky for the hat and shred a bit of cornhusk to make a few wisps of hair. Wiggle a toothpick through the center of the cooky. If the cooky is too hard, make a hole with a stout needle before putting the toothpick through. Spear the toothpick through the cornhusk hair and into the potato. Arrange the wispy hair into a coiffure "becoming" to Potato Pete. Then stick a marshmallow on the other end of the toothpick to make the crown of the hat.

LEMON PIG

You will need a lemon, a pipe cleaner, and 4 toothpicks. Make the ears by cutting two slits in the lemon rind and peeling the rind back. Do not cut off the strips but fashion them into ears. Stick the long end of cloves into the lemon for eyes. Make the tail from a piece of pipe cleaner and stick in toothpicks for legs. Anchor the legs at an angle so that the pig can stand on all fours.

CELERY SPOOK

Turn a bunch of celery upside down. Trim the leafage to resemble the "skirts" of a ghost. Press in cloves for the eyes and nose.

MISS EAR OF CORN

Supply yourself with an unhusked ear of corn, a round onion, several toothpicks and cloves, and a slice of red radish. Use the ear of corn for the body. Peel off a swath of the husk on one side of the ear to form the front of the dress. Use the onion for the head. On one side cut away several layers for the face, and loosen the rest of the cut layers enough to form the hair. (To keep your eyes from watering, hold the onion under water while cutting.) Make a slit in the onion for the mouth and press in a slice of radish for the lips. Use cloves for eyes. With a pointed tool, such as an ice pick, make a hole in the end of the ear of corn to support the head. For additional strength, use two toothpicks and spear into the onion with one end of the toothpicks and push the other end into the hole in the corn.

THE VIRGINIA REEL

The Virginia reel is known as a colonial dance and also as an English country-dance. Any number of couples may take part. The music for the Virginia reel should have a clearly defined 4-4 rhythm, such as "Irish Washerwoman" or "Possum in the 'Simmon Tree."

The dancers form two lines with perhaps five people in each line. The girls stand in one line, the boys in the other; partners face each other, as in the illustration at the top of the next page. The time required for each step is clearly indicated by the music, the usual time being four measures.

286

5 4 3 2 1

5 4 3 2 1

The directions for the dance follow below.

1. The first girl and the fifth boy skip toward each other diagonally across the set and bow to each other; then they skip back to place.

2. The fifth girl and the first boy do the same.

3. The first girl and the fifth boy skip toward each other and join right hands facing each other; then they skip around each other clockwise and back to place.

4. The fifth girl and the first boy do the same.

5. The first girl and the fifth boy repeat with a left-hand turn.

6. The fifth girl and the first boy do the same.

7. The first girl and the fifth boy repeat with two-hand turns.

8. The fifth girl and the first boy do the same.

9. The first girl and the fifth boy repeat with a dos-à-dos; that is, they pass each other back to back.

10. The fifth girl and the first boy do the same.

11. The first girl and her partner, the first boy, join hands and sashay; that is, skip lightly, down between the two lines of the set and back again.

12. The same two, the first girl and the first boy, reel down the two rows of the set person by person. To do this, they turn around each other clockwise, linking right elbows. Then the girl reels left elbow with the second boy; the first boy with the second girl. The first two reel together again and progress to the third couple. They dance with each couple, after whirling with each other, until they reach the foot of the set.

13. The first couple sashays to the head of the set.

14. Each turns outward and leads his or her line down to the foot of the set. They form an arch. The other couples pass under it to their new positions.

15. The dance begins again from the beginning, but with a new head couple.

VIVID SPEECH

Helping boys and girls to develop their vocabularies is the aim of every teacher. Point out, for example, that carefully chosen words add color and variety to speech and that the ability to use vivid and exact words greatly increases the effectiveness of a person's everyday speech.

To add to a child's store of words, encourage him to watch for clear, colorful word pictures in his reading and to listen for them in the speech of others. Ask him to jot down the words and to use them the next time he tells an incident or story.

Notice these exact and vivid words:

a purple patch	the rustle of paper
a grazing cow	the ticking of a clock
a narrow vacant lot	the train whistle

Perhaps the pupil can tell about the sounds he heard on a picnic.

crackling fire	excited voices
sizzling meat	splashing water
curly bacon	rustling leaves

Can the pupil make others see his pet dog or cat? There may be something in his room such as a football, a doll, a view from his window that he can describe.

WAITING ROOM

A GAME FOR ANY NUMBER OF PLAYERS

To play Waiting Room, the group chooses someone to be "it." The players sit in a large circle with one extra seat. Allow about 1½ feet between the chairs. The person chosen to be "it" goes to the center of the circle and calls either "Everyone left!" or "Everyone right!" The players move in the direction called. The object of the game is for "it" to steal the vacant seat from the person about to move in. His chance comes when a player starts in the wrong direction. If he succeeds in moving in, the unseated player is the next "it" and moves to the center to continue the game. Waiting Room requires alertness and agility on the part of the person who is "it."

WALNUT SHELL BUTTONS

Attractive buttons may be made from black walnuts. To cut a walnut into buttons, fasten the nut in a vise and with a coping saw cut the walnut into cross sections thin enough for buttons. Remove the meat from the shell. Sandpaper the edges smooth and then shellac.

Make a small loop from string to serve as a fastener for the button. With rubber cement fasten the ends of the loop to any substantial part of the center of the button.

WASTEBASKETS

Neatness in the schoolroom can be encouraged easily by having an adequate supply of wastebaskets on hand. These may be made from articles, such as nail kegs, large ice-cream containers, hat and cardboard boxes. The ice cream containers are usually available at places selling ice cream. Decorate the baskets with left-over pieces of wallpaper, chintz, or colored paper or cloth.

WAX PAPER TRANSPARENCIES

Making transparencies from wax paper is an interesting art project. Work out on paper a silhouette of a subject that lends itself to this type of treatment, such as flowers, skiers descending a mountain, people skating, children playing with their sleds, a Maypole dance. Then transfer the design to colored paper and cut out.

Arrange the cutouts between two pieces of wax paper. Press with a warm iron (not with a hot iron) so that the cutouts "set" into the wax paper.

The pictures may have a holiday theme, such as an Easter lily, a Christmas candle, a shamrock for St. Patrick's Day, and so on.

WEATHER VANE

To make a weather vane, work out a paper pattern of an arrow. Make the arrow 6½ inches long, the shaft ½ inch wide, and the head and tail 1½ inches at their widest parts. Then cut the arrow from balsam or other lightweight wood. Work a long thin nail or  a large stout pin through the center of gravity; that is, the center on which the arrow will rotate. To determine the center of gravity, make a loop with a 6-inch string or use a thin rubber band. Slip it on the arrow and slide it along until the arrow balances when you hold it up with the loop. Mark the point as the center. It will be off center as far at the eye is concerned. Work the nail through. Then turn the arrow around and around many times on the nail until the hole is large enough so that the arrow rotates easily.

Place the nail on the end of a 12-inch stick. Drive in the nail lightly with a hammer, but allow enough play on both sides of the arrow so that it can rotate with the least possible friction. Paint the arrow and stick. Then post the weather vane in a place where the wind can strike it from any direction.

WEAVING A BERET

Berets are a "good old standby" and their popularity seldom wanes regardless of changes in the styles of other types of hats. Yarn, cord, or narrow ribbon are suitable materials. Make a loom by cutting a circle from cardboard 9 inches in diameter. The 9-inch diameter merely gives you a starting point. Vary the size to make the beret you need. Label the two sides of the cardboard loom with letters and numbers as in the diagram.

Thread a large needle with a length of yarn as long as can be handled without tangling, or with whatever material you are using. Tie a knot in the end or allow a 2-inch length in the yarn, which later may be fastened to the weaving. Holding the front side of the loom toward you, start on the back and sew through A^1 on the front. Go to C^1 and through C^1 to C^2 on the back. Down toward the center to E^2 and through to E^1. Over to F^1, through to F^2, up to D^2. Then through to D^1, down the center to B^1. Through to B^2, over to A^2, through to A^1, and to E^1, etc.

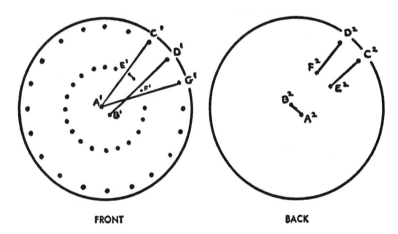

FRONT   BACK

After the loom has been threaded, begin at the center front and weave outward. Complete one side. Then turn the loom over and now weave *toward* the center. When you reach the end of the yarn, tie it to another length and continue to weave. When you have finished, break the cardboard away. Finish the head opening with a band of grosgrain ribbon.

WEAVING A BELT

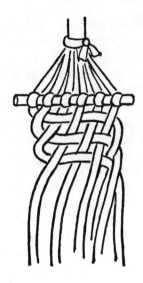

To weave a belt you will need a piece of broomstick about 6 inches long and 8 yards of raffia or heavy cord or leather thong. Divide the 8 yards into 6 lengths each 1⅓ yards long. Tie the six strands of raffia or cord or leather strips into slip knots on the stick as in the illustration. Allow enough to tie a knot around a doorknob, chair arm, or other object substantial enough to hold the weaving.

Start to weave with the strand at the left. Carry it crosswise, under the second strand, over the third, under the fourth, over the fifth, and under the sixth. For the second row, start with the second strand. Then with the third, etc.

WEAVING A PURSE

A practical coin purse may be woven with yarn. Make a loom 6 x 9 inches from a piece of board or from heavy cardboard. The end of an orange crate also makes a satisfactory loom. Sandpaper

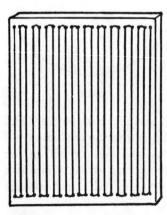

it smooth. Pencil a row of dots ¼-inch apart across the ends of the board. Allow ½-inch space at each end and at the sides of the loom. This makes the weaving surface 5 x 8 inches. Space the dots carefully and be sure to have the same number at each end. Now drive in a small headed nail in each dot. Let about ⅜-inch of the nail stick up.

Place the loom lengthwise in front of you. Tie an end of the yarn to the first nail in the upper left-hand corner. Bring the yarn down and around the first nail in the lower left-hand corner. Now around the second nail at the top. Continue until the loom is threaded. Thread a large needle with a length of yarn, as long as can be handled without tangling. Begin to weave at one end and continue across and back until the entire 8-inch length has been woven.

Remove the rectangle from the loom and fold across the middle making a purse approximately 5 x 4 inches. Sew up the two sides with yarn and turn inside out. Line the purse if you prefer to do so. Add a zipper to close the purse at the top.

WEAVING A SEWING BAG

A practical and unusual sewing bag may be woven with raffia. Follow the instruction given on page 291 for making a round loom and for weaving a beret.

Lining the bag is optional. It, however, adds to the attractiveness of the bag. Select a striking color, such as kelly green or a small-figured material. Use either cotton or rayon. Cut two circles the size of the sewing bag. The second circle will not be solid since you need to allow for an opening corresponding to that of the bag. Sew the outer edges of the circles together. Put the lining in place and sew the edge of the opening to that of the raffia bag.

Around the opening make a hem large enough for a drawstring. Use ribbon, cord, or braided raffia for a drawstring. If you use raffia, use enough for each strand to make a substantial braid. The ideal way is to make two drawstrings and put them through from opposite sides. Tie the ends of each string together.

WHAT AM I?

This is an activity in identifying objects, such as leaves, flowers, bugs, insects, rocks, seeds. Include seeds of flowers, vegetables, and grains. Put the seeds in cellophane envelopes so that they can be seen through the envelope. Be sure to include nuts, pods, and acorns in your collection.

Set aside a table for a collection of specimens. Make a sign for the table reading, "What Am I?" Anyone who can or who wishes to identify an object, removes it from the table and labels it. If he cannot identify it on sight, he may do some research on the subject by consulting an encyclopedia or his science textbook. Before long every object will be identified and arranged systematically on the exhibition table.

A WHEEL OF FORTUNE

FOR ST. PATRICK'S DAY

To make a fortune wheel, cut a cardboard circle 15 inches in diameter, or larger if you prefer. Use green cardboard. If you cannot get it, use white cardboard and cover the finished wheel with green crepe paper. Make a rim for the wheel by drawing a circle 2½ inches from the outer edge. Draw the spokes and hub. Then cut out the cardboard between the spokes and you will have an artistic wheel.

Make a shamrock from green construction paper for everyone in the room. Write fortunes on the shamrocks and tie them to the rim of the wheel with green yarn. Then on St. Patrick's Day everyone chooses a shamrock and reads his fortune.

WHEN AUNT ESTHER TALKS

AN INDOOR GAME FOR ANY NUMBER OF PLAYERS

When Aunt Esther Talks is a jolly, wriggling, winking, and tapping game. The players sit in a circle. Someone is designated to start play by saying to his neighbor, "When Aunt Esther talks, she goes like this": Whereupon the first player pats his knee or performs a similar rhythmical motion. The second player copies the action and passes it on to his neighbor, who in turn does likewise until everyone is patting his knee.

Then, continuing with the first motion, Player 1 again says, "When Aunt Esther talks she goes like this": Player 1 adds a second motion, such as winking his left eye. This, too, is passed from neighbor to neighbor around the circle. Actions are added, until finally all the players are tapping, wiggling, and rocking.

A WHITE ELEPHANT "PIE"

FOR THE PRIMARY GRADES

Toys and trinkets that are no longer used or wanted may be used for the ingredients of a white elephant "pie." Encourage the children to collect and wrap the toys and trinkets, and to attach a long string to each package.

For a pie tin use a bushel basket or a round clothesbasket. Put the "ingredients" into the "pie tin" and make a "crust" of brown wrapping paper. Crimp the crust around the edges and cut perforations in the top for air holes in true pie-crust fashion. Thread the strings attached to the packages through the perforations and the pie is ready.

The fun is on as everyone pulls a string to get a prize.

WHO IS HUMMING?

A GAME FOR THE PRIMARY AND ELEMENTARY GRADES

Who is Humming? is an excellent classroom game as the entire group participates. It is also a good game for a rainy recess. One of the players is chosen to leave the room while the others choose a hummer. Then everyone, including the hummer, rests his head on his desk. The first player returns and the hummer starts to hum a tune. The object of the game is for the player to locate the hummer. The game is more fun if the hummer stops humming when the guesser approaches. The guesser is given a reasonable time in which to locate the hummer. Whether or not he succeeds in identifying the hummer in a reasonable length of time, the hummer becomes the next guesser to leave the room.

WHO IS THE LEADER?

A GAME FOR THE PRIMARY AND ELEMENTARY GRADES

Who Is the Leader? is an excellent classroom game. One of the players is chosen to be "it." He leaves the room while the others agree upon a leader who can lead them in rhythm patterns, such as scratching your ear, tapping the desk, or winking an eye. The first player is called back and the rhythms begin. The leader, from his accustomed seat, deftly leads the group from one rhythm into another. The players slyly watch the leader as he tries to change the rhythm pattern without being detected by "it." "It," of course, tries equally hard to determine who is leading the group. Whether or not "it" succeeds in a reasonable length of time, the leader becomes the next "it." He leaves the room and the game begins again.

A WHO'S WHO SCRAPBOOK

FOR THE INTERMEDIATE AND UPPER GRADES

An interesting scrapbook project is a who's who of people who have achieved some prominence. To work effectively on a project of this type, divide the class into committees with a chairman for each committee to guide his group. One committee, for example, may work up a scrapbook about local people who have achieved some prominence; a second group, about people in the state; a third group, about people in the region, which may include several states; a fourth group, about people in the nation; and, a fifth group, about people in other countries. Encourage the group to collect biographical data and pictures, accomplishments, personal interest items, and anecdotes. Include people in all fields of endeavor, such as statesmen, congressmen, businessmen, workingmen, doctors, lawyers, teachers, dentists, artists, musicians, singers, writers, athletes. The best scrapbooks may be added to the school library.

A WHO'S WHO OF COLONIAL AMERICA

The early colonists who came to America—to Virginia, Massachusetts, Maryland, Connecticut, Rhode Island, New Hampshire, North and South Carolina, New York, New Jersey, Delaware, Pennsylvania, Georgia—helped to make our country what it is today. Overcoming hardships never before experienced, the early settlers subdued the forest, fought the Indians, hunger, disease, and poverty. They built homes and churches, and they had very definite ideas about the laws under which they should live.

Compile a who's who of these sturdy people who gave America its start. Select a group of colonists—men, women, and children—to include in the study. Be sure to include some of the Indians, both hostile and friendly, whom the early white men encountered. Work up short stories of the lives of the colonists and arrange the material into a scrapbook. To work on a project of this type, divide the class into committees and assign a part of the project to each group.

Here are listed some of the people who you will want to include. There are many others equally interesting.

Virginia Dare (1587–?), the first child born of English parents in America.

Captain John Smith (1580–1631), an able leader of the first group of settlers in Virginia. Smith put everybody to work, including the lazy people, saying, "If you will not work you shall not eat." Captain Smith loved to sail up and down the Atlantic coast and name everything, Cape Charles, Cape Henry. He was interested in starting things in a new world. He was a great storyteller and enjoyed advertising America in England after his return there.

Pocahontas (1595?–1617), an Indian princess, who was fascinated by the white-skinned newcomers to America. She was converted to Christianity, and married John Rolfe, a colonist.

William Bradford (1590–1657), governor of Plymouth Colony. He came to Plymouth on the *Mayflower* and was one of the Pilgrim Fathers. He was a quiet, able scholar. The Narragansett Indians threatened to make war and sent Bradford a rattlesnake skin filled with arrows as a challenge.

William Brewster (1567–1644) also came to America on the *Mayflower*. He was a preacher and teacher, a dear old gentleman, the bone and sinew of a new country.

Captain Miles Standish (1584–1656), a rough soldier who liked the quiet life of the Pilgrims. He, too, came on the *Mayflower*. He was practical and useful to the Pilgrims.

Squanto (?–1622), an Indian born on the site where the Pilgrims settled. Pestilence swept his people, the Pawtuxet tribe, away while Squanto was on a fishing trip. When he came back, he found the Pilgrims settled there. Squanto was friendly to the Pilgrims and taught them to plant corn and squashes and what oysters were good to eat.

King Philip (?–1676), an Indian and chief of the Wampanoag tribe. He united the neighboring tribes and attacked the whites. They were too strong for him and he was killed.

John Winthrop (1588–1649), governor of Massachusetts Bay Colony for many years, and important in the Puritan group.

Thomas Hooker (1586?–1647) was a Congregational minister who left Massachusetts Bay Colony in 1636 and led his flock to Connecticut where he made an important settlement. He and his followers founded homes where the capitol of Connecticut now stands. Hooker also came from England and lived with the Puritans a few years.

Roger Williams (1603?–1683) was the father of religious toleration. He had long chestnut locks which he loved to toss back. He liked controversy and spoke so convincingly that he swept people "off their feet." In 1636 he left Massachusetts and moved to Rhode Island where he founded a settlement.

Anne Hutchinson (1591–1643) was a liberal in her thinking. She, like Roger Williams, left Massachusetts and started a neighboring settlement.

Peter Stuyvesant (1592–1672) was a fiery, one-legged governor sent over from Holland to govern the Dutch colony in New York. He became a distinguished ancestor.

Lord Baltimore (1580?–1632, George Calvert) was a Catholic. He obtained a grant of land from the king of England to establish a colony in what is now Maryland. He wished to make a home for English Catholics, but he died before his wish could be carried out. His oldest son, the second Lord Baltimore, Cecil Calvert, carried out the plan. Protestants as well as Catholics were allowed to settle in Maryland.

William Penn (1644–1718) belonged to the Society of Friends, or Quakers, in England where they were treated harshly. The king gave Pennsylvania to Penn in payment of a debt and Penn founded a colony there.

James Oglethorpe (1696–1785) was interested in prison reform. He was a rich man and with the help of rich friends received permission from the king to start a colony in Georgia. He established a settlement at Savannah and made it possible for unfortunate people to start life anew.

Benjamin Franklin (1706–1790) lasted a long time. He belonged to the colonial period but he helped to draft the Declaration of Independence. He was a member of the Constitutional Convention and lived to see the new government in operation. He was a printer, scientist, statesman, diplomat, and philanthropist. He did so many things well that you can write a long biography about him.

WIGS

Powdered wigs were common in colonial America, and so the need for wigs arises in costuming a play or an informal dramatization. In fact, a wig is all that is needed in carrying out the spirit of colonial times for an informal dramatization. Children in the early elementary grades often enjoy "just wearing a wig" as they imagine themselves a Benjamin Franklin or George Washington.

Use a skull cap for the foundation of a wig. Cover the cap by sewing on tufts of cotton batting. Fluff the cotton.

Instead of using a skull cap for a base, you may make a cap from an old stocking. Hair may be made from raveled rope, white yarn, or fringed crepe paper.

A WILLOW WHISTLE

For a willow whistle you will need a smooth piece of green willow three or four inches long and one-half inch thick. You may also use any kind of sapling—birch, hickory, sassafras, sycamore—on which you can loosen the bark.

(1) Cut one end of the stick on the diagonal. (2) With your knife, cut around the stick about an inch from the diagonal end.

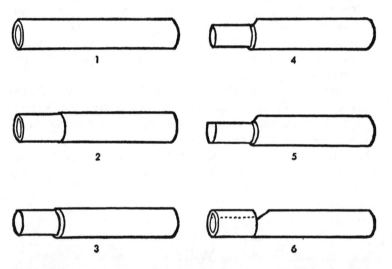

Be careful to cut through the bark only; cut no deeper. (3) With the handle of your knife, tap the bark lightly on the short end of the stick until you have loosened the bark enough to slide it off the stick all in one piece. You should moisten the stick. This will help you to work off the bark without breaking it. (4) Cut a notch in the long end at the point where it meets the part from which you have removed the bark. Slant the notch away from the short end. (5) Starting at the notch, slice a layer about an eighth of an inch thick down the length of the short end. (6) Slide the bark back on, and the whistle is ready to blow.[1]

WINDOW SHADE PULLS

FOR A GIFT

Interesting and attractive window shade pulls may be made from felt, raffia, fruit pits, and walnuts.

FELT SHADE PULLS

Here's a use for old felt hats. Select areas of felt that are not too faded. Work out patterns on paper of the pulls on this page. For the heart-shaped one, both pieces may be made from felt of

contrasting colors, or the smaller heart may be outlined in yarn or cord. The eyes and wings of the bird and the eyes, ears, and tusk of the elephant may be worked in yarn. Keep the elephant small, about 1½ inches long. If you wish to put out a finished product, make both sides of the pulls alike. Fasten a shade string to the top with a needle large enough to take the string.

[1] Harry A. Greene and Kate Ashley. *Building Better English*, Grade VII, pages 79–80 (adapted somewhat). Evanston, Illinois: Row, Peterson and Company, 1944.

RAFFIA SHADE PULLS

To make a raffia tassel, cut 20 to 25 strands of raffia into 6-inch lengths. Tie them together at the center with the end of the shade

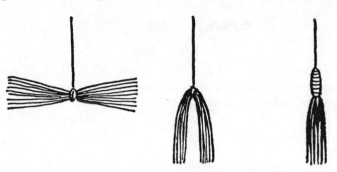

string. Draw the ends of the raffia down. Tie the tassel tightly **1** inch from the top with colored yarn. Wind the yarn around the raffia working up until you reach the shade string. Cut off the yarn and fasten the end securely with needle and thread.

SHADE PULLS MADE FROM WALNUTS AND FRUIT PITS

Black walnuts are especially suitable for shade pulls because of the thick shells. Screw a small screw eye into the top of the walnut. Lacquer the walnut and allow to dry. Fruit pits, such as peaches and avocado, work equally well. Clean them thoroughly, twist in the screw eye and then lacquer.

A WITCH'S HAT

The need for a witch's hat arises often, especially around Halloween time. A hat may be easily made from black cardboard. Work out a pattern on paper, basing the brim of the hat on an oval, which in turn may be based on a circle. Draw a circle 12 inches in diameter and narrow the sides and extend the ends slightly as in the diagram. Make the head opening oval, using the same procedure as for the brim. Make the opening nearly 7 inches across at the narrow part of the oval and more than **7** inches at the wide part. These dimensions, however, are approximate; adjust the size to fit the wearer. Place the pattern on black cardboard and cut out.

Make the crown from black carboard by fashioning a cone 12½ inches high (12 inches when finished). Make the base or perimeter

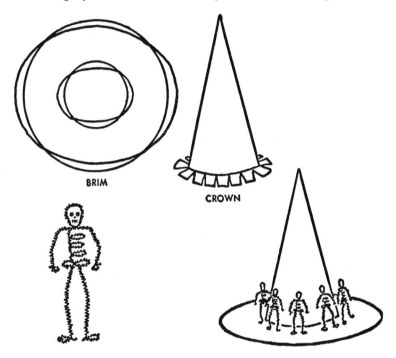

BRIM

CROWN

of the crown to fit the head opening in the brim (about 21 to 22 inches in circumference). Fasten the sides of the cone-shaped crown together with roundheads (brass paper fasteners) and glue. To make an edge for fastening the crown to the brim, mark off a strip ½-inch wide at the bottom of the crown and slash at intervals. Bend back and paste to the under side of the brim.

Make skeletons from pipe cleaners and put them around the brim. You will need three pipe cleaners: one for the head and torso, one for the legs, and another for the arms and shoulders. Sew the feet of the skeleton to the brim and anchor the body to the crown.

A WORD ACTIVITY

FOR THE ELEMENTARY GRADES

This activity involves finding words that are hidden in longer words. It may be used for seatwork or as a game. Select a long word or name like Washington. Using the letters of the word only once, the children make as many words as they can. They may work out a list for "Washington" similar to the one below. The list is given as a timesaver for the teacher.

ah	hash	now	stag	two
an	hat	oats	sting	wag
anoint	haw	oh	stow	wagon
anon	ho	on	swain	wain
ant	hog	sag	swan	waist
anti	hoist	sago	swat	wait
as	host	sang	swath	wan
ash	hot	sat	tan	want
awing	how	satin	tag	wanton
gain	in	saw	tang	was
gait	ingot	shag	tango	wash
gas	inn	shot	than	what
gash	iota	show	thaw	whist
gat	is	sin	thin	whit
gnat	it	sing	tin	who
go	its	snag	tog	whoa
got	nag	snow	toga	win
gown	nation	so	ton	wing
ha	night	son	tow	wish
hag	no	song	town	wit
hang	not	sow	twain	with
has	nothing	sown	twang	won

WORD TREASURE CHEST

The treasure chest idea may be used to help boys and girls develop their vocabularies. On slips of paper they write down the unfamiliar words that they come upon during the day and drop the slips into a box that has been decorated as a treasure chest. At the end of the day, the chest is opened, and the words are discussed with the guidance of the teacher.

A WORK PARTY

Tidying up the classroom provides an opportunity for a practical lesson in democracy. Discuss with the class what needs to be done to tidy and to clean the room. Suggestions are written on slips of paper and dropped into a box. Everyone draws an assignment from this box and acts upon it. The task may continue to be that of the drawee for a set period of time.

YARN PATTERNS

If a boy or a girl thinks that he cannot draw, encourage him with this device. Have him fold a piece of drawing paper into four squares. Drop a piece of yarn or string about fifteen or twenty inches long on one of the squares. He then draws the pattern into which the yarn has fallen and copies the same pattern on the other three squares. He will be surprised and pleased at the artistic design that he has made.

MATERIALS TO SAVE FOR HANDICRAFT PROJECTS

Handicraft projects are a joy to carry on if, early in the school year, you enlist the co-operation of the boys and girls to collect and to save materials. If storage space is inadequate at school, keep as many of the materials as possible at home. Here are some of the more helpful items worth saving.

Boxes
  apple and orange crates
  cigar boxes
  ice-cream and milk cartons
  packing boxes
  pill and match boxes
Broom handles
Brushes of all kinds
Candles, beeswax, paraffin
Cellophane
Chamois skins
Cloth and materials
  cotton cloth and scraps
  feed sacks
  flour and sugar sacks
  burlap sacks
  lace and trimmings
  ribbons
Clothespins
Corks and cork materials
Cornhusks
Drinking straws
Electric light bulbs (old)
Fingernail polish
Glass bottles and jars
Matches (burned kitchen matches)
Newspapers and magazines

Paper products
  cardboard
  colored paper
  corrugated paper
  paper bags
  paper plates
  paper towels
  wallpaper
Peanut Shells
Phonograph records (old)
Rubber inner tubes (old)
Sawdust
Soap scraps
Spools
Sucker sticks
Tinfoil, leadfoil
Toothpicks
Twine
Wallboard
Walnut shell halves
Wire
Wire screening
Wood
  blocks and scraps
  barkwoods
  softwoods
  strips of wood

WHERE TO WRITE FOR FREE MATERIALS

AETNA LIFE COMPANIES. Booklets on the prevention of fires and accidents in the home, entitled "Friend or Foe?" and "Home, the Most Dangerous Place in America." Hartford, Connecticut: Aetna Life Companies.

AMERICAN CAN COMPANY. Booklet, entitled "The Story of Food," telling how man has preserved food through the ages. New York: American Can Company (100 Park Avenue).

AMERICAN FORESTS PRODUCTS INDUSTRY, INC. Booklets, charts, films, teacher's manual on wood products. Washington, D. C.: American Products Industry, Inc. (1319 Eighteenth Street).

AMERICAN INSTITUTE OF BAKING. Weight record and diet charts, wheel of good eating, posters and leaflets on nutrition. Chicago: American Institute of Baking (400 East Ontario Street).

AMERICAN IRON AND STEEL INSTITUTE. Descriptions of some of the important steps in the manufacture of steel. New York: American Iron and Steel Institute (150 East Forty-second Street).

AMERICAN PETROLEUM INSTITUTE. Material on oil and the oil industry. New York: American Petroleum Institute (50 West Fiftieth Street).

AMERICAN WORLD FOOD. Booklets on food. Washington, D. C.: American World Food (800 Twenty-first Street).

ASSOCIATION OF AMERICAN RAILROADS. A set of 56 pictures showing the history and development of railroads and booklets, entitled "The Stories behind the Pictures" for primary and intermediate grades; "Railroads at Work." Washington, D. C.: Association of American Railroads (Transportation Building).

AUSTRALIAN NEWS AND INFORMATION BUREAU. Pictures, maps, and booklets on Australia. New York: Australian News and Information Bureau (636 Fifth Avenue).

BELDING HEMINWAY CORTICELLI COMPANY. Booklet, entitled "The Romantic Story of Silk." Putnam, Connecticut: Belding Heminway Corticelli Company (P. O. Drawer 32).

BELL TELEPHONE COMPANY. Booklets on the use of the telephone and on telephone topics, entitled "A Guide for Teaching Correct Telephone Usage"; "The Telephone and How We Use It," for pupils in the middle and later elementary grades; "The Telephone in America"; "The Magic of Communication"; "The Telephone Almanac," which gives an account of the development of communication by the spoken word; "Alexander Graham Bell." New York: Bell Telephone Company (195 Broadway); or Chicago (212 West Washington Street; or your local Bell telephone office.

BICYCLE INSTITUTE OF AMERICA. Bicycle safety tests and safety rules; bicycle safety posters in color. New York 17: Bicycle Institute of America (122 East Forty-second Street).

BITUMINOUS COAL INSTITUTE. Stories and films on coal and the coal industry. Washington, D. C.: Bituminous Coal Institute (Southern Building).

BRISTOL-MYERS COMPANY. Material on dental health: wall charts, score sheets, teacher's manual, individual dental health certificates. New York: Bristol-Myers Company (630 Fifth Avenue).

BRITISH INFORMATION SERVICES. Material on the following subjects: Industrial (labor, industry, agriculture), economic (business, tariffs, controls, trade), sociological (social legislation, health, education, housing), British Empire and international affairs. New York: British Information Services (30 Rockefeller Plaza).

CALIFORNIA DAIRY INDUSTRY ADVISORY BOARD. Material on health education for the primary and intermediate grades. Los Angeles, California: California Dairy Industry Advisory Board (670 South Lafayette Park Place).

CALIFORNIA FRUIT GROWERS EXCHANGE. The story of oranges and lemons from bud to consumer; a set of 18 pictures about oranges. Los Angeles, California: California Fruit Growers Exchange (Educational Division, Sunkist Building).

CANADIAN INFORMATION SERVICE. Up-to-date information about Canada. Washington, D. C.: Canadian Information Service (1205 Fifteenth Street, N. W.).

CEREAL INSTITUTE INC. "A Classroom Breakfast Party and Other Classroom Activities," Grades I, II, III; "Two Breakfast Plays and Other Classroom Activities," Grades IV, V, VI. Chicago: Cereal Institute Inc. (135 South La Salle Street).

GENERAL MOTORS CORPORATION. "The Automobile Story," includes a short history of travel and story accounts of the use of automobiles. Good for the elementary grades. Detroit, Michigan: General Motors Corporation (Public Relations Department, 3044 West Grand Blvd.).

HAWAIIAN PINEAPPLE COMPANY. Booklet, entitled "The Story of Pineapples." Honolulu, Hawaii: Hawaiian Pineapple Company (P. O. Drawer 3380).

H. J. HEINZ COMPANY. Material on food processing, history of foods, wall charts, films. Pittsburgh, Pennsylvania: H. J. Heinz Company.

ILLINOIS DEPARTMENT OF PUBLIC HEALTH. Booklets on communicable diseases, food poisoning, cancer, athletes foot, leukemia, tetanus, malaria. Springfield, Illinois: Illinois Department of Public Health.

ILLINOIS NATURAL HISTORY. Material on collecting and preserving insects. Urbana, Illinois: Illinois Natural History Survey.

LAMBERT PHARMACAL COMPANY. Dental hygiene helps. St. Louis, Missouri: Lambert Pharmacal Company (2117 Frankline Avenue).

LANCE COMPANY. Leaflet, entitled "The Peanut and How It Is Processed." Charlotte, North Carolina: Lance Company (P. O. Box 2389).

LIBRARY OF CONGRESS. Material on (1) Declaration of Independence, (2) the Constitution of the United States, (3) Library of Congress, (4) the Lincoln Collection. Washington, D. C.: Library of Congress (Publications).

LURAY CAVERNS IN VIRGINIA. Booklet and films on the Caverns of Luray. Luray, Virginia: Luray Caverns (Education Department).

LOUISIANA STATE DEPARTMENT OF AGRICULTURE AND IMMIGRATION. Samples of sugar cane, rice, cotton bolls, and lint cotton (exhibit). A class should be considerate in its request and should not ask for more than one. Baton Rouge 1, Louisiana: Louisiana State Department of Agriculture and Immigration.

MAHOGANY ASSOCIATION, INC. Films and booklets on mahogany. Chicago: Mahogany Association, Inc. (666 North Lake Shore Drive).

G. & C. MERRIAM COMPANY. Dictionary games and exercises, vocabulary quiz. Springfield, Massachusetts: G. & C. Merriam Company.

NATIONAL COTTON COUNCIL OF AMERICA. Material on growing and processing cotton. Memphis, Tennessee: National Cotton Council (P. O. Box 18).

NATIONAL FOOT HEALTH COUNCIL. Pictures, charts, pamphlets on foot health and care. Rockland, Massachusetts: National Foot Health Council (Phoenix Building).

NATIONAL NOISE ABATEMENT COUNCIL. Booklets on noise abatement. New York: National Noise Abatement (9 Rockefeller Plaza).

NEW YORK, NEW HAVEN AND HARTFORD RAILROAD. Booklets on New England, entitled "The New England People and Their Heritage," "The New England Region and Its Resources," "The Role of Industry in New England Life." Boston, Massachusetts: New York, New Haven and Hartford Railroad Company (South Station).

PLANTERS NUT AND CHOCOLATE COMPANY. Material on the peanut and its uses. Wilkes-Barre, Pennsylvania: Planters Nut and Chocolate Company (632 South Main Street).

PUBLIC HEALTH SERVICE. Dental Posters. Single sample copy sent free. Washington, D. C.: Public Health Service.

ROBERTS, JOHNSON, AND RAND. Booklets and pictures, entitled "Shoes through the Ages." St. Louis, Missouri (1501 Washington Avenue).

UNION BAG AND PAPER CORPORATION. Booklet describing forest conservation. Elementary grade level. Savannah, Georgia: Union Bag and Paper Corporation.

UNITED AIR LINES. Kit containing maps, pictures, and pamphlets. Chicago 38: United Air Lines (5959 South Cicero Avenue).

UNITED FRUIT COMPANY. Story about bananas from tree to consumer; poster of fruit to be colored (for the primary grades). New York: United Fruit Company (Educational Division, Pier 3, North River).

UNITED STATES BEET SUGAR ASSOCIATION. A large poster on the story of sugar. Washington, D. C.: United States Beet Sugar Association.

UNITED STATES DEPARTMENT OF AGRICULTURE. A large chart, "What We Get from Trees." Washington, D. C.: United States Department of Agriculture.

WEST COAST LUMBERMAN'S ASSOCIATION. Information on fir trees and the practical uses made of wood; Paul Bunyan's Quiz booklets. Portland, Oregon (1410 S. W. Morrison).

WORLD CALENDAR ASSOCIATION. Leaflets, booklets, calendars. New York: World Calendar Association (650 Fifth Avenue).

STATES (OF THE UNITED STATES)

Free materials that are put out by some of the state governments are listed below. Practically every state, however, puts out similar materials on the state's historic sites, landmarks, and state parks. For descriptive and pictorial materials about your state write to the State capitol. If you know the department or bureau that will handle your request, direct your letter to that department. If you do not, direct your request to the Information Bureau.

Many business concerns also put out free materials about the natural features, resources, industries, occupations, and unique features of their state. The names and addresses of several of these sources are given in the list.

ALABAMA. A history of the Alabama State capitol; a description of Alabama's historic spots and parks. Montgomery, Alabama: State of Alabama (Division of Records and Reports).

CALIFORNIA AND COLORADO. Pictures and materials on cities and other points of interest. Omaha, Nebraska: Union Pacific Railroad (Department of Traffic, 1416 Dodge Street).

LOUISIANA. Information about the state's agriculture, industries, natural resources, etc. Baton Rouge, Louisiana: Louisiana Department of Agriculture and Immigration.

MAINE. "Facts about Maine." Augusta, Maine: State House (Maine Development Commission).

MASSACHUSETTS. Description and interesting facts about the state. Boston, Massachusetts: Massachusetts Development and Industrial Commission, State House.

NEW ENGLAND. "The New England People and Their Heritage," "The New England Region and Its Resources," "The Role of Industry in New England Life." Boston, Massachusetts: The New York, New Haven, and Hartford Railroad Company (South Station).

OREGON. "Oregon the Beaver State." Salem, Oregon: Oregon State Highway Commission (Travel Information Department).

TENNESSEE. "Tennessee: Perhaps This Answers Your Question," answers to questions most frequently asked about the state. Nashville, Tennessee: Department of Conservation (Division of Information).

TEXAS. "Texas: Facts and Imaginary Tour." Austin, Texas: Texas Highway Department.

GENERAL INDEX

315